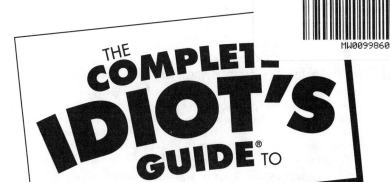

THE
COMPLETE
IDIOT'S
GUIDE® TO

5-Minute Appetizers

by Tod Dimmick

ALPHA

A member of Penguin Group (USA) Inc.

For Jen

This is a CWL Publishing Enterprises Book created for Alpha Books by CWL Publishing Enterprises, Madison, WI, www.cwlpub.com.

Most Alpha books are available at special quantity discounts for bulk purchases for sales promotions, premiums, fund-raising, or educational use. Special books, or book excerpts, can also be created to fit specific needs.

For details, write: Special Markets, Alpha Books, 375 Hudson Street, New York, NY 10014.

Publisher: *Marie Butler-Knight*
Product Manager: *Phil Kitchel*
Senior Managing Editor: *Jennifer Chisholm*
Senior Acquisitions Editor: *Renee Wilmeth*
Development Editor: *Nancy D. Lewis*
Senior Production Editor: *Christy Wagner*
Copy Editor: *Nancy Wagner*
Illustrator: *Chris Eliopoulos*
Cover/Book Designer: *Trina Wurst*
Indexer: *Brad Herriman*
Layout/Proofreading: *Angela Calvert, Rebecca Harmon, Donna Martin*

Contents at a Glance

Contents

Appendixes

Foreword

An appetizer is essential. It is the *seduction* to a meal, or any festivity.

Appetizers are conversation starters. As everyone marvels at your bite-size gifts, your occasion is off to a memorable start. To serve an appetizer is to serve that all-important first impression.

The only protest I have ever heard against serving appetizers is, "But they take so long to prepare."

Well, not only does chef-author Tod Dimmick deliver almost every appetizer recipe imaginable in this new book, *The Complete Idiot's Guide to 5-Minute Appetizers*, but time becomes a nonissue.

Why?

Because Tod delivers.

Our magician in the kitchen offers us more than 300 fast, tasty, appealing alternatives to that ubiquitous bag of chips dumped in a bowl.

Tod serves up recipes with variety, versatility, and fun, including the classics, the new, and the revisited—delectable little bites with big flavor for any party. And he even gives us around-the-world recipes to munch on.

Throughout this book, Tod reminds us why everyone loves a great appetizer. These irresistible nibbles bring tremendous value when we entertain. Appetizers stimulate your guests' palate in anticipation of what is to come. They set a mood of festivity, a welcome to a party, and the tone for a meal—matching whether the rest of the menu is fancy, casual, or in between.

Tod shows us how appetizers make any occasion into a celebration, whether served at a party, a meal, or any other social gathering.

As he writes: "Appetizers are the multi-taskers of the kitchen. They help satisfy those urgent premeal hunger pangs, of course, but they also help us shake off the outside world and relax. Served at a party or social gathering, they set the tone for whatever is to come. Through taste, smell, and visual appeal, appetizers make the transition from work to play, between the everyday and a celebration. That's a big responsibility for a small bite of food, but that's perhaps why we all love appetizers so much."

Tod Dimmick delivers the answer to home entertaining's biggest quandary: how to make delicious, crowd-pleasing appetizers that are complete and ready-to-serve in only 5 minutes!

Mara Reid Rogers,
cookbook author and host of "The Midday Dish with Mara Reid Rogers"

Introduction

Appetizers set the stage. Of course, an appetizer is only food, but food is endowed with symbolism far beyond mere calories. That tiny, flavorful bite is a magic portal to the "time-off frame of mind." Through appearance, smell, and taste, all in the context of our friends, we start to kick back and enjoy ourselves.

With that in mind, envision throwing down on the table a plastic container of dip and a bag of chips or a plastic tray with shrimp, sauce, and that wilted piece of lettuce it comes with as a "garnish." This just doesn't quite do the trick, does it?

How about, instead, blue cheese spread with toasted walnuts, served with freshly sliced apples; or bruschetta, the Italian-style toasted bread with savory tomato topping, served fresh from the oven? The smells are irresistible, the tastes delicious, and suddenly the conversation picks up and people have a good time. These are the foods that appetizer dreams are made of, and they are here in these pages.

Appetizers can be simple yet elegant and packed with flavor. They can be fun to make and even more fun to serve, because of the glowing response you receive as the cook. There are so many possibilities that, unless you're a fanatic about that recipe for Mock "Guac" (Spicy Asparagus Dip) in Chapter 19, you can serve something different from this book every night for almost a year. In my book, that's a recipe for fun and maybe even learning.

In these pages, you'll find simple combinations—what I call "pairs" of ingredients that together create a sum much greater than their separate parts, such as figs with prosciutto or goat's milk cheese and toasted pine nuts. You'll find dips and spreads, a multitude of toasts, vegetable- and meat-based appetizers, and hors d'oeuvres that pay homage to cuisines from around the globe.

I hope you find this book helpful as both a reference and as inspiration. Give some of these appetizers a try. Once you do, your party will really get started!

How This Book Is Organized

The book is divided into four parts:

Part 1, "Time-Honored Classics," reviews some appetizer basics, from common terminology and tips about presentation to sure-fire preparation methods (even quick cooking) for 5-minute fare. Then I review some of the appetizer classics, from high-quality cheeses to dips, spreads, and bread-based appetizers, as well as seafood and meat hors d'oeuvres.

Part 2, "A 5-Minute World Tour," explores the dishes, seasoning, and ingredients that make cuisines of the world unique. I'll start "South(west)," and then visit Europe, Asia, and other parts of the world to find some of the best quick appetizers around.

Part 3, "Vegetable- and Fruit-Focused Appetizers," investigates the undiscovered country—appetizers that are tasty, quick, yet for the most part reasonably healthful. What a concept! I'll look at vegetable starters (can you say "crudité"?), fruit-driven hors d'oeuvres, vegetarian appetizers, and more.

Part 4, "Practical Secrets," exposes the things you need to know to succeed with hors d'oeuvres—from recipes that travel well (for an appetizer you're taking to a friend's house) to the case in which a few drips in the name of delicious flavor are okay (a sit-down dinner). I'll discuss quick yet attractive dishes based on store-bought goodies and talk about wines (and wine-friendly appetizers) to make your party complete.

Extra Bites of Information

In each chapter, I've included a number of helpful hints in small boxes with information related to the topic at hand. Here's what to look for:

Gourmet Glossary
Words and phrases used in cooking or in recipes.

Unappetizer
An alert about a common misunderstanding, mistake, or potential hazard.

Hors D'oeuvre History
Information about an appetizer, or background that helps an ingredient, a recipe, or a method make sense ... and even more fun.

Savoir Starter
Tips and secrets, from one cook to another, on how to make something simpler, quicker, faster, and easier.

Acknowledgments

As you might imagine, the research for this book was a lot of fun. During parts of this project, appetizers were coming out of the kitchen morning, noon, and night. Even so, there was much more to do than one person could hope to accomplish alone, and I am in debt to the people who helped out with suggestions, advice, and testing. Thanks to John Woods of CWL Publishing Enterprises, who recruited me for my first book, *The Complete Idiot's Guide to 20-Minute Meals* and then called again to ask me to write a similar but time-reduced (from 20 minutes to 5 minutes) guide to appetizers. Thanks also to Renee Wilmeth of Alpha Books for the original idea.

This book would not have been possible without the help of several dear friends (and skilled cooks), including Jean Burke (New England Test Kitchen), Anya Dorst (Northwest), and Marcia Friedkin (Gotham City), who came back for more after surviving *20-Minute Meals*. I am also grateful to Irene Carrick, Ann Marie Kott, Berinder Singh, and Aileen Zogby, who cheerfully joined the test kitchen melee.

Thanks also to Renee Crockett Rehn, Italo DeMasi, Freddie Dimmick (Mom), Dave Dimmick (Dad), Elaine Early, Anne and Derek Footer, Dos Frazee, Valerie Gates, Marci Goldberg, Steve Gorski, Anne Schaller, Simon Waller, and many others for inspiration, recipe suggestions, and support.

Finally, thanks to my sons Spencer (8) and Kurt (5), who expressed enthusiasm for Gruyère and curiosity about chickpeas. (Unfortunately, the peas didn't grow like they were supposed to—must have something to do with being cooked.) To my wife, Jen, who made this book possible by picking up the many loose ends as I was immersed in writing and who supported the whole process. I love you.

And to Lexie the dog, who helpfully ate all the leftovers and licked her chops, although I don't think her love for the food had anything to do with my culinary skills.

Special Thanks to the Technical Reviewer

The technical reviewer for *The Complete Idiot's Guide to 5-Minute Appetizers* was Karen Berman, a Connecticut-based writer and editor who specializes in food and culture. She is a contributing editor to *Wine Enthusiast* magazine, and her work has appeared in magazines, newspapers, and newsletters. She is the author of an illustrated history book, *American Indian Traditions and Ceremonies*, and has worked in various editorial capacities on numerous cookbooks.

Trademarks

All terms mentioned in this book that are known to be or are suspected of being trademarks or service marks have been appropriately capitalized. Alpha Books and Penguin Group (USA) Inc. cannot attest to the accuracy of this information. Use of a term in this book should not be regarded as affecting the validity of any trademark or service mark.

Part 1

Time-Honored Classics

A world of elegant, flavorful cheeses exists out there that, carefully selected, can provide an awe-inspiring appetizer tray in seconds, not minutes. We'll then dip into dips—those creamy, savory mixes that we might have first tried as kids. But the dips—and us—have grown up a lot since then. We'll look at rich, savory spreads, then move on to bread-based recipes such as crostini, bruschetta, and canapés. We'll bow to royal salmon, the flavorful food that can be elegant served practically naked but is delicious combined with other ingredients. Further on the seafood theme, we'll look at crab recipes (talk about rich and delicious) and say hello to shrimp (the quintessential hors d'oeuvre bite). Finally, we'll visit the deli for a jump-start on a range of meat-based appetizers.

Yes, You Can Do This at Home!

In This Chapter

- ◆ What's so exciting about appetizers?
- ◆ Set expectations
- ◆ Presentation is everything
- ◆ Let the ingredients do the work
- ◆ Hors d'oeuvres and other fancy words

Appetizers, in all their exciting forms, are a favorite food around the world. Whether passed for casual nibbling or plated and served as a first course, these small portions of food are tantalizing and tasty. But many require extensive preparations. And because we want to spend our precious time with friends and family, the last thing we need is something to take us away from our guests.

The purpose of this book is to explore this rich universe of appetizers and to highlight those that are delicious and easy to prepare, yet take little enough time so (what a thought) we can enjoy our own party.

Tall order? Not at all. A huge number of appetizer possibilities exist, and even by limiting that field to only those that take 5 minutes to prepare, we still have ample opportunity to explore and pick only the best.

Start a Celebration in Style

Appetizers, also known as starters and *hors d'oeuvres*, are meant to tantalize the taste buds. For this reason, small bites often carry big flavor. This flavor comes from herbs, spices, salt, and rich ingredients. Not only is it by design that these morsels are small, but it's also a necessity, so our palate is not overwhelmed.

Gourmet Glossary

One of my favorite cooking terms is **hors d'oeuvre**. From the French, it literally means "outside of work"; in this case, outside of the main work (or main course) of the meal. Perhaps a bit of license with the word *work* is in order. Appetizers, indeed, serve as a transition—for the palate and in our minds—to help us move from work to celebration. The term is perfect for us!

Whether we're talking about starting a party, a meal, or a social gathering, appetizers are the multitaskers of the kitchen. They help satisfy those urgent pre-meal hunger pangs, of course, but they also help us shake off the outside world and relax. Served at a party or social gathering, they set the tone for whatever is to come. Through taste, smell, and visual appeal, appetizers make the transition from work to play, between the everyday and a celebration. That's a big responsibility for a small bite of food, but that's perhaps why we all love appetizers so much.

The other night, my wife and I were invited to a friend's house for dinner. What, we asked, could we bring? "Well, an appetizer would be nice," was the reply. We could, I suppose, have arrived with a bag of tortilla chips and a jar of salsa. In fact, for some laid-back occasions that ol' bag of chips is just what the doctor ordered. But for other occasions, especially when, as in this case, our friend had worked hard to prepare a meal for us, it's only right to respond by bringing something that people will enjoy, that might be the least bit unusual, and that helps set the mood. In this case the weather was miserable, so I brought an appetizer to make people think of summer in Tuscany—Bruschetta with Roasted Red Peppers (see Chapter 6 for both recipes). They disappeared in about a minute.

Whether you're visiting friends, hosting a party, or preparing a dinner for friends or family, the appetizer is, in many ways, the start of the event ... the "cover of the book." And although the old saying warns, "don't judge a book by its cover," we all do it. The starting taste, the presentation, the colors, the textures, and the evidence of your care (and the *impression* of the time you've spent) are what bring people to a heightened level of pleasure and enjoyment of the event ... or not. It's up to you.

Next time you need to put together an appetizer for some friends, whether the event is at your place or theirs, think about what kind of a reaction you'd like to cause with your gift. Will your appetizer be simple fuel? Or will your fellow guests devour what you've made and beg for the recipe? Which is the better way to start off a party? You set the tone by the choices you make.

Simple Is Good

We've all seen those cookbooks. You know the ones I mean. The photographs are stunning; the ingredients are exotic. These books make fascinating reading, but there's only one problem. Each recipe takes 12 hours to make. That 12-hour recipe is easy as pie when all you're doing is reading it!

Reading one or two of these books, I remembered something that cookbook publishers know well: Different types of readers exist out there. Some buy cookbooks *only* to read.

Then there are folks like you and me, who crack open a guide for practical help— not for 12 hours later, but for *now*. For this type of cookbook reader (count me in), there are books like this one, designed to be easy and quick to use.

One of the persistent myths I want to dispel right away is that for an appetizer to be appealing, it must be complex and time-consuming. Nothing could be further from the truth. Of course, there are those time-consuming specials, but most people are like you and me: We want fun and unique flavor combinations, but we need to be able to prepare them in just a few minutes. Otherwise, what's the point? We wouldn't be able to enjoy the occasion at hand.

The focus on 5-minute preparation is an opportunity. The time requirement means that we have to be smart about ingredients, equipment, and preparation methods (more on that in the next chapter). For example, consider the following version of a classic Italian-style appetizer using figs, goat's milk cheese, and prosciutto. Many of the recipes in this book will make similar use of flavorful, somewhat unusual ingredients that together create sublime taste sensations.

Figs with Goat's Milk Cheese and Diced Prosciutto

I like dried figs for their intense flavor, but this will also work with fresh fruit.

Serves 6 (can be scaled as needed)

1 (8-oz.) pkg. fresh goat's milk cheese

9 dried figs, cut in half lengthwise

4 oz. diced *prosciutto* (available in many grocery stores)

Gourmet Glossary

Prosciutto is aged, typically salty, dry-cured ham that originated in the Parma region of Italy. It is usually purchased sliced very thin, although this recipe calls for diced.

Using a bread knife or a spoon, spread about 1 teaspoon goat's milk cheese on the cut side of each fig half and arrange figs, stem end out, in a wreath shape on a round serving platter. Sprinkle diced prosciutto over figs, being sure that a few pieces cling to each piece of fig and cheese.

To add a little more atmosphere, float a single flower (a daisy, rose, chrysanthemum, or your favorite) in 1 inch water in a bowl or round vase on the serving platter inside your "wreath." The presentation once again evokes summer in Tuscany, even if it's February in Boston.

Now that we've agreed that an appetizer is an important and valuable way to help everybody—yourself included—enjoy a party, let's make sure we don't ruin that pleasure by attempting to build the *Titanic* when a much smaller (and less accident-prone) vehicle will get us there.

From the Ordinary ... Extraordinary

Everybody these days serves chips and salsa or cheese and crackers. There's nothing wrong with that; the reason many people serve these items is because most everyone likes them. But in barely more time than it takes to slice cheese and arrange crackers on a tray, you can create something delicious, new, and interesting.

A sage once said that variety is the spice of life. Even a basic twist on the ordinary piques interest and stimulates the appetite. When you and your guests are interested in the food, suddenly everybody starts having more fun.

Interesting appetizers come from the most ordinary of ingredients used in slightly different ways. For example, do you have carrots and celery in your fridge? If you do and if you have a food processor (an indispensable tool for 5-minute appetizers), you're so close to an appetizer that, well, you can almost taste it.

Crunchy Creamy Vegetable Spread

A minute in the food processor works wonders in this vegetable-intensive spread. If you have the time, make this in the morning and let the flavors meld in the fridge for a few hours.

1 stick celery	8 oz. cream cheese, softened
1 large carrot	½ cup light sour cream
2 scallions, dark green leaves removed, 1 tablespoon finely chopped green leaves reserved for *garnish*	½ cup shredded Parmesan cheese
	Dash hot pepper sauce, such as Tabasco (optional)

Using a food processor fitted with a shredder wheel or a hand shredder (although this will probably put you over the 5-minute mark), shred celery, carrot, and scallions. Mix vegetables in a serving bowl with cream cheese, sour cream, Parmesan cheese, and hot pepper sauce (if using). Top with a sprinkling of chopped scallion. Serve with crunchy breadsticks or pita bread sliced into pie-shape wedges. Ordinary vegetables suddenly seem extraordinary!

Note: Nonfat cottage cheese can be substituted for the cream cheese for a lower-fat recipe.

> **Gourmet Glossary**
>
> In the context of food, a **garnish** is an embellishment, something added to enhance the appeal of a dish. The green scallion pieces atop the light-colored vegetable spread create an appealing contrast and evoke freshness and flavor—sensations that help your guests fully enjoy what you've made.
>
> With 5-minute appetizers, we'll take full advantage of presentation aides like garnishes to make even the simplest dish look fresh and appealing (and look like you've been working on it for a long time).

Dressing Up Store-Bought

Throughout this book, you'll find recipes that empower you to make things from scratch using basic ingredients, as well as suggestions for making good use of some of the delicious ready-made options from the grocery store. The key is presenting these preprepared foods in ways that will dazzle your guests. That's "dressing up store-bought," and there's no shame in making good use of high-quality prepared foods, especially if doing so enables you to include otherwise time-consuming appetizers in your 5-minute repertoire. You'll find these recipes throughout the book and especially in Chapter 23. High-quality sushi, which follows, is just one example.

Sushi Platter

This is a terrific, unusual appetizer for a dinner party.

Serves 6 (easily scaled using the rule of 3 portions per person)

Handful fresh chives

18 pieces sushi (tuna, octopus, crab, and cucumber rolls are all popular choices)

2 TB. wasabi paste (Japanese horseradish paste)

2 TB. pickled ginger

¼ cup soy sauce

Arrange chives in a checkerboard pattern on a large serving platter and place sushi pieces in the resulting squares.

Place wasabi and ginger on small complementary serving plates with small spoons, and pour soy sauce into a shallow bowl. Give your guests small plates, and invite them to take a bit of wasabi and ginger and dip their sushi pieces in soy sauce. Add a small amount of wasabi and ginger (to taste) to each sushi bite when eating. Take care; wasabi is powerful. Traditional accompaniments are a light-style beer or sake (Japanese rice wine) served warm in small glasses.

Unusual and delicious, sushi from a high-quality vendor is a treat that will wow your guests. Many restaurants and grocery stores offer delicious, freshly prepared sushi. This recommendation is for a starter platter, but there are many varieties, so feel free to explore. The sushi vendor will often include the wasabi, soy sauce, and pickled ginger. If that's the case, you're ahead of the game!

Be sure to purchase seafood products such as sushi from a reputable source. Most sushi vendors these days offer only the freshest, highest-quality produce, but it's always a good idea to be sure so your appetizer isn't, well, *unappetizing*.

Vegetables, Fruit, and Healthful Appetizers

Appetizers with loads of flavor and texture often come with a corresponding load of fat and calories. This reality has long been a challenge for cooks who seek to create delicious starters but who also want to keep their food as healthful as possible. Although this book is not explicitly about eating healthfully, I suspect we all want healthful alternatives. For that reason, where possible in this book, I've provided light or low-fat alternatives where a "full-fat" primary ingredient is given. Often I've suggested low-fat ingredients as the base in cases where I found little or no benefit in using the full-fat ingredients. This vegetable- and fruit-focused section contains many appetizers low in fat, especially Chapter 19.

All that said, we must recognize that many appetizer favorites, were they to be eaten as an entrée, would not be very healthful. Perhaps that's another benefit to the fact that appetizers come in small portions!

Time Is of the Essence

In this book, I focus on finding the very best flavor and ingredient combinations you can accomplish darn quickly—in 5 minutes, to be precise.

To keep sane, I'll do my best to avoid the mad dash. Successful appetizers are possible through the use of the right ingredients, equipment, methods (see Chapter 2), and *reasonable expectations*. Accordingly, on these pages you will find that I …

- ◆ Avoid complicated menus. Entertaining as they might be, just reading the recipe could take 5 minutes!
- ◆ Keep things simple in terms of preparation and cleanup.
- ◆ Focus on ingredients that are tasty, interesting, and easy to use.
- ◆ Keep the ingredients to a minimum in the interest of saving time.
- ◆ Make good use of dramatic or occasionally unusual seasonings, as these are an integral part of many exciting appetizers.
- ◆ Avoid expensive ingredients—for the most part.
- ◆ Identify preparation methods that are quick and appropriate for our 5-minute goal.

Even with these so-called "limits," we have a world to explore. Think of Hot Crab-Parmesan Dip, Smoked Salmon and Roasted Red Pepper Spread, or Sautéed Garlic Shrimp. Your guests will rave, but you don't have to tell them your prep only took 5 minutes.

With these parameters set, I think you'll be surprised to see all you can accomplish. As I was researching the recipes to use in this book, I found that there were so many I had to *cut* some. The problem was not finding enough to fit in the book; the problem was keeping the number low enough so you wouldn't have to buy a two-volume set.

Appetizer Attitude

In these pages, I'll do my best to equip you with the tools (methods, equipment, and knowledge of what goes with what) to really get started. My hope is that many of the appetizers here will become your favorites. I also hope you'll use some of my recipes as starting points as you begin to create recipes on your own. If you do, I'll be one very happy author.

In *The Complete Idiot's Guide to 20-Minute Meals*, I wrote that it's our choice whether we view the time we spend on food as a chore or a pleasure—and I suspect most of us are ready for a little more pleasure. For this reason, my not-so-secret theme in this book is to invite you along on an enthusiastic tour of an exciting area of exploration. Many people find a great deal of joy comes in creating something for the table. It might be revisiting an old favorite (a good aged cheddar with fresh crusty bread) or a new twist (such as the following recipe for Warm Smoked Gouda with Crisp Apple). Almost regardless of the content, though, the result is satisfaction for the cook (that's you) and delight for your guests.

Warm Smoked Gouda with Crisp Apple

The magic in this incredibly easy appetizer is the contrasting texture and flavors—the warm creaminess of the cheese with the tart crunch of the apple. (And the presentation masks the fact that this took you 3½ minutes to prepare.)

Serves 6 to 8 (can easily be scaled)

2 Granny Smith apples (or other fresh, crisp apples), cut lengthwise into slices about ½ inch thick

4 oz. smoked Gouda cheese, cut into ½ by ½ by 1-inch pieces (approximating the proportion of an apple slice)

Several sprigs fresh parsley for garnish

On a circular, microwave-safe serving platter, arrange apple slices so they nest each other like crescents—without quite touching—in a circle around the plate. Top each apple slice with a piece of smoked Gouda. Microwave for 20 to 30 seconds or until Gouda pieces just start to soften. (Heating time will vary according to the power of your microwave.) Apple pieces will be warm but will maintain their crunch. Place sprigs of parsley in the center of the circle, stems inward to form a decorative "leaf-only" view, and serve your apples to appreciative crunching.

Now that we've reviewed the parameters of 5-minute appetizers and are focused on what's realistic, we can really begin to play. And even in 5 minutes, there's a lot of potential. Let's get started!

The Least You Need to Know

- Fast, tasty appetizers are not only possible, but they're also easy … with a bit of knowledge and preparation.
- Take advantage of the flavors inherent in fruits, vegetables, cheeses, and meats to create something that is, simply, a masterpiece.
- Healthful appetizers need not require any sacrifice in flavor.
- Even in 5 minutes, there are hundreds of appetizer options.

2

5-Minute Foundation

In This Chapter

- ◆ Ingredients to set you up for success
- ◆ Seasonings to please the palate
- ◆ 5-minute methods
- ◆ Time-saving equipment

I've included in this chapter my suggestions for the ingredients, methods, and equipment necessary to get a running start. I love fresh ingredients—vegetables and fruits are a wonderful source of natural, quick flavors—but I've also recommended many canned or jarred ingredients. These preserved ingredients have a long shelf life, and you won't have to devote a fridge exclusively to appetizers (although that sounds like a great fridge).

I've also included a short list of seasonings particularly useful for hors d'oeuvre prep, many of which you might already have. Methods and equipment will also likely be familiar, as this is a subset of the repertoire of most kitchens. All the ingredients, methods, and equipment, of course, focus on enabling you to achieve the 5-minute appetizer as I refer to them in the recipes in this book.

Key Ingredients for 5-Minute Appetizers

With appetizers in mind, you should always have these indispensable ingredients on hand. At any given time, I try to have several of the following vegetables and fruits, as well as a number of the preserved ingredients. One of my favorite pastimes is to peer into the pantry, see what I've got, and use that as the inspiration to create something. Some items I don't tend to stock unless I've purchased them for a special occasion. But if you always have caviar in your kitchen, I want to see what else you've got!

Fresh Vegetables

Fresh vegetables work magic with your appetizers. They bring flavor, texture, and visual appeal with little or no prep time. Here's a short list of my favorites, but please add your own to the list.

Gourmet Glossary
Belgian endive resembles a small, white, elongated, tightly packed head of romaine lettuce. The thick, crunchy leaves can be broken off and used as a terrific vehicle for dips and spreads.

Unappetizer
Although fresh vegetables will speed you on your way, many, such as mushrooms, should also be used in a hurry. Old mushrooms won't be on your guests' "favorites" list.

- *Belgian endive*
- Carrots (both large carrots for recipes and "baby" carrots to serve)
- Celery
- Chives (also available dried in the herbs and spices section of your grocery store)
- Cucumbers
- Mushrooms (sliced or whole white button and portobello)
- Scallions
- Spinach (fresh for wrapping appetizers and frozen as an ingredient in dips and spreads)
- Sweet onions (such as Vidalia)
- Tomatoes (grape and cherry)
- Zucchini squash

Fruits

Fruits also bring freshness, flavor, and visual appeal. Some such as avocados and coconut bring an exotic richness, and others (apples, dates, etc.) add sweetness to appetizers.

- Apples (Fuji and Granny Smith)
- Avocados

- Coconut (shredded; most have added sugar, the recipes in this book allow for that)
- Dates
- Figs (dried)
- Grapefruit
- Grapes
- Lemons (for fresh lemon juice, a critical component in many recipes)
- Limes
- Melons (cantaloupe and honeydew)
- Pears (Bartlett)
- Pineapple (canned pieces are the easiest with the 5-minute time frame)

Savoir Starter

In botanical terms, a fruit is the seed-bearing section of a plant, which includes not only apples and other obvious "fruits," but also tomatoes and other vegetables with seeds. Because we're cooks, not botanists, I've listed tomatoes (and other seeded edibles) according to the way we use them, with the vegetables. A tomato pie, though, is an interesting thought.

Canned, Dried, and Preserved Items

Preserved items lurk in the pantry, instantly available when you need them. Here are some of my favorites:

- Almonds
- Canned chickpeas (also known as garbanzo beans)
- Hearts of palm
- Marinated artichoke hearts
- Marinated mushrooms
- Olives (I like whole Kalamata olives and green olives, both with pits, as well as canned sliced black olives for quick olive mixes.)
- Pasta sauce
- Roasted red peppers
- Sun-dried tomatoes (oil-packed)
- Walnuts
- Water chestnuts

Meats and Seafood

Keep an open mind about seemingly commonplace items like deli-counter or canned chicken and ham or canned tuna. These items can be used to create unusual and delicious appetizers, and these ready-to-use ingredients can be the basis of recipes that would otherwise take far too long. I won't tell anyone you got it from a can.

- *Anchovies*
- Bacon and/or bacon bits
- Canned clams (chopped)
- Canned crabmeat
- Canned ham
- Canned tuna fish (chunk white)

- Chicken chunks (canned white meat)
- Capers
- Pâté
- Prosciutto
- *Sardines*
- Shrimp (cocktail size)
- Smoked salmon

Gourmet Glossary
Anchovies and **sardines** are tiny, flavorful preserved fish that typically come in cans. The strong flavor from these tiny salted fish is a must in many recipes ... even if you don't like them on your pizza.

Cheese and Other Dairy Products

These are cheeses intended as base ingredients in recipes. For much more on cheeses as an appetizer on their own, see Chapter 3.

- Blue cheese, crumbled
- Butter
- Cheddar cheese (shredded)
- Cottage cheese (light or nonfat)
- Cream cheese or light cream cheese
- Eggs (hard-boiled)
- Feta (crumbled)
- Goat's milk cheese
- Mayonnaise

Unappetizer
The reduced-fat variety of mayonnaise will work, but I prefer to keep the full-fat mayo and try to minimize the amount, rather than using more of a substitute that is lighter in calories but also lighter in flavor.

- Mozzarella (fresh)
- Parmesan (shredded)
- Ricotta (part skim)
- Sour cream or light sour cream
- Yogurt, plain (nonfat)

Condiments, Sauces

These flavorsome sauces, seasonings, and cooking liquids play an important role in the recipes in this book:

- Balsamic vinegar
- Bruschetta topping mixture (containing tomatoes, garlic, peppers, and other ingredients; available in jars in many grocery stores)
- Canola oil
- Chunky blue cheese dressing
- Chutney
- Cocktail sauce
- Dijon-style mustard
- Extra-virgin olive oil
- Honey
- Horseradish
- Hot pepper sauce
- Italian salad dressing or mix
- Minced garlic (available at grocery stores)
- Olive tapenade
- Peanut butter
- Salsa (your favorite varieties, including a fruit salsa; I'll also discuss making salsa [Chapter 10], but there's nothing wrong with a backup)
- Soy sauce
- Teriyaki sauce
- Worcestershire sauce

Savoir Starter
There's a big difference between shredded mozzarella used on your pizza and fresh mozzarella from the deli or gourmet store—the kind that is shaped like golf balls and comes packed in water. Creamy and luxuriant, fresh mozzarella is, for the most part, the mozzarella for us appetizer lovers.

Savoir Starter
For the sublime, rich flavor of peanuts to shine through in dips and sauces, choose all-natural peanut butter. You have to stir the peanut oil back in to the mix the first time you open the jar, but the overwhelming upside is flavor and the knowledge that you're bypassing a big dose of preservatives.

Seasoning for Smiles

Appetizers are all about intense flavor. The source of flavor might be the main ingredient itself (for example, a strong cheese), or the main ingredient might serve as a willing platform for added flavors (for example, is it the shrimp you crave or the highly seasoned cocktail sauce?). Spices and herbs also add flavor and interest *without* fat or calories.

Seasonings to Have on Hand

With the following seasonings in your pantry, you will be equipped to prepare most of the menus described in this book and many more besides.

Herbs and Spices

Basil

Chives

Cilantro

Dill

Ginger

Ground black pepper

Ground cumin

Ground red pepper

Kosher salt

Marjoram

Oregano

Paprika

Rosemary

Sage

Tarragon

Thyme

Blends

Cajun seasoning

Chili powder

Curry powder

Garlic salt

Italian seasoning

Unappetizer _____

With unfamiliar seasonings and combinations, stick close to a recipe the first several times you use it until you're comfortable with ratios and "what goes with what." There's a big difference between 1 teaspoon and 1 tablespoon curry powder. After that, experiment and have fun!

I've included several popular seasoning blends in this list. These mixes, evocative of a particular region or cooking style, are ready to go and are indispensable for reducing prep time. For a list of some of my favorite spice vendors, see Appendix B.

Gourmet Glossary
Italian seasoning, the ubiquitous grocery store blend including oregano and thyme, is a useful tool for quick flavor that evokes the "Old Country."

Seasonings That "Match"

Each seasoning is distinctive, and some combinations work better than others. Although the following chart shows some general guidelines for matching ingredients with seasonings, keep in mind that the inclusion of one herb might push out another.

	Vegetarian	Seafood	Chicken	Pork	Beef	Vegetables
Basil	XX	X	XX	XX		
Chili powder	XX	X	XX	X	XX	X
Chives	XX	XX	XX	XX	X	X
Dill	XX	XX	XX			
Ginger	X	X	X	X	X	X
Ground black pepper	XX	XX	XX	XX	XX	XX
Ground red pepper	XX	X	XX	XX	XX	XX
Marjoram	X	X	XX	XX	XX	X
Paprika	X	X	XX	X	X	X
Parsley	XX	XX	XX	XX	XX	XX
Sage	X	X	XX	XX	X	
Tarragon	X	XX	X	X	X	
Thyme	XX	XX	XX	XX	XX	XX

XX = Best match

X = Works

Recipes are formulas, but keep in mind the possibilities of substitutions to improve them to your taste and give you more freedom to make use of ingredients you actually have on hand. With seasonings, substitutions can also be made between herbs and some spices with similar flavor and texture. That's

Unappetizer
Some herbs, such as cilantro, bring a strong flavor that should be substituted with caution. It's probably fine to use basil in place of cilantro in a recipe, but not the other way around.

where some basic knowledge is important. Among the herbs, those that contribute a distinctive but not overpowering flavor—oregano, basil, rosemary, for example—can be experimented with freely.

Prep Tools for 5-Minute Appetizers

You will note that this list of prep tools is short and sweet, focusing only on cookware that enables a 5-minute dish by utilizing high heat. Some items (you probably already have them) are essential for the fast-moving cook. With these in your arsenal, you'll be in good shape:

♦ Baking tray

♦ Food processor (with the shred, slice, and standard purée blades)

♦ Microwave oven

♦ Skillet (10 inch)

♦ Wok (if you have a gas cook top)

As for the food processor, well, that's as close as we're going to get to an appetizer panacea. This remarkable device makes most of the recipes in Chapters 4 and 5 (dips and spreads) and many other recipes possible.

Serving Appetizers

Appetizers are different from most other foods in several ways. I've discussed seasoning and ingredients, but, of course, one of the most notable characteristics is portion size. Small, bite-size appetizers don't need a knife and fork, but other "tools" are a good idea:

♦ Cutting boards (which can double as serving trays) for cheeses, fruits, and other things that come under the knife

♦ Knives for serving, such as cheese knives (sharp) and rounded spreading knives

♦ Platters (varying sizes) for serving solid items

♦ Serving bowls for dips, spreads, and other dishes, as well as for grain platforms (crackers, chips, and so on)

♦ Skewers (wooden)

♦ Toothpicks

   Unless we're talking about a dinner party, your guests will most likely be standing. This means that consistency (its ability to hold its shape) is critical so what's being offered won't disintegrate between the serving tray and your guests' mouths. (Your hard-to-clean carpet will thank you, too.) I'll talk more of form in Chapter 21, where I dig deeper into the differences between appetizers for dinner parties and for bringing to a friend's house.

5-Minute Appetizer Cooking Methods

Of the many cooking methods, these work best with 5-minute appetizers. (You'll see these referenced throughout the book. No time for baking here!)

♦ Broiling

♦ Frying, stir-frying, and sautéing

♦ Grilling

♦ Microwave cooking

♦ No cooking at all—raw (puréeing, mashing, slicing, stacking, etc.)

> **Savoir Starter**
> A raw deal is a good deal! One of the greatest benefits of quick appetizers is that—how can I put this delicately—you don't have time to ruin things. This is the place for all those ingredients that shine when they aren't cooked at all. Think of fresh garden vegetables that sing with flavor and feelings of health, of creamy dips and spreads, or of a combination of the two.

The Least You Need to Know

♦ Careful selection of key ingredients will quickly set you on your way to delicious, quick hors d'oeuvres.

♦ Creative use of seasonings brings new and irresistible flavors without the addition of fat and calories.

♦ Several handy pieces of kitchen equipment (the food processor is at the top of the list) are well suited to speedy appetizers.

♦ Even in 5 minutes, there are methods of cooking that add sizzle to your starters, including grilling, wok cooking, and sautéing.

♦ A short time frame is the perfect opportunity to take advantage of fresh, raw ingredients such as vegetables and fruits, where natural flavors are allowed to shine.

Chapter 3

Say Cheese!

In This Chapter

- Cheese—a classic
- The timeless cheese board
- Pairing cheese with other flavors
- Taking advantage of texture

Long before human beings had the luxury of serving appetizers before a meal, cheese was a coveted part of man's diet in many parts of the world. Whether from the milk of a cow, a sheep, or a goat (or other creatures, although we won't spend much time on yak cheese here), cheese, like bread and wine, is something akin to magic. From one everyday ingredient—milk—comes something new, different, and exciting, the creamy, flavorful experience of cheese.

There are hundreds of varieties and textures, each representative of its region of origin. Cheese is a broad category of food that encompasses hundreds and hundreds of varieties—and as with other such foods, it offers a tremendous opportunity to explore and learn. There's a vast universe of cheese beyond that block of store-brand cheddar served with a plate of crackers.

In this chapter, we'll look at cheese from two general perspectives. The first is that of cheese boards, where the focus is, front and center, on high-quality cheeses. The second is on simple combinations of cheese and fruit, cheese and herbs, and other pairing delights in which the flavor of cheese, like a work of art, is highlighted by its frame (the accompanying food).

A Cheese Tray Is Definitely the Way

A cheese board is a casual, fun way to sample several different cheeses. A typical cheese board, or cheese tray, is a collection of three or four cheeses—more than that might put the palate on overload.

A cheese tray offers an opportunity to learn about cheeses by comparing their similarities and differences (while having fun). This "tasting" can be similar in many ways to a wine tasting, as formal or informal as you like, but always classy, with the added interest of a learning experience. A visit to a dedicated cheese shop or deli will offer a peek at the many varieties across the flavor and texture spectrum, from soft to hard, from mild to deeply flavorful.

One classic example of a cheese tray is a sampling of cheeses made from cow's, sheep's, and goat's milk. Another way to go is to select cheeses based on a theme.

A more formal alternative to the self-serve tray is to prepare a plate for each guest—each with an individual-size portion of each cheese. With this approach, guests actually sit at a table with a standard dinner table place setting around the plate.

Savoir Starter

Knowing where a cheese originates can be very helpful in deciding what to serve with it. A cheese from a particular part of France, for example, is likely to pair beautifully with a wine from that same area. In a way, both were grown from the same soil (only the cheese comes by way of the cow and the grass she grazes on).

Recently I served a cheese board with a "Vermont cheeses" theme, including Putney Tomme (cow's milk), Vermont "shepherd cheese" (sheep's milk), Aurora (cow's milk), and a sharp cheddar (cow's milk), all accompanied by pieces of warm, crusty wheat bread. After working their way around the four types several times, our guests remarked that although each individual cheese was tasty, together they provided not only a delicious variety but also a perspective on a particular cheese-producing region.

Short List of Cheese Board Favorites

I won't attempt to provide a comprehensive glossary of great cheeses in this space; rather, I'll relay some of my favorites and provide some serving suggestions. I'll also make an impassioned plea that you befriend the proprietor of your local cheese shop or the manager of a well-stocked cheese department at a good grocery store. These people can recommend some terrific cheeses based on their own stock or what they can obtain for you.

For our purposes here, I've divided these cheeses into two categories: mild and flavorful. I suggest that you include one or more from the mild list, both to balance the flavorful (stronger) ones and to accommodate guests who prefer mild flavors. The cheeses on the flavorful list are delicious and all "must-try"s, but they might take some getting used to. This does *not* imply that there is any similarity between any two of the cheeses on the flavorful list, but simply that they are distinctive in their own ways.

Mild cheeses:

- **Brie** (France, with some good U.S. versions): Creamy, with a soft, edible rind. Tasty with almost anything, from bread to fruit to nuts.
- **Cheddar** (originally United Kingdom, also United States): The ubiquitous hard cheese with a rich, buttery flavor ranges from mellow to sharp. Look for cheddars from England or from small producers in the United States for unique tastes that are very different from mass-market brands.
- **Cheshire** (England): A fruity, crumbly, cheese that is delicious with bread as well as with toasted almonds. Cheeses similar in taste and consistency and that might make for an entertaining tasting include Leicester and Double Gloucester.
- **Emmental** (Switzerland) Also Emmantaler, Emmantal, Emmenthaler: A nutty, rich, "Swiss" cheese.
- **Gouda** (the Netherlands or the United States): A mild cheese most popular (at least in my house) when it's "smoked" Gouda.
- **Gruyère** (Switzerland): A rich, sharp cow's milk cheese with a nutty flavor.
- **Fontina D'Aosta** (Italy): Buttery, nutty, and delicious.
- **Havarti** (United States and Denmark): A creamy mild cheese perhaps most enjoyed in its herbed versions (Havarti with dill).
- **Jarlsberg** (Norway): A famous cousin of "Swiss" cheese, also with holes but perhaps a riper flavor.
- **Port Salut** (France): Creamy, rich, and irresistible.
- **Provolone** (Italy): Not the kind from the deli! This is a rich-tasting, yet still mellow delight.

- **St. Andre** (France): Decadent and creamy, delicious with nuts. You don't want to know the butterfat content. (*Hint:* It's higher than 75 percent.)
- **Taleggio** (Italy): A creamy, nutty, rich cheese.

Hors D'oeuvre History

I once sampled a cheese tray focused exclusively on cheddar. Similar to a tasting of competing wines made from the same grape, this tray was a learning adventure. Cheddars from their birthplace (England), as well as Oregon, Wisconsin, and Vermont, aged and sharp, showed that even within a single cheese family, variety is a beautiful thing and that even an expansion on cheddar and crackers can offer education and interest.

Flavorful cheeses:

- **Cabrales** (Spain): A pungent, earthy blue cheese with a distinctive, knock-your-socks-off flavor. It makes a dream combination with slices of crisp apple or fresh pear.
- **Chevre, fresh** (France and United States): Creamy with a slight astringency characteristic of goat's milk, chevre is a creamy-salty soft cheese delicious by itself and dreamy paired with fruits or chutney. There are many varieties of chevre; for cheese aficionados, the varieties most often available in the States would likely be considered mild, but for those who have never tried it, it is a taste experience. Nor is all chevre created equal; artisan-produced cheeses are usually more expensive and sold in smaller quantities. These are often delicious by themselves. Other chevres produced in quantity are less expensive and often more appropriate for combining with fruit or herbs.
- **Feta** (Greece and United States): The white, crumbly, salty cheese of Greek salads, this cheese is also tasty on its own and pairs beautifully with Kalamata olives. Typically made from sheep's milk and brined.
- **Gorgonzola** (Italy): The "sweet" style is creamy and rich with that musty tang associated with all blue cheese.
- **Munster** (France): A rich, nutty cheese not to be confused with Muenster, the ever-so-mild stuff in American grocery stores.
- **Parmigiano-Reggiano** (Italy): A hard, dry, flavorful cheese.
- **Pecorino-Romano** (Italy): A hard sheep's milk cheese with a delightful salty-savory taste. Delicious.

- **Roquefort** (France): A world-famous (French) creamy but sharp sheep's milk cheese containing blue lines of mold, making it a "blue cheese."
- **St. Marcellin** (France): Unctuous, creamy with a slight hint of lemon. Delicious with toasted nuts or bread.
- **Stilton** (England): The famous English blue cheese. Delicious with toasted nuts and renowned for its pairing with port wine.
- **Tomme de Savoie** (France): Nutty, rich, and delicious with bread and toasted nuts.

Keep in mind that, as with every food, presentation is important, as is serving size. Allow about 4 ounces per person total. If you're serving four cheeses, that would mean an ounce of each cheese per person. So if you have 8 guests, that would mean 32 ounces, or 4 half-pound (8-ounce) pieces of cheese.

Cheese Board Ideas

I've included here some potential combinations. Feel free to assemble these cheese boards as described, but also feel free to "mix and match" with the advice of your local cheese shop personnel. You'll find that assembling a cheese board is not only entertaining and fun, but it's also a learning experience, precisely analogous to the pleasure many people take from a well-organized winetasting. (I've had people whip out a pen and start taking notes on what they like, and that's a great thing to see.)

Try a cheese board with one of the following themes:

- Cheeses from three or four different countries
- Cheeses from a particular region within a country
- Cheeses from cow's, goat's, and sheep's milk
- Several cheeses from the same animal but from different producers or even different countries
- Several cheeses of differing styles (young, soft, aged, hard, blue)
- Several cheeses of the same style (several types of blue cheese would be fascinating, although probably best served to real cheese lovers)

Don't Forget the Accoutrements

An accoutrement is an accompaniment, a trapping, a garnish in the food context, for example:

Savoir Starter _____
You won't go wrong with serving fresh, crusty bread with cheese. This is not the mass-market sliced stuff, but bakery bread, usually long loaves that you cut into thick, crusty slices or wedges.

- Dried fruits (dates and apricots pair nicely with many cheeses)
- Fresh orchard fruits (especially apples and pears)
- Fresh, crusty bread
- Olives
- Toasted nuts

And from the Beverage Department ...

I've found that wine is a natural accompaniment to many cheeses. In general, wines from the region in which a cheese is produced are likely to match well. Another rule of thumb I've found works well is to match "relative weight" (a lighter wine with a mild cheese, and so on). Try these:

- Soft, fresh cheese will be buried under flavors of a hearty red wine such as Cabernet Sauvignon, so instead serve with a white wine, such as a Riesling or Sauvignon Blanc.
- Blue (moldy) cheeses often pair well with sweet wines, such as Port, Madeira, or Sauternes.
- Firm, aged cheeses are likely to match well with those complex reds—Rhones, Bordeaux, Cabernet from California or Australia.
- Chevre, I think, goes best with either Sauvignon Blanc or a dry French-style unoaked Chardonnay.

However, if you have a small number of people tasting four different types of cheese, you'll be unlikely to have four different types of wine. In that case, strike a middle ground. With the focus on the cheese, just be sure your wine is not a monster that smothers cheesy subtleties.

Classic Cheese Trays

A traditional cheese tray contains cheeses made from cow's, goat's, and sheep's milk. Some other types of cheese trays follow; give them all a try.

Artisanal Cheese Board

Artisanal refers to a small producer, often a family business, where care and attention are lavished on the product, whether it be cheese, bread, or something else. These cheeses will often be a bit more expensive but are also almost certain to be more enjoyable than their less-expensive cousins in brand-name packaging. Each region has its own producers. This is an example of a cheese board from a New England cheese-lover's dream in suggested tasting order:

- Camembert Vermont (Blythedale Farms)
- Baby Gouda (Smith's Country Cheese, Massachusetts)
- Cheddar Classic Reserve Extra Sharp (Grafton Village Cheese Company, Vermont)
- Hubbardston Blue (goat's milk), (Westfield Farms, Massachusetts)

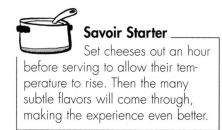

Savoir Starter

Set cheeses out an hour before serving to allow their temperature to rise. Then the many subtle flavors will come through, making the experience even better.

Serve these cheeses with fresh bread, and, for the blue, sliced apple or pear. For information on these cheeses, visit www.newenglandcheese.com.

French Sampler

France produces hundreds of different cheeses across the entire range of styles. This selection picks a few shining examples in suggested tasting order:

- Saint Andre
- St. Marcellin ("Fermier")
- Tomme de Savoie
- Roquefort (sheep's milk)

Fresh bread or plain wheat crackers will allow the flavors of these cheeses to shine through; perhaps supply a sliced pear for the Roquefort.

Savoir Starter _____
    Most cheeses go beautifully with crusty bread. It's an ultimate cheese vehicle. The combination of textures creates interest, and the mellowness of the bread allows you to focus on the unique cheese flavors. This is the same concept with crackers; they are all about adding texture without distraction from the main show. However, spiced crackers should be treated with caution unless you have a specific spice-cheese combination you want.

Italian Cheese Tray

Italy also has a centuries-old cheese-making tradition. These examples will give you a sense of the range, but again, work with your local cheese shop.

Savoir Starter _____
    "Serve with bread"—emphatically—does not mean off-the-shelf sliced white bread. Instead, select a baguette or other loaf that has a thick, chewy crust and the flavor of a home-baked loaf. Each piece of that crust is just perfect with a piece of cheese.

In suggested tasting order:

- Fontina D'Aosta
- Taleggio
- Pecorino Romano (sheep's milk)
- Gorgonzola

Toasted pine nuts, figs, and sliced pear for the Gorgonzola will make this a tasting to remember.

Mellow Yellow

Mild, creamy cheeses each with a slightly different flavor and texture.

In suggested tasting order:

- Brie (U.S. is fine)
- Double Gloucester (England)
- Port Salut (France)
- Vermont "shepherd cheese" (sheep milk)

Dried fruits and crusty bread will make this board complete.

Old World and New World

An opportunity to compare and contrast the unique (but still delicious) flavors of cheeses sourced from Italy and the United States.

In suggested tasting order:

♦ Aged Provolone (Italy)
♦ Parmigiano-Reggiano (Italy)
♦ Vintage white cheddar (Tillamook, United States)
♦ Cookeville Parmesan (Blythedale Farms, Vermont, United States)

Add crisp pear, bread, and toasted nuts.

European Union

A cross-section of delicious cheeses in different styles from four different European countries.

In suggested tasting order:

♦ Crottin de Chavignol (goat's milk, France)
♦ Cheshire (England)
♦ Gruyère (Switzerland)
♦ Cabrales (Spain)

Add toasted pine nuts (pecans or almonds will also be great), sliced pear, and crusty bread.

Matching Cheese with Other Ingredients

Testing your favorite cheeses with fruits, nuts, bread, and other ingredients will give you a whole new perspective on your old friends. How about Melted Brie with Crisp Apple Slices (see the recipe later in this chapter), chevre with apricot, or homemade herbed cheese (similar to Boursin)? These quick cheese-based hors d'oeuvres take advantage of the familiar rich, creamy texture of cheese but take enjoyment to new levels.

Many cheese vehicles not only carry the cheese but also marry it. This is the concept known as "pairing," where, at least in theory, two flavors go so well together that the sum is considered greater than the two parts. Here are some of my favorites (you'll find many others in this book).

Parmigiano and Roasted Piquillo Pepper Canapés

A fast appetizer with toasted bread (see Chapter 6 for more of this melody).

Serves 6, easily scaled for larger groups

1 baguette or long loaf of bread, sliced into ½-inch thick pieces

1 (12 oz.) jar roasted piquillo or red peppers, drained and cut into 1 by 2 inch pieces

6 oz. Parmigiano-Reggiano, cut into flat 1 by 2 by ¼-inch pieces

¼ cup chopped fresh chives for garnish (optional)

Unappetizer

The broiler is an invaluable tool for the cook in a hurry, but watch your food carefully. With bite-size servings, the difference between "extremely delicious" and "burnt to a crisp" can come within a matter of seconds.

Preheat the broiler. Place bread slices on a baking sheet and broil until lightly browned, about 1 minute on each side. Remove the baking sheet from the oven and top each piece of toast with a piece of red pepper and a piece of Parmigiano-Reggiano. Return the baking sheet to the broiler and heat for about 1 minute. Remove from the broiler and arrange toasts on a serving platter, topping with a sprinkling of chives (if using).

Melted Brie with Crisp Apple Slices

Decadent and delicious, the creamy texture of melted brie is set off perfectly by the tart crunch of the Granny Smith apple.

Serves 8

1 (16 oz.) wheel brie (available in cheese shops or in the cheese section of many grocery stores)

3 Granny Smith apples, cored and cut lengthwise into slices about ⅓-inch wide

Savoir Starter

If you need to set out the apple slices in advance (for longer than 15 minutes), browning can be prevented by rubbing the apple pieces with a piece of lemon. The acid in the lemon juice prevents the unappetizing oxidation (browning).

Unwrap brie and place it on a microwave-safe serving plate that has room for a ring of apple slices as well. Microwave on high for 2 minutes, remove, and test for softness. A knife should easily cut through the rind, and cheese should be slightly oozy. (With most foods, this is not a good quality, but with brie, oozy is heaven.) Surround brie with apple slices, and pass with a very sharp knife. To serve, cut a piece of cheese about ¼-inch thick, place it on a slice of apple, and enter the realm of taste bud delight.

Herbed Cheese Spread

This classic cheese spread is simple to make and tasty as a spread for appetizers or on sandwiches.

Serves 4 to 6

8 oz. cream cheese, softened

½ tsp. garlic salt

½ tsp. dried dill

1½ tsp. Italian seasoning

¼ tsp. freshly ground black pepper

Dash hot pepper sauce

Place cream cheese, garlic salt, dill, Italian seasoning, black pepper, and hot pepper sauce into a serving bowl and mix thoroughly. If possible, chill for several hours to allow the flavors to meld. Serve with crisp pita crackers or melba toasts.

Tip-of-the-Iceberg Seasonings

Some recipes are what I consider to be "tip-of-the-iceberg" recipes—you can see a small part, but you know there's a lot more below the surface. Herbed cheeses such as Boursin and cheese-plus-X combinations such as cheese plus chutney are representative of this type of recipe. I've chosen one or two popular combinations, but there are many others that will work. For your taste, they might even work better!

This is an at-a-glance list of seasonings that work with cream cheese. In a simplistic sense, you can pick a seasoning or two, mix, and have something that resembles a recipe. Keep in mind, though, that some herb and spice combinations are better than others, both with each other and with specific cheeses. Cream cheese is a natural candidate for mixing with herbs, but similarly mild cheeses, such as fresh chevre, can be delicious with herbs. Cheeses that bring their own strong flavor (think blue cheese) risk fighting with herb flavors and should be avoided.

- Basil
- Chili powder
- Chives
- Cilantro
- Coriander
- Cumin
- Dil
- Fennel
- Garlic
- Ginger
- Ground black pepper
- Ground red pepper
- Marjoram
- Onion
- Paprika
- Rosemary
- Tarragon
- Thyme

Savoir Starter

The combination of cheese and a sweet and/or spicy fruit mixture can be pure magic. Using fresh fruit is one method, as in the recipe for Melted Brie with Crisp Apple Slices. Another is to take advantage of the wealth of intensely flavored fruit mixtures such as chutney on the grocery shelf to serve as the counterpoint to your cheese. At a cocktail party years ago, I was introduced to a smoky aged Italian hard cheese, a bowl of sweet and spicy Major Grey's Chutney, and an assortment of wheat crackers. Each cracker, topped with cheese and chutney, was a flavor delight. Although homemade chutney can be made from a variety of fruits, for our 5-minute purposes here, I suggest buying one of the ready-made versions such as Major Grey's, which are available at most grocery stores.

Hard Cheese and Chutney

Serves 6 to 8

¾ lb. aged flavorful hard cheese, such as Asiago or sharp cheddar

1 (7- to 9-oz.) pkg. wheat crackers

1 (9-oz.) jar Major Grey's *Chutney*

Gourmet Glossary

Usually the consistency of relish, **chutney** is a combination of sweetened fruits and spices that originated on the Indian subcontinent. It is somewhat unusual in this country and is a delicious pair with many cheeses.

Arrange cheese and crackers on a cutting board with a sharp cheese knife, and pour chutney into a serving bowl. Prepare several crackers topped with cheese and then a scant spoonful chutney to get people used to the idea.

Variation: Try your favorite marmalade in place of chutney.

Olive and Cheese Ball

How can so much flavor fit into such a small package?

Serves 4 to 6

8 oz. cream cheese, softened

4 oz. crumbled blue cheese

1 cup pitted black olives

3 scallions, dark green leaves removed, chopped coarsely

1 TB. fresh lemon juice

¼ tsp. ground black pepper

Parsley to garnish

Place cream cheese, blue cheese, olives, scallions, lemon juice, and black pepper into a food processor and process until just coarsely blended. Scrape out cheese, and form into a ball; chill to set. Garnish with parsley, and serve with crisp wheat crackers and a sturdy spreading knife.

Savoir Starter

Throughout this book when I suggest lemon or lime juice, I'll always specify fresh. Although you can buy lemon and lime juice bottled, there's just no flavor comparison, and not much time saved. When it comes to appetizers, where flavor and quality is critical, that freshness is essential. Do a taste test, and you'll see what I mean.

Gruyère and Gherkins

This rich, flavorful cheese pairs well with the small, slightly sweet "cocktail pickles," creating a quick appetizer that mimics that flavor of a *raclette*.

Serves 6 to 8

1 baguette or long loaf of bread, sliced into ½-inch thick pieces

3 TB. Dijon-style mustard

1 cup gherkins, sliced in half lengthwise

8 oz. Gruyère cheese, sliced into ¼-inch-thick pieces

2 TB. fresh chives, finely chopped

Preheat the broiler. Place bread on a baking sheet and broil until lightly browned, about 1 minute on each side. Remove the baking sheet from the oven, and spread about ½ teaspoon mustard on each piece of toast. Place a half gherkin on each piece, cover with a piece of sliced Gruyère, and broil for an additional minute or until cheese begins to melt. Arrange on a serving tray. Sprinkle a pinch of chives on each and serve.

Variation: Replace gherkins with sliced pickled sweet onions.

Gourmet Glossary _____

Raclette is a famous cheese-intensive Swiss and French dish using the cheese of the same name (a richly flavored relative of Swiss cheese). A hunk of cheese is heated by holding it near a fire or placing it into a special flame-heated container. As the heat softens the cheese, it is scraped off and served with potatoes, pickles, tiny onions, and crusty dark bread. Talk about comfort food! I first tried this on a summer trip through Switzerland and afterward felt like I didn't need to eat for a week.

As with the other "tip-of-the-iceberg" foods in this book, treat these suggestions as starting points and create your own set of flavor delights.

The Least You Need to Know

♦ Cheeses are made across the world and in huge variety. France alone produces hundreds of different cheeses.

♦ There are high-quality cheeses to please every palate—from mild, soft Port Salut to pungent, earthy Cabrales.

♦ A cheese board is not only a fast, elegant hors d'oeuvre, but is also an opportunity to explore the styles of cheese from different countries and different production methods. It's an opportunity for creativity!

♦ Many cheeses pair beautifully with other ingredients such as fresh fruits, nuts, and crusty bread. These ingredients are critical components in winning appetizers featuring cheese.

♦ Cheese and wine are often a terrific combination, particularly if the wine is of a similar character or from the same region as the cheese.

Chapter 4

Your Friend Is a Dip!

In This Chapter

- Varying textures and flavors to make dips that satisfy your senses
- Food processor magic
- Favorite recipes—from classics to new twists
- Vehicles and passengers
- Fabulous flavor sources

Dips and spreads exist on a continuum. Dips are, for the purposes of this book, a creamy flavorful appetizer component that varies from almost fluid to almost solid but are always soft enough to be scooped with something edible—the other component that makes the appetizer complete. If something is too thick to be scooped, I call it a spread, more appropriate for use with a knife (see Chapter 5).

The Usual Dippy Suspects

The base ingredient has everything to do with the consistency and "mouthfeel" of a dip; cream cheese and sour cream have that rich, creamy feeling as opposed to a dip based on yogurt or ricotta cheese, which tends to feel rather light. Mayonnaise is another dip base that gives a light, creamy consistency.

Beans are yet another base ingredient for dips, and they offer a low-fat alternative to dairy- and mayonnaise-based dips.

Keep in mind that often a combination of ingredients can achieve the right texture.

Here are some of the usual suspects:

♦ Beans, such as chickpeas, kidney beans, or white beans

♦ Cottage cheese, light or nonfat

♦ Cream cheese or light cream cheese

♦ Mayonnaise

♦ Mozzarella, fresh

♦ Ricotta, part skim

♦ Sour cream or light sour cream

♦ Yogurt, plain (nonfat)

> **Hors D'oeuvre History**
>
> Mayonnaise is an emulsion of vegetable oils, egg yolks, and vinegar. A basic in French cooking and an important element of many Western cuisines, its high fat content makes its consistency and taste very attractive to us fat-loving humans. Mayo is a delicious dip base. Because of the fat content, however, I try to minimize how much I recommend in these recipes.

Warm Dips

Warm dips, just for starters, are the epitome of comfort food and are always a hit at parties, especially if it's mid-winter in New England.

Warm Crab Dip with Scallions, Ricotta, and Cheddar

Serves 6

1 (6-oz.) can flaked crabmeat

1 cup part-skim ricotta cheese

¼ cup shredded cheddar cheese

¼ cup mayonnaise

1 scallion, dark green leaves removed, sliced into ½-inch pieces

> **Savoir Starter**
>
> When a recipe calls for softened cream cheese, I've found that about 25 seconds in the microwave does the trick. Alternatively, use "whipped" cream cheese, which is ready to use as is.

In a food processor fitted with a metal blade, process crabmeat, ricotta cheese, cheddar cheese, mayonnaise, and scallion until smooth. Scrape dip into a microwave-safe serving bowl, and microwave on high for 90 seconds or until dip just begins to bubble. Stir and serve with pita or tortilla chips.

Warm Cheddar-Bacon Dip

Health food this isn't, but for comfort, it's off the scale.

Serves 4 to 6

4 slices bacon, or 1 (3-oz.) jar real bacon bits

8 oz. shredded mild cheddar cheese

1 cup cream cheese or light cream cheese, softened

¼ cup *Madeira*

3 scallions, sliced into ¼-inch pieces (about ⅓ cup)

Cook bacon in a 10-inch skillet over medium heat; remove when crispy, drain on paper towels, and crumble into small pieces. (Or as an alternative, use bacon bits.)

While bacon is cooking, combine cheddar cheese, cream cheese, and Madeira in a microwave-safe serving dish. Microwave on high for 90 seconds or until bubbly (cooking time will vary according to microwave power). Stir in bacon pieces, top with scallions, and serve with thin slices of baguette or other crusty bread.

Gourmet Glossary
Madeira is a fortified wine, similar to port and sherry, with sweet flavors of caramel, nuts, and honey.

Be sure to serve warm dips, well, *warm*. You can do this by preparing and serving them for immediate consumption using a heat source such as an electric hot pad/tray or a heatproof container suspended over special candles or "canned" heat such as Sterno. You can even gather your guests around a stovetop if your kitchen is conducive to such an arrangement. Some warm appetizers include normally solid ingredients such as cheddar cheese, for example, that solidify as they cool, meaning that before long the "dip" will require a knife and fork.

Just Add Seasoning

Herbs and spices often form the backbone of flavor in dips. But other dips draw their flavor from naturally tasty main ingredients such as sun-dried tomatoes.

Chickpea and Sun-Dried Tomato Dip

A close cousin of hummus, this rich, savory dip is tasty and unusual. You can use the oil from the sun-dried tomatoes as a nice replacement for an equal amount of the olive oil, provided you are satisfied it is the kind of oil you like to eat.

Serves 6

1 (15½-oz.) can chickpeas, drained

⅔ cup sun-dried tomatoes (oil-packed), oil reserved

½ cup olive oil (or oil from sun-dried tomatoes, if desired)

Juice of ½ lime

Savoir Starter
Chickpeas (also known as garbanzo beans), the base ingredient in the Middle Eastern dip hummus, are high in fiber and low in fat, making them both a delicious and healthy component of many appetizers.

In a food processor fitted with a metal blade, process chickpeas and sun-dried tomatoes until smooth. While the machine is running, slowly add oil and process until the mixture reaches a creamy consistency. Scrape the dip into a serving bowl, stir in lime juice, blend thoroughly, and serve with pita bread.

Variation: Add ½ to 1 cup nonfat plain yogurt for a creamier, slightly milder dip.

Spinach-Parmesan Dip

You will remember the dramatic green color of this dish. Although a close relative of the earlier Chicken-Parmesan Dip, the taste is all its own.

Serves 6 to 8

1 (10-oz.) pkg. frozen chopped spinach, thawed and drained

1 cup sour cream or light sour cream

½ cup mayonnaise

1 cup shredded Parmesan cheese

½ tsp. garlic salt

Dash hot pepper sauce (such as Tabasco)

Tortilla chips for serving

Combine spinach, sour cream, mayonnaise, Parmesan cheese, garlic salt, and hot pepper sauce in a serving bowl and mix thoroughly. Serve with tortilla chips.

Chicken-Parmesan Dip

This creamy and satisfying dip raises the question: Is it a dip, or is it a meal? I like using shredded Parmesan cheese for the texture, but grated cheese can also be used.

Serves 6 to 8

1 (12½-oz.) can chunk white chicken meat, broken up in the bowl with a spoon

1 cup sour cream or light sour cream

½ cup mayonnaise

1 cup shredded Parmesan cheese

½ tsp. garlic salt

½ tsp. ground black pepper

Dash hot pepper sauce (such as Tabasco)

Chopped scallion pieces for garnish (optional)

Tortilla chips for serving

Combine chicken, sour cream, mayonnaise, Parmesan cheese, garlic salt, black pepper, and hot pepper sauce in a serving bowl and mix thoroughly. Top with scallion pieces (if using), and serve with tortilla chips.

Out-of-the-Box Spinach Dip

As you can see, variation is the name of the game with dips. Even on the spinach theme, there are several options. This classic, even though it's out of the box, is worth knowing because it's so quick (although it does need fridge time for the flavors to *meld*).

Serves 6 to 8

1 (10-oz.) pkg. frozen chopped spinach, thawed and drained

1 cup sour cream or light sour cream

½ cup cottage cheese or light cottage cheese

½ cup mayonnaise

1 pkg. dry vegetable soup mix

Tortilla chips for serving

Combine spinach, sour cream, cottage cheese, mayonnaise, and soup mix in a serving bowl and mix thoroughly. Chill for several hours, and serve with tortilla chips.

> **Gourmet Glossary**
>
> **Meld** (a combination of *melt* and *weld*-no kidding) is the term many cooks use to describe how flavors blend over time. Dips (and spreads) are prime examples of this process. Taste a dip immediately after making it and then after it's been in the fridge several hours, and you'll see what I mean.

Chive Dip

Although this dip takes only a few minutes to make, if possible, give it several hours in the fridge to allow the flavors to meld.

Serves 6 to 8

1 cup sour cream or light sour cream

⅔ cup plus 2 TB. finely chopped fresh chives

½ cup mayonnaise

½ cup (4 oz.) cream cheese or light cream cheese, softened

¼ cup finely chopped sweet red onion (such as Vidalia)

½ tsp. garlic salt

Tortilla or ridged potato chips for serving

Combine sour cream, ⅔ cup chives, mayonnaise, cream cheese, onion, and garlic salt in a serving bowl and mix thoroughly. Top with remaining 2 tablespoons chives, and serve with tortillas or ridged potato chips.

Savoir Starter _____

You can use low-fat alternatives for cottage cheese, cream cheese, and sour cream in these recipes. With mayo, however, substitute with caution, as lower-fat mayonnaise has a very different flavor than its high-octane cousin.

Bagna Cauda

From the Italian for "hot bath," this classic is at the saucy end of the dip spectrum but at the bold end for taste. It requires quick cooking to bring the flavors together.

Serves 4 to 6

⅔ cup olive oil

⅓ cup cream cheese or light cream cheese, softened

5 tsp. chopped garlic

6 anchovies

Pieces of crusty bread and vegetables such as jicama, baby carrots, and celery sticks for dipping

In a food processor fitted with a metal blade, process olive oil, cream cheese, garlic, and anchovies until smooth. Pour into a small saucepan (6 inches if you have one that small) and heat over medium-high heat for 3 minutes, stirring constantly.

Place the saucepan into the serving area on a trivet or heatproof surface, and serve with pieces of crusty bread and vegetables for dipping.

Creamy Blue Dip

Blue cheese dip is a hearty and flavorful guest favorite.

Serves 6 to 8

1 cup sour cream or light sour cream

⅔ cup crumbled blue cheese

½ cup (4 oz.) cream cheese or light cream cheese, softened

¼ cup mayonnaise

2 TB. chopped walnuts for garnish (optional)

3 pears or apples, sliced, or 4 Belgian endive heads, separated, for serving

Combine sour cream, blue cheese, cream cheese, and mayonnaise in a serving bowl and mix thoroughly. Top with walnuts (if using). Serve with fresh pear or apple slices for a flavor and consistency taste treat, or serve with Belgian endive leaves.

As with other recipes that include fresh-cut orchard fruit, a quick rub with a cut lemon will keep pear and apple slices fresh if they are to be set out more than a few minutes in advance.

Dill-Tarragon Dip

Intense herb flavors make this a terrific dip.

Serves 4 to 6

1 cup sour cream or light sour cream

1 cup (8 oz.) cream cheese or light cream cheese, softened

3 scallions, dark green leaves removed, finely chopped

2 tsp. dried dill weed

½ tsp. dried tarragon

½ tsp. garlic salt

Additional chopped scallion pieces for garnish (optional)

Cucumber slices for serving

Combine sour cream, cream cheese, scallions, dill, tarragon, and garlic salt in a serving bowl and mix thoroughly. Refrigerate, if possible, for an hour or more. Stir after dip has chilled, garnish with scallion pieces (if using), and serve with cucumber slices for a match made in heaven—or rather, a match made in the garden.

The Dip Is a Passenger—but What Is the Vehicle?

In a simple sense, appetizers such as dips and spreads are all about passengers and *vehicles*. The passenger is the focus of your attention (the dip), and the vehicle is the means by which you get that passenger to your mouth. Vehicles should be chosen carefully to either complement the dip (crisp, salty chips with creamy dip) or to serve primarily as transportation. Corollary unappetizer: Competition between one and the other is to be avoided. (Picture chili-spiced tortillas with a curry dip. Ugh!)

The more fluid the dip, the lighter the "dipper" you should use to pick it up—think of a potato chip for a yogurt-based dip as opposed to a sturdy bread stick or carrot stick with a thicker, cream cheese–based dip.

Big dippers are as follows:

- Belgian endive leaves
- Breadsticks
- Potato chips
- Slices of baguette or other crusty bread
- Tortilla chips and chips made from other types of bread such as pita or even bagel "chips"
- Vegetables such as broccoli, carrots, celery, cauliflower, radishes, green beans, *blanched* asparagus, and many others
- Wedges of pita bread or store-bought pita crisps

> **Gourmet Glossary**
>
> A **vehicle** (in tongue-in-cheek use in this book!) is a food that is used to scoop or dip another ingredient such as vegetables or pitas with dip.

> **Unappetizer**
>
> You might, like me, have chastised your children about "double dipping"—dipping a chip in dip, biting off part of the chip, then reinserting that same chip back in, with all the cold-germ-spreading implications. Prevent the double-dipping syndrome by serving your dip with small dippers that don't encourage a second trip.

> **Gourmet Glossary**
>
> **Blanching** is a culinary technique in which you plunge vegetables such as asparagus, broccoli, or green beans into a pot of boiling water for 30 to 60 seconds and then into a bowl of ice water for about 30 seconds. Use a slotted spoon to transfer the vegetables directly from one to the other. The boiling water cooks them just enough so they are slightly tender but still pleasantly crisp. It also renders them a brilliant green color. The cold water stops the cooking process and sets that beautiful color.

When serving dips with crisp dippers such as chips and crisps, avoid the temptation to artfully arrange them in the dip for guests to take. In just a few minutes, those pita crisps will become pita *sogs*. Serve dip in a bowl on a platter surrounded by your dippers or with the dippers alongside in a cloth-lined basket.

Warm Romano-Bacon Dip with Pita Crisps

Serves 6 to 8

1 cup (8 oz.) sour cream or light sour cream

1 cup (8 oz.) part-skim ricotta cheese

½ cup grated Pecorino-Romano cheese

½ cup grated Parmesan cheese

2 scallions, dark green leaves removed, finely chopped

3 TB. real bacon bits, 1 TB. reserved for garnish

1 (6-oz.) pkg. pita crisps

Combine sour cream, ricotta cheese, Pecorino-Romano cheese, Parmesan cheese, scallions, and all but 1 tablespoon bacon bits in a serving bowl and mix thoroughly. Heat for a minute in the microwave, and top with remaining bacon bits. Serve with a basket of pita crisps, and watch it disappear.

Warm Crab-Parmesan Dip

This will be the favorite of those people who claim not to like seafood. (*Evil idea:* Serve it first; tell them what it is later.) Light cream cheese may be substituted for the mayo.

Serves 6

2 (6-oz.) cans flaked crabmeat

2 cups shredded mild cheddar cheese

1 cup mayonnaise

1 tsp. garlic salt

¼ tsp. hot pepper sauce (such as Tabasco) (optional)

Crisp wheat crackers or breadsticks for serving

Combine crabmeat, cheddar cheese, and mayonnaise in a microwave-safe serving bowl, and heat on high for 90 seconds or until it just begins to bubble. Stir in garlic salt and hot pepper sauce (if using), and serve with crisp wheat crackers or breadsticks.

Onion Dip

A twist on the traditional onion dip, this recipe includes Parmesan cheese and the green of scallion and chives for color and texture. The flavor secret: Give this dip time in the fridge for the flavors to meld.

Serves 6 to 8

1 cup (8 oz.) cream cheese or light cream cheese, softened

¾ cup sour cream or light sour cream

¼ cup mayonnaise

2 TB. minced sweet onion (such as Vidalia)

2 TB. grated Parmesan cheese

3 scallions, dark green leaves removed, finely chopped

¼ tsp. garlic salt

Additional scallion slices for garnish (optional)

Ridged potato chips for serving

Combine cream cheese, sour cream, mayonnaise, onion, Parmesan cheese, scallions, and garlic salt in a serving bowl and mix thoroughly. Refrigerate for several hours. Garnish with scallion slices (if using), and serve with (what else?) ridged potato chips.

The Least You Need to Know

- From Onion Dip to Bagna Cauda, dips are a perennial favorite for parties.
- The use of base ingredients, including dairy products such as sour cream and cream cheese, mayonnaise, beans, and oils, controls the texture and consistency of dips.
- Low-fat alternatives are possible for the base ingredients of most dips.
- Dips can be served at temperatures ranging from warm to cold, creating multiple opportunities to tantalize the taste buds.
- The flavor of a dip comes from both its seasonings (herbs and spices) and its flavorful main ingredients (such as sun-dried tomatoes).
- Dips present an opportunity to evoke a wide range of ethnic sources.

Chapter 5

Spread It Around

In This Chapter

- Key ingredients
- Let herbs do the work
- Add a touch of class
- Spread it on thick

On the continuum of formality, spreads are perhaps a bit higher than dips. With dips, you use your fingers and stick food right into the bowl. Spreads are served with a spreading knife, and often guests will hold a serving plate with several hors d'oeuvres. The overall effect is to set the tone just a bit higher but still have fun.

As with dips, spreads usually gain their texture and consistency from their base ingredients. There are also other ways to obtain that thick, rich texture while bringing in flavor. Read on …

Spread the Bases

Base ingredients for spreads are thicker and used in different proportions than those used for dips; they include goat's milk cheese, cream cheese, or light cream cheese, mayonnaise, ricotta (part skim), sour cream, or light sour cream. These starter recipes will show you just how easy, fast, and delicious spreads can be.

Chutney and Cream Cheese Spread

Although there are plenty of recipes that make this dish more complicated, the essence is right here to enjoy. Make this in about a minute and watch it disappear. Pretend it took you hours to cut the mangoes, distil the vinegar, and combine the spices for the chutney.

Serves 6, easily doubled

1 cup (8 oz.) cream cheese or light cream cheese, softened

1 (9-oz.) jar Major Grey's Chutney, half for mixing, half for topping

Sliced brown bread for serving

Sliced apples

Combine cream cheese and half chutney in a serving bowl and mix thoroughly. Spread remaining chutney on top of cream cheese. Serve with slices of brown bread or crunchy apple slices (cut them just before serving, or rub with lemon juice to prevent browning). Use the spreading knife to scoop up some chutney and cheese-chutney mixture each time.

Variation: Mix 1 teaspoon aged balsamic vinegar into the spread for added zing.

Unappetizer

As with all appetizers, the flavor of your vehicles (crackers, chips, and so on) is just as important as the seasoning in your passenger (the spread). Highly seasoned chips or crackers will affect the overall taste. I know it's obvious, but consider for a minute serving this chutney and cream cheese (with its sweet taste) with garlic crackers.

Cream Cheese and Chive Spread

Simple is good. Fresh chives taste better and are less expensive, but dried will work.

Serves 6 to 8

1 bunch fresh chives, finely chopped, or 1 (.25-oz.) jar dried chives

2 cups (16 oz.) cream cheese or light cream cheese, softened

Assorted fresh vegetables cut into finger-food size or assorted baby vegetables for serving

Crisp wheat crackers for serving

If you are using fresh chives, set aside 1 tablespoon for garnish. Combine cream cheese and remaining chives in a serving bowl and mix thoroughly. Sprinkle reserved chives on top as a garnish if using. Although this spread will taste good immediately, an hour or more in the fridge will make it taste even better. Serve with an assortment of fresh vegetables or crisp wheat crackers.

Hors D'oeuvre History

Because of the thick consistency of spreads, a spreading knife is a necessary tool for serving most of the recipes in this chapter. A spreading knife is typically short, with a broad, blunt blade. Regular table knives you use for spreading butter on bread are also fine, but sharp knives such as steak or paring knives are less useful.

Warm Dijon-Ham Spread

If you have leftover ham, there is no better destination for it than this spread. If you don't have leftovers, head for the deli for the honey ham.

Serves 6 to 8

½ lb. sliced honey ham

8 oz. mild cheddar cheese, shredded

¼ cup Dijon-style mustard

Wheat crackers for serving

In a food processor fitted with a metal blade, process ham and cheddar cheese until ham is reduced to small pieces. Scrape the mixture into a microwave-safe serving bowl, and heat on high power for 1 minute or until cheese begins to bubble. Remove from microwave, stir in mustard, and serve with wheat crackers. Sighs of appreciation will follow.

Apple and German Sausage Spread

When people rave about the beauty of pairing certain foods, they're talking about matches like apples and German sausage.

Serves 6 to 8

½ lb. cooked German sausage such as bratwurst, cut into ½-inch sections

½ cup shredded Swiss cheese

1 crisp Granny Smith apple, cored and cut into slices

2 tsp. prepared mustard

1 tsp. fresh lemon juice

Dash hot pepper sauce

Salt and black pepper to taste

Belgian endive leaves or *toast points* for serving

In a food processor fitted with a metal blade, process sausage, Swiss cheese, apples, mustard, lemon juice, hot pepper sauce, salt, and pepper until almost smooth. Scrape into a microwave-safe serving bowl, heat for 2 minutes, stir, and serve with Belgian endive leaves or toast points.

Gourmet Glossary

Toast points are quick and easy to make. They are, quite simply, pieces of bread with the crusts removed and toasted for about a minute on each side. They are then cut on the diagonal from each corner, resulting in four triangle-shape pieces—an elegant platform.

Pea and Mint Spread

The brilliant green of this spread and the surprisingly refreshing taste will have people asking you for the recipe.

Serves 4 to 6

½ lb. peas

3 TB. fresh mint leaves, chopped

2 TB. fresh lemon juice

¼ tsp. salt

Dash hot pepper sauce (such as Tabasco)

1 cup (8 oz.) cream cheese or light cream cheese, softened

Toast points for serving

Gourmet Glossary

A **dash** refers to a few drops, the amount (usually of a liquid) that is released by a quick shake of, for example, a bottle of hot sauce.

In a food processor fitted with a metal blade, process peas, mint, lemon juice, salt, and hot pepper sauce until completely mixed. Scrape pea mixture into a serving bowl, add softened cream cheese, and mix thoroughly. Serve with toast points.

Whole-Grain Mustard Spread

Another this-is-too-simple-to-be-this-good spread. I won't tell.

Serves 4 to 6

1 cup (8 oz.) cream cheese or light cream cheese, softened

½ cup (4 oz.) whole-grain mustard

1 TB. olive oil

1 TB. chopped fresh chives for garnish (optional)

½ lb. thinly sliced ham, each piece rolled into a cylinder, for serving

Melba toast for serving

Combine cream cheese, mustard, and olive oil in a serving bowl and mix thoroughly. Scatter chives over the top (if using), and serve with rolled pieces of ham and/or melba toast.

> **Gourmet Glossary** _____
> **Melba toasts** are small pieces of crisp bread available in the cracker section of the grocery store. In a pinch, they can serve as the platform for bruschetta or canapés. Avoid the seasoned versions, though, to keep the focus on *your* ingredients.

Blue Cheese and Chopped Pecan Spread

This is comfort food in a spread.

Serves 4 to 6

1 cup (8 oz.) cream cheese or light cream cheese, softened

1 cup (4 to 6 oz.) crumbled blue cheese

⅔ cup plus ⅓ cup chopped pecans

Belgian endive leaves for serving

Sliced pears for serving

Wheat crackers for serving

Combine cream cheese, blue cheese, and ⅔ cup pecans in a serving bowl and mix thoroughly. Top with remaining ⅓ cup pecans, and serve surrounded by a combination of Belgian endive leaves, pear slices (rub with lemon juice if setting out in advance), and/or wheat crackers.

Greek Islands Feta and Herb Spread

Have a bite of crusty bread with this savory herb spread, lean back, and imagine a sunset over the Aegean.

Serves 6

1½ cups (6 oz.) crumbled feta cheese

⅔ cup (8 oz.) plain yogurt

2 TB. olive oil

2 tsp. fresh lime juice

½ tsp. chopped fresh rosemary

1 tsp. Italian seasoning

¼ tsp. garlic salt

Sprig parsley or fresh rosemary as garnish (optional)

Carrots, cut into 2½-inch pieces and sliced lengthwise for serving

Hunks of crusty bread for serving

Combine feta cheese, yogurt, olive oil, lime juice, rosemary, Italian seasoning, and garlic salt in a serving bowl and mix thoroughly. Chill for several hours to allow herb flavors to meld, and top with parsley or rosemary sprig (if using) for garnish.

To serve, I've found this spread to be delicious with fresh carrots, peeled, cut into pieces about 2½ inches long, and sliced lengthwise. Put the spread on the flat side. It also works with hunks of fresh crusty bread.

There's no extra charge for the sunset.

Unappetizer

Vehicles for spreads should be strong enough to stand up to the pressure of a knife pressing down on them with a thick substance. Good candidates are toasts, thick crackers, fruits, and vegetables. Thin crackers and chips might turn into crumbs!

Ginger-Lemon Goat's Milk Cheese

Here's a delicate, elegant spread for your summer cocktail party out under your spreading oak.

Serves 6

1 (8-oz.) pkg. fresh goat's milk cheese, softened

2 TB. extra-virgin olive oil

2 tsp. fresh lemon juice

1 tsp. peeled, chopped fresh ginger

¼ cup chopped walnuts

¼ cup raisins or other chopped dried fruit such as cranberries

Belgian endive leaves for serving

Wheat crackers for serving

Combine goat's milk cheese, olive oil, lemon juice, and ginger in a serving bowl and mix thoroughly. If possible, refrigerate for an hour or two or even all day. To serve, top with chopped walnuts in a single layer, followed by raisins, and serve surrounded with Belgian endive leaves or wheat crackers.

Goat's Milk Cheese with Black Olives

The black of the olives and the white of the cheese make for an appealing color contrast, followed by an appealing set of flavors.

Serves 6

1 (8 oz.) pkg. fresh goat's milk cheese, softened

½ cup plus 3 TB. sliced black olives

2 TB. extra-virgin olive oil

1 tsp. fresh lemon juice

Pinch ground black pepper

Slices of crusty bread for serving

Combine goat's milk cheese, ½ cup olives, olive oil, lemon juice, and black pepper in a serving bowl and mix thoroughly. To serve, top with remaining 3 tablespoons olives and surround with pieces of crusty bread.

Gourmet Glossary _____

A **pinch** is yet another of those highly unscientific cooking terms that refers to the amount of a substance (typically a dry, granular substance such as an herb or seasoning) that can be held between finger and thumb. (I guess it follows that the bigger the person's fingers, the bigger the pinch …)

Red Caviar Spread

This delicious spread was inspired by the Caviar Dip created by Julee Rosso and Sheila Lukins for *The Silver Palate Cookbook* (a classic, by the way). This dip makes use of the less-expensive but still delicious red caviar.

Serves 6

1 cup (8 oz.) cream cheese, softened

½ cup sour cream

2 TB. finely chopped fresh dill or 2 tsp. dried dill

Pinch black pepper

1 scallion, dark green parts removed, finely minced

1 TB. fresh lemon juice

2 oz. red caviar

White or wheat toast points for serving

Combine cream cheese and sour cream in a serving bowl and mix thoroughly. Mix in dill, black pepper, scallion, and lemon juice. Finally, *carefully* mix in caviar, trying not to break the delicate eggs. Serve with white or wheat toast points. This spread can be refrigerated for several hours.

Savoir Starter

One of the many reasons people love caviar is the multitude of tiny, distinct bubbles (the eggs). The reason a caviar recipe uses terms like *carefully* is to avoid, as much as possible, bursting those little bubbles.

Some recipes, like Red Caviar Spread, are perfect celebratory foods and a bit of a splurge. If you're buying caviar, I suggest doing it justice by also using fresh herbs (rather than dried). If you need an excuse to use full-fat versions of sour cream and cream cheese as well, this is the place!

Ricotta and Roasted Red Pepper Spread

This is a lighter-tasting spread because of the ricotta base.

Serves 4 (easily doubled)

1 cup (8 oz.) part-skim ricotta cheese

½ cup roasted red peppers, cut into 1-inch pieces

¼ tsp. garlic salt

Dash hot sauce (such as Tabasco)

1 TB. chopped fresh chives for garnish (optional)

Pita crisps for serving

In a food processor fitted with a metal blade, process ricotta, red peppers, garlic salt, and hot sauce until almost smooth—a bit of texture is good. Scrape spread into a serving bowl, sprinkle chives on top (if using), and serve with pita crisps.

Mushroom "Pâté"

This quick version preserves much of that irresistible *pâté* texture and flavor.

Serves 6

1 (13½-oz.) can mushroom stems and pieces, drained

½ cup plain breadcrumbs

¼ cup mayonnaise

2 scallions, dark green parts removed, cut into ½-inch pieces

1 TB. fresh lemon juice

1 tsp. Worcestershire sauce

¼ tsp. hot pepper sauce (such as Tabasco)

Toast triangles for serving

In a food processor fitted with a metal blade, process mushrooms, breadcrumbs, mayonnaise, scallions, lemon juice, Worcestershire sauce, and hot pepper sauce until smooth. Scrape mixture into a serving bowl and chill. Serve with toast triangles.

Gourmet Glossary

Pâté is a savory loaf containing meats, fish or vegetables, spices, and often a lot of fat. It's served cold.

Roasted Pepper Salmon Spread

Here is just one example of a spread with seafood. If this floats your boat, look for more on this theme in Chapters 7 and 8.

Serves 4 to 6

1 can (6 oz.) boneless, skinless canned salmon, or cooked fresh salmon, bones removed

½ cup (4 oz.) cream cheese or light cream cheese, softened

½ cup roasted red pepper pieces

2 TB. margarine

2 tsp. fresh lemon juice

1 tsp. capers, drained

Dash hot pepper sauce (such as Tabasco)

1 thin slice of lemon for garnish (optional)

Several additional capers for garnish (optional)

Toast points or wheat crackers for serving

Savoir Starter
This Roasted Pepper Salmon Spread recipe can use canned salmon or leftover salmon (one benefit of cooking extra).

In a food processor fitted with a metal blade, process salmon, cream cheese, red pepper, margarine, lemon juice, capers, and hot pepper sauce until almost smooth. Scrape spread into a serving bowl, place lemon slice in the center (if using), and scatter a few capers over the top (if using). Serve with toast points or plain wheat crackers.

Swiss Cheese and Cherry Spread

This fun spread will start conversations at any party.

Serves 6 to 8

1 (8-oz.) can tart, pitted cherries (not Maraschino), drained (1 cherry reserved for garnish)

1 (8-oz.) pkg. shredded Swiss cheese

1 cup (8 oz.) cream cheese or light cream cheese, softened

1 tsp. prepared horseradish

Wheat crackers for serving

In a food processor fitted with a metal blade, process cherries for 10 seconds or until they are reduced to pieces.

In a serving bowl, combine Swiss cheese, cream cheese, cherry pieces, and horseradish and mix thoroughly. Place reserved cherry in the center. Serve with plain wheat crackers.

Variation: Combine only Swiss cheese, cream cheese, and horseradish, and serve in two bowls—one with the spread, one with cherries. Guests take a cracker, spread on cheese mixture, top it with cherries, and enjoy.

Derek's Curry Ball

I have received rave reviews for this recipe, which I adapted from my book *The Complete Idiot's Guide to 20-Minute Meals*. It's an unusual, flavorful appetizer that benefits from being made ahead. It can be eaten right away if it just looks too good or if you don't have the time to wait!

Serves 4 to 6

1 cup (8-oz.) cream cheese or light cream cheese, softened

2 TB. sour cream

2 tsp. curry powder

½ cup chopped scallions

½ cup coarsely chopped dried peanuts

½ cup raisins (optional)

Dried or flaked coconut

1 cup chutney such as Major Grey's Mango

Wheat crackers for serving

Combine cream cheese and sour cream in a mixing bowl and mix thoroughly. Blend in curry powder. Add chopped scallions, peanuts, and raisins (if using). Mix thoroughly, form into a ball, and chill.

To serve, roll ball in coconut and pour chutney over the top. Serve with wheat crackers.

The Least You Need to Know

- The texture and consistency of spreads, like dips, is largely dependent on base ingredients, which can include cream cheese, goat's milk cheese, ricotta cheese, and mayonnaise. Spreads also rely on other solid ingredients for their texture.

- As with dips, low-fat alternatives are possible for most base ingredients.

- Flavors in spreads come from herbs and spices as well as flavorful main ingredients such as cheeses, vegetables, seafood, and even fruits.

- The vehicles for spreads (toasts, crackers, vegetables, and so on) should be sturdy enough to stand up to the pressure of spreading a thick substance.

Chapter 6

The Spread on Bread

In This Chapter

- ◆ Bread recipes from the Old Country—bruschetta, canapés, and crostini
- ◆ Bread soul mates
- ◆ Other grain-based appetizers
- ◆ When is a sandwich not just a sandwich?

Imagine the aroma of grilled bread and garlic wafting from your warm kitchen, the same smells that might emanate from the ovens of a villa in the Italian countryside as the host prepares for your arrival for a dinner party. If that wonderful aura doesn't start a party on the right foot, nothing will! This is what this chapter is all about—creating that warm welcome and those tantalizing aromas. Your guests will be enjoying themselves even as they walk through the door.

Bread Classics

The crunchy, savory appetizers *bruschetta*, *canapés*, and *crostini* are classy and irresistible. These recipes capture that delicious taste in short order. As noted in an earlier chapter, bruschetta is an Italian favorite that consists of grilled bread rubbed with garlic and drizzled with olive oil, although this definition has been embellished by contemporary cooks. Crostini, another Italian classic, consists of toasted bread topped with a spread—the classics are chicken liver, artichoke, or olives. Canapés are the French version of this kind of appetizer—small pieces of bread that hold a variety of delectable toppings.

> **Gourmet Glossary** _____
>
> Bruschetta, canapés, and crostini are very similar in composition. **Bruschetta** is an Italian favorite; in the classic version, slices of good bread are toasted or grilled, rubbed with garlic, and drizzled with olive oil. Another Italian favorite, **crostini,** is toasted bread spread with pastes made of chicken liver, olives, or artichokes. Modern chefs have adapted both bruschetta and crostini to hold all kinds of flavorful toppings. We can do that! **Canapés** (French in origin) are hors d'oeuvres made up of small pieces of bread topped with your favorite ingredients (commonly cheese, vegetables, and herbs) that sometimes are broiled or toasted, sometimes not. We can do that, too.

Although the base ingredient is bread, the ingredients used in toppings for contemporary bruschetta, canapés, and crostini are limited only by the imagination. Here are some of my favorites:

> **Savoir Starter** _____
> Use your imagination with toppings. Are there slightly unusual toppings that will add fun and interest? Try them out. (Okay, maybe chocolate is going too far. On the other hand, maybe not!)

> **Savoir Starter** _____
> As with many of the recipes in this book, a jar of chopped garlic in the fridge will help speed your bruschetta on its way.

- Artichoke hearts
- Asparagus tips (blanched)
- Cream cheese and combinations
- Fresh basil and tomato
- Fresh mozzarella slices
- Goat's milk cheese
- Parmesan cheese
- Prosciutto
- Roasted peppers
- Scallions
- Sliced olives
- Sun-dried tomatoes (drained oil-packed ones are best; regular dried are tough)
- Sweet onion
- Various forms of ham

Crostini and Bruschetta Mania

Flavor, texture, and the aura of the Italian countryside—need I say more? The challenge is limiting such delicious dishes to be "only" appetizers; I'm always tempted to add a salad and call them dinner.

Quick Bruschetta

This quick take on the classic is a favorite everywhere.

Serves 4 to 6

1 baguette or slender loaf of crusty bread, sliced into ½-inch-thick rounds

2 tsp. chopped garlic

⅓ cup olive oil

1½ tsp. Italian seasoning

1 (8-oz.) jar bruschetta mixture (chopped tomatoes and garlic, available in many grocery stores ready to go)

⅓ cup shredded Parmesan cheese

Kosher salt to taste

Preheat the broiler. Arrange bread on a baking sheet in a single layer. Mix garlic and olive oil in a small cup, and brush each slice of bread with the mixture. Sprinkle with Italian seasoning, and broil for 1 minute on each side.

Remove baking sheet from broiler, leaving the broiler on. Spoon a little bruschetta mixture onto each slice of bread, and sprinkle with Parmesan cheese. Broil again for 1 minute. Transfer bruschetta to a serving platter, sprinkle with kosher salt, and serve.

Gourmet Glossary
Kosher salt, with its large grains, adds texture and visual appeal as well as flavor to savory appetizers.

Quick Bruschetta Topping

Although you can buy bruschetta topping in the store, satisfaction and taste are the winners if you've made it yourself.

Serves 6 to 8

2 fresh tomatoes, chopped into ¼-inch pieces

2 tsp. chopped fresh basil

1 TB. olive oil

1 tsp. chopped garlic

1 tsp. kosher salt

1 baguette or slender loaf of crusty bread, sliced into ½-inch rounds

Combine tomatoes, basil, olive oil, garlic, and salt in a mixing bowl and toss. Spoon a little of the mixture onto each piece of bread and serve.

Roasted Red Pepper

Another favorite from my book, *The Complete Idiot's Guide to 20-Minute Meals*, these glistening red peppers topped with rich Romano cheese make this appetizer irresistible.

Serves 6 to 8

1 baguette or slender loaf of crusty bread, sliced into ½-inch rounds

1 TB. chopped garlic

2 TB. olive oil

2 cups roasted red peppers, chopped into ½-inch pieces

⅓ cup shredded Romano or Parmesan cheese

1 tsp. kosher salt

Preheat the broiler. Arrange bread on a baking sheet in a single layer. Mix garlic and olive oil in a small cup, and brush each slice of bread with the mixture. Broil for 1 minute or until lightly browned. Turn the slices, brush the other side with garlic-olive oil mixture, and broil for 1 more minute.

Remove baking sheet from the broiler, leaving broiler on. Spoon some red peppers onto each slice of bread, and sprinkle with Romano cheese.

Broil again for 1 minute or until cheese begins to melt. Sprinkle with salt, transfer to a large platter, and serve.

The Canapé Connection

One of the differences between the bruschetta and canapés I make is the shape of the bread. For bruschetta, I like round slices from a baguette or similarly slender loaf. For canapés, I like to use triangular toast points.

Cream Cheese and Prosciutto

This is easy and classy. The saltiness of the cured ham is a nice contrast to the cream cheese.

Serves 6 to 8

8 slices white or wheat bread, crusts removed, cut into 4 triangles per slice

1 cup (8-oz.) cream cheese or light cream cheese, softened

1 cup (about 4 oz.) diced prosciutto

2 TB. finely chopped fresh parsley for garnish

Preheat the broiler. Arrange bread slices on a baking sheet in a single layer, and broil for about 1 minute on each side or until lightly browned. Meanwhile, combine cream cheese and prosciutto in a mixing bowl and mix thoroughly.

Remove toast points from the broiler. Spread about 1 tablespoon cream cheese-prosciutto mixture on each, and arrange on a serving tray. Sprinkle a pinch of parsley on each and serve.

Variation: Use diced ham or other meat. I've even seen this work with thin slices of roast beef.

Savoir Starter
To save time, take a close look at your grocery store shelves. Some stores sell prosciutto already diced, and—*shh*—it's usually cheaper than the full-size version.

BBQ Canapés

Not exactly French seasoning, these are surely tasty.

Serves 4 to 6

8 slices white or wheat bread, crusts removed, cut into 4 triangles per slice

¼ cup barbecue sauce

1 cup (8-oz.) cream cheese or light cream cheese, softened

2 TB. finely chopped fresh chives for garnish

Preheat the broiler. Arrange bread on a baking sheet in a single layer and broil for about 1 minute on each side until lightly browned. Meanwhile, combine barbecue sauce and cream cheese and mix thoroughly.

Remove the baking sheet from the oven, and arrange toast points on a work surface. Spread about 2 teaspoons cream cheese mixture on each. Top each with a pinch of chives, arrange on a serving tray, and serve.

Savoir Starter
Have fun with the sauce you use for BBQ Canapés. Try your favorite traditional sauce, but also some of that Hawaiian Guava BBQ hiding in the fridge. You could even use chutney.

Unappetizer
Although it might be tempting, be careful with tasty ingredients that don't balance well atop that toast platform. Fresh cherry tomatoes or chunks of feta on toasted bread create an interesting image, but the reality is the amazing rolling appetizer. If you attached that tomato to the toast with a bit of goat's milk cheese, on the other hand, that's a delicious (and stable) possibility.

Goat's Milk Cheese and Cherry Tomato

Here you will find beautiful colors and textures. I cut the cherry tomatoes in half to avoid the rolling appetizer syndrome.

Serves 6 to 8

8 slices of white or wheat bread, crusts removed, cut into 4 triangles per slice

8 oz. fresh goat's milk cheese

½ pint (about 12) cherry tomatoes, halved

2 TB. finely chopped fresh chives for garnish

Preheat the broiler. Arrange bread on a baking sheet in a single layer and broil for about 1 minute on each side until lightly browned.

Remove the baking sheet from the oven and arrange toast points on a work surface. Spread about 2 teaspoons goat's milk cheese on each, and top each with cherry tomato half, cut side down. Arrange on a serving tray. Sprinkle a pinch of chives on each and serve. *Ah!*

Cucumber and Tomato

This tasty combination is especially quick because it requires no heating or mixing. Just slice the ingredients and assemble.

Serves 6 to 8

1 cup (8-oz.) cream cheese or light cream cheese, softened

8 slices white or wheat bread, crusts removed, cut into 4 triangles per slice

1 English-style cucumber (about 12 oz.), ends removed, *striped*, and sliced into ⅛-inch rounds

8 grape tomatoes, sliced into ¼-inch rounds

2 TB. finely chopped fresh chives for garnish

Kosher salt to taste

 Gourmet Glossary
Striped simply refers to using a vegetable peeler to peel the skin in lengthwise strokes along the cucumber, leaving "stripes" of skin between the peeled sections.

Spread about 2 teaspoons cream cheese on each slice of bread, and top each with slices of cucumber and tomato. Arrange on a serving tray. Sprinkle a pinch of chives and a few grains of salt on each and serve.

Olive and Feta

This recipe provides a delicious flavor combination evocative of the Mediterranean. The cream cheese anchors the feta.

Serves 6 to 8

8 slices white or wheat bread, crusts removed, cut into 4 triangles per slice

1 cup (about 4 oz.) crumbled feta cheese

½ cup (4 oz.) cream cheese or light cream cheese, softened

1 (4¼-oz.) can chopped black olives

½ tsp. dried chopped rosemary

⅛ tsp. garlic powder

2 TB. finely chopped fresh chives for garnish

Preheat the broiler. Arrange bread on a baking sheet in a single layer, and broil for about 1 minute on each side until lightly browned. Meanwhile, combine feta cheese, cream cheese, olives, rosemary, and garlic powder in a bowl and mix thoroughly. Remove the baking sheet from the oven, and arrange toast points on a work surface. Spread about 2 teaspoons feta mixture on each. Arrange on a serving tray. Sprinkle a pinch of chives on each and serve.

Big Dippers

There's something just plain fun about dipping crisp bread into a savory sauce.

Garlic-Basil Toasts with Dipping Sauce

The grilled-bread method will be familiar from the bruschetta recipes; the difference is that the sauce comes from dipping instead of topping. I like to use crusty baguette slices that are cut in half. The pointed end is perfect for dipping, and the crust holds up to the sauce. Make it in 5 minutes, but watch it disappear even more quickly. This recipe makes the most of prepared pesto, that savory combination of basil, garlic, olive oil, and pine nuts.

Serves 4 to 6

⅓ cup olive oil

1 TB. chopped garlic

1 TB. dried basil

1 baguette or slender loaf of crusty bread, sliced crosswise into ½-inch rounds, each piece then cut in half

1½ cups pizza sauce

1 TB. shredded Parmesan cheese, for garnish (optional)

Unappetizer
Many high-quality pasta sauces will also work as a dipping sauce. Feel free to experiment, but avoid those prepared sauces with a lot of added sugar. (Sugar will be near the top on the ingredient list.) These overly sweet sauces could strike an incongruous note in your savory "starter symphony."

Preheat the broiler. Combine olive oil, garlic, and basil in a small cup and mix thoroughly. Brush each piece of bread on both sides with some olive oil mixture, and broil for 1 minute on each side until lightly browned.

Heat pizza sauce in a small (about 2 cup), microwave-safe serving bowl for about 1 minute or until very warm but not boiling, and stir to ensure even temperature. Sprinkle Parmesan cheese (if using) on the surface of sauce, place the bowl in the center of a serving platter, and surround it with toasted bread arranged pointing outward like spokes on a wheel.

Variation: Replace garlic and basil with 2 tablespoons prepared pesto. These toasts are also delicious with Bagna Cauda (see recipe in Chapter 4).

Appetizer Sandwiches

Sandwiches are not just for the main course. Because you eat them with your hands, they're ideal for appetizers. Appetizer sandwich ingredients span the spectrum—from fillings you might expect in a "normal sandwich" to specialty items like those I've used in earlier recipes.

To avoid the message of "this appetizer is the meal," serve small sandwiches, offer fun shapes (like triangles), and remove the crusts. A combination of white and whole-wheat bread adds to the visual appeal. Arrange the sandwiches in a tempting pyramid or circle. I've even seen a platter of finger sandwiches encircling a small vase of fresh herbs. This arrangement can truly set the mood, and afterward you can eat the bouquet!

In just reviewing these ingredients, don't you start to taste the possibilities? Pick a cheese as a base, add one of the fun, complementary ingredients, and you're on the way to a great appetizer sandwich. Or make up your own combinations.

Unappetizer
Appetizer sandwiches are quick and easy, but don't make them too far in advance! Fresh, soft bread will quickly absorb the moisture from your fillings, making those delicate sandwiches unappetizingly soggy.

Here are some of my favorite sandwich ingredients and combinations. Note that not all of them need to have a cheese—good news for those of us watching our diets.

- Brie
- Cream cheese and chutney
- Cream cheese and cucumber
- Cream cheese and watercress

- Cucumber slices
- Fresh mozzarella slices
- Goat's milk cheese and chives
- Goat's milk cheese and prosciutto
- Goat's milk cheese and roasted pepper
- Goat's milk cheese and tiny shrimp
- Goat's milk cheese and black olive
- Mozzarella and black olive
- Mozzarella and tomato
- Provolone
- Roast beef (thinly sliced)
- Roasted peppers
- Scallions
- Sliced olives
- Sliced sweet onion
- Sun-dried tomatoes
- Swiss cheese
- Tomato (thinly sliced)
- Tomato and fresh basil
- Tomato and sweet onion (thinly sliced)

If you're planning to use fresh vegetables in your appetizer sandwiches, check to see what's good and in season. Fresh, local tomatoes, for example, are irresistible. Their tasteless counterparts that have been shipped across the globe are, well, *resistible*.

The Least You Need to Know

- In these recipes, bread moves from a supporting to a starring role to make appetizers that are classic, quick, and tasty.
- Some bread-based appetizers, such as bruschetta and canapés, use broiling to add flavor and irresistible texture.
- Sandwiches, prepared just a bit differently than their mealtime brethren, can be tempting appetizers.
- As with many other appetizers, simple, compelling combinations of flavor and texture create unusual and appealing hors d'oeuvres.

Chapter 7

Fish Food: Salmon and Other Finny Appetizers

In This Chapter

- The wonders of smoked salmon
- Fish-based spreads
- Other smoked fish dishes
- Favorite recipes

For many people, seafood, and especially fish, form the flavor backbone for appetizers. If there's a table with several choices, one of which is a fish dish, that's the one they visit first. Distinctive seasonings, color and texture, and a slightly out-of-the-ordinary flavor all contribute to making these hors d'oeuvres a classy addition to any event.

Salmon Starters

Whether used as an appetizer or a main course, salmon is one of the most popular fish in America. Its distinctive pinkish color and pleasingly mild flavor are a welcome component in many unique appetizers. And its slightly firm texture means it won't fall apart on you. Here are some of my favorites.

Creamy Salmon Caper Spread

This is a fast and easy salmon spread.

Serves 4

1 (6-oz.) can boneless, skinless pink salmon, drained

½ cup mayonnaise

½ cup (4 oz.) cream cheese or light cream cheese

1 tsp. capers, drained

1½ tsp. fresh lemon juice

¼ tsp. ground black pepper

Dash hot sauce (such as Tabasco)

Crusty bread or crisp wheat crackers for serving

In a food processor fitted with a metal blade, process salmon, mayonnaise, cream cheese, capers, lemon juice, black pepper, and hot sauce until smooth. Scrape spread into a serving bowl, and serve with crusty bread or crisp wheat crackers.

Savoir Starter

Salmon is a favorite in our household. Sometimes, in spite of our best efforts, we end up with leftovers. But we don't really mind—the leftover salmon, with any spices or seasonings (but with the skin and bones removed), is just perfect as a base for salmon dips and spreads.

Teriyaki Salmon Dip

This dip marries ingredients from East and West: Japanese-style teriyaki sauce and the dairy products prized in Western cuisines. The resulting fusion is delicious.

Serves 4

1 (6-oz.) can boneless, skinless pink salmon, drained

¾ cup sour cream

¼ cup (2 oz.) cream cheese or light cream cheese, softened

1 TB. teriyaki sauce

1 tsp. fresh lemon juice

2 TB. chopped fresh chives for garnish

Wheat crackers for serving

In a food processor fitted with a metal blade, process salmon, sour cream, cream cheese, teriyaki sauce, and lemon juice until smooth. Scrape into a serving bowl, sprinkle with chives, and serve with wheat crackers.

Variation: Mix with a spoon instead of a food processor for a chunky, farmhouse-style spread.

Smoked Salmon and Cream Cheese Wheels

Here's an easy and festive starter. Don't forget to stock up on toothpicks.

Serves 6 to 8

1 (8-oz.) pkg. smoked salmon, thinly sliced

1 cup (8 oz.) cream cheese or light cream cheese, softened

2 TB. chopped fresh chives for garnish (optional)

Arrange salmon slices on a work surface in a single layer, with the narrow ends facing you. Spread each with a thin layer (¼ inch or less) of cream cheese. Working from one end, roll salmon evenly over cream cheese. When salmon is completely rolled, insert toothpicks spaced at ½-inch intervals along the roll. Using a very sharp knife, slice the roll at the midpoint between each toothpick. Repeat with other pieces of salmon. Arrange finished wheels on a serving plate, and sprinkle with chopped chives (if using).

Savoir Starter _____
Grocery stores all carry canned salmon, a quick and convenient starting point for salmon dips and spreads. Grocery stores and specialty food stores also offer smoked salmon, packaged in flat, thin slices—perfect as a topping and for rolling those wheels.

Smoked Salmon and Cantaloupe Bites

Simple to make, this unusual combination delivers a terrific contrast in flavor.

Serves 4 to 6

½ ripe cantaloupe, seeds removed, formed into balls with a melon baller or cut into 1 by ½-inch wedges

1 (8-oz.) pkg. thinly sliced smoked salmon, cut into 1 by 3-inch strips

2 TB. fresh lemon juice

1 tsp. Kosher salt

Parsley sprigs for garnish

Thin lemon *twists* for garnish

Wrap each piece of cantaloupe in a smoked salmon strip, and fasten with a toothpick. Arrange on a serving plate, drizzle with lemon juice, and sprinkle with salt. Garnish with parsley and lemon twists and serve.

Gourmet Glossary

A lemon **twist** is an attractive way to garnish an appetizer or other dish. Cut a thin (about ⅛-inch-thick) round slice of lemon. Then place the tip of your knife at the center of the round and make a cut from the center out to the edge. Pull the two cut ends apart in opposite directions, and place where desired on your serving surface.

Salmon and Sun-Dried Tomato Spread

The rich, sunny taste of the tomatoes blends beautifully with the flavor of salmon, and the red and green colors are very cheerful. If possible, chill this spread for an hour or so to let the flavors meld. If you wish, you can substitute oil from the sun-dried tomatoes for the called-for olive oil.

Serves 4 to 6

1 (6-oz.) can boneless, skinless pink salmon, drained

½ cup (4-oz.) cream cheese or light cream cheese, softened

⅔ cup (about 5 oz.) chickpeas

½ cup (about 4 oz.) sun-dried tomatoes (oil-packed), drained, oil preserved

2 TB. olive oil plus more for processing if needed

1 tsp. fresh lemon juice

1 sliced scallion for garnish

Pita bread wedges or crisps for serving

In a food processor fitted with a metal blade, process salmon, cream cheese, chickpeas, tomatoes, olive oil, and lemon juice until smooth. If necessary, add a little more olive oil to achieve a thick, smooth consistency. Scrape spread into a serving bowl, top with scallion slices, and serve with pita bread or pita crisps.

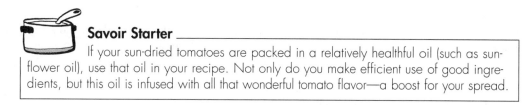

Savoir Starter _____

If your sun-dried tomatoes are packed in a relatively healthful oil (such as sunflower oil), use that oil in your recipe. Not only do you make efficient use of good ingredients, but this oil is infused with all that wonderful tomato flavor—a boost for your spread.

Teriyaki Salmon Mozzarella Bites

This is one of the easy "bite" recipes in this book, with a combination of flavors that work magic when you pop it in your mouth. Use fresh mozzarella that comes packed in brine in balls about the diameter of a quarter.

Serves 4

1 (8-oz.) pkg. thinly sliced smoked salmon, cut into 1 by 3-inch pieces

1 (about 8-oz.) pkg. fresh mozzarella balls packed in brine, each ball cut in half

2 TB. teriyaki sauce

2 TB. chopped fresh chives for garnish (optional)

Arrange salmon on a work surface in a single layer and top each with 1 mozzarella piece. Roll salmon around mozzarella and fasten with toothpicks, arranging the "bites" on a serving platter as you go. Drizzle with teriyaki sauce, sprinkle with chives (if using), and serve.

Variation: Use feta cheese in place of mozzarella.

Unappetizer _____

The herbs and seasonings used in this chapter—lemon juice, scallions, chives, dill, teriyaki sauce, capers, hot pepper, and so on—have a time-honored place as seafood accompaniments. Many other seasonings and flavors also work well with seafood, but others work less well. Be cautious about introducing sweet flavors (some work and some don't), as well as spices associated with sweetness (casual use of cinnamon could be hazardous to your palate).

Salmon with Cucumber and Dill

This is the place for store-brand, mild goat's milk cheese.

Serves 6 to 8

8 oz. fresh, mild goat's milk cheese, softened

2 TB. plus ¼ tsp. chopped fresh dill or 2 tsp. dried dill

1 English-style cucumber (about 12 oz.), ends removed, peeled in stripes, and sliced into ⅛-inch rounds

1 (8-oz.) pkg. thinly sliced smoked salmon, cut into 1-inch squares

Kosher salt to taste

Lemon wedges

Combine goat's milk cheese and 2 tablespoons fresh or 2 teaspoons dried dill in a small bowl and mix thoroughly. Spread about 2 teaspoons goat's milk cheese mixture on each cucumber slice, top each with a piece of salmon, and arrange on a serving platter. Sprinkle remaining fresh dill (if using) and a few grains of salt on each, and serve with lemon wedges for guests to squeeze a few drops on each bite.

Smoked Salmon Platter

This simple dish wins the prize for lightning-fast elegance.

Serves 4 to 6

1 (9- or 10-oz.) box good-quality plain wheat crackers

1 cup (8 oz.) cream cheese or light cream cheese, softened

1 (8-oz.) pkg. thinly sliced smoked salmon, cut into 1 by 2-inch pieces

2 TB. capers, drained

2 TB. chopped fresh parsley for garnish

Lemon wedges

Arrange crackers on a serving platter. Spread about 2 teaspoons cream cheese on each cracker, top each with a piece of salmon, and scatter capers and parsley on top. Serve with lemon wedges.

Spicy Mayonnaise

Try this as a spread for smoked salmon!

Serves 4 to 6

½ cup mayonnaise

2 TB. Worcestershire sauce

2 TB. Dijon mustard or brown mustard (not too strong a Dijon, and not a yellow mustard)

1 tsp. hot pepper sauce (such as Tabasco)

1 tsp. paprika

¼ tsp. freshly ground black pepper

Juice of 1 lemon

Whisk together mayonnaise, Worcestershire sauce, mustard, hot pepper sauce, paprika, black pepper, and lemon juice, and use as a spicy condiment for on seafood, from appetizers to seafood steaks.

Savory Tuna Spread

Forget tuna sandwiches. This is tuna like you've never seen it before.

Serves 4

1 (6-oz.) can white tuna packed in water, drained

¼ cup mayonnaise

¼ cup (4 oz.) cream cheese or light cream cheese, softened

¼ cup Italian-style breadcrumbs

2 scallions, dark green parts removed, cut into ½-inch pieces

1 TB. fresh lemon juice

1 tsp. Worcestershire sauce

Dash hot pepper sauce (such as Tabasco)

Thinly sliced scallions for garnish (optional)

Belgian endive leaves and/or melba toast for serving

In a food processor fitted with a metal blade, process tuna, mayonnaise, cream cheese, breadcrumbs, scallions, lemon juice, Worcestershire sauce, and hot pepper sauce until almost smooth (some texture adds to the appeal). Scrape spread into a serving bowl, top with scallion slices (if using), and chill for several hours. Serve with Belgian endive leaves or melba toast.

Savory Fishes

Savory fish like sardines and anchovies bring not only rich and sunny flavor but also evoke whole cultures. A sardine is a small fish, packed in oil and salt. An anchovy is an even smaller, more flavorful fish. These tiny fish bring to mind villages by the ocean and warm climes. Have a bite and travel to the seaside.

Sardines on Garlic Toast

People don't serve sardines as much as they used to, so a dish like this takes on the aura of novelty. The flavor is a knockout.

Serves 4 to 6

5 slices white or wheat bread, crusts removed, each cut into 4 long pieces of equal size (20 pieces total)

3 TB. olive oil

2 tsp. chopped garlic

1 (3¾-oz.) can sardines (about 20), drained

2 TB. chopped fresh parsley or chives for garnish

Pepper to taste

Preheat the broiler. Arrange bread on a baking sheet in a single layer. Mix olive oil and garlic in a small cup, and brush over bread. Broil bread for 1 minute on each side or until bread is crisp and oil is sizzling. Arrange bread on a serving platter, and place 1 sardine lengthwise on each piece. Arrange on a large round platter with the long sides out like spokes on a wheel. Sprinkle with parsley or chives, and pepper to taste, and serve. (This is another of those opportunities for placing something creative and thematic in the middle, such as that scallop shell you picked up at the beach on vacation but haven't used since.)

Spicy Fish Pâté

Want a hearty, fragrant appetizer? Look no further!

Serves 4

1 (6½-oz.) can skinless, boneless pink salmon

2 anchovies

½ cup plain breadcrumbs

¼ cup (2 oz.) cream cheese or light cream cheese, softened

2 TB. olive oil, plus more as needed

2 scallions, dark green parts removed, cut into ½-inch sections

1 tsp. fresh lemon juice

1 tsp. dried dill

Dash hot pepper sauce (such as Tabasco)

4 slices white or wheat bread, crusts removed, cut on the diagonal to form triangles

In a food processor fitted with a metal blade, process salmon, anchovies, breadcrumbs, cream cheese, olive oil, scallions, lemon juice, dill, and hot pepper sauce until smooth. If necessary, add a little more oil to achieve a thick, smooth consistency. Scrape mixture into a serving bowl and, if possible, chill for several hours. Shortly before you are ready to serve, preheat the broiler. Arrange bread on a baking sheet, and broil for 1 minute on each side until lightly browned. Serve spread with toast triangles.

Unappetizer

Many fish-based appetizers are quick and easy to make, but unless the recipe calls for chilling, make them just before you need them. Old fish tastes like, well, old fish.

Sardine Spread

This is a savory, delicious spread that will disappear all too quickly.

Serves 6 to 8

1 (3¾-oz.) can oil-packed sardines, drained

1 (15½-oz.) can chickpeas

¼ cup fresh parsley, chopped

3 TB. fresh lemon juice

2 TB. olive oil, plus more if needed

½ tsp. salt

¼ tsp. freshly ground black pepper

¼ tsp. hot pepper sauce

4 pieces white or wheat bread, crusts removed, cut on the diagonal to form triangles

In a food processor fitted with a metal blade, process sardines, chickpeas, parsley, lemon juice, olive oil, salt, black pepper, and hot pepper sauce until blended but still chunky. (The texture adds to the appeal.) If necessary for processing, add a little more olive oil. Scrape mixture into a serving bowl and, if possible, chill for several hours. Shortly before you are ready to serve, preheat the broiler. Arrange bread on a baking sheet, and broil for 1 minute on each side until lightly browned. Serve spread with toast triangles.

Sardine, Olive, and Sun-Dried Tomato Spread

Talk about a flavor explosion! If you wish, you can substitute oil from the sun-dried tomatoes for the called-for olive oil.

Serves 4 to 6

1 (3¾-oz.) can sardines, drained

1 cup (8-oz.) cream cheese or light cream cheese, softened

½ cup (about 4 oz.) sun-dried tomatoes (oil-packed), drained, oil reserved

½ cup (about 4 oz.) pitted Kalamata olives, drained

2 TB. olive oil (or oil from tomatoes), plus more for processing if needed

1 TB. fresh lemon juice

Sprig parsley for garnish

In a food processor fitted with a metal blade, process sardines, cream cheese, tomatoes, olives, oil, and lemon juice until blended but still chunky. If necessary for processing, add a little more olive oil. Scrape mixture into a serving bowl, and garnish with parsley. Serve with crisp wheat crackers.

Not Your Ordinary Tuna Fish Sandwich

Canned tuna is a readily available, affordable, and reliable resource for quick appetizers. Try a few of these and surprise yourself.

Tuna Pâté

This *pâté*like appetizer offers pâté texture but is based on inexpensive ingredients and has a quick prep. It's delicious, especially with warm, crisp toast points.

Serves 6

1 (6-oz.) can white tuna packed in water, drained

½ cup Italian-style breadcrumbs

½ cup (4 oz.) cream cheese or light cream cheese, softened

2 TB. olive oil, plus more if needed

2 scallions, dark green parts removed, cut into ½-inch pieces

1 TB. fresh lemon juice

2 tsp. soy sauce

4 pieces white or wheat bread, crusts removed, cut on the diagonal to form triangles

Sprig parsley for garnish (optional)

In a food processor fitted with a metal blade, process tuna, breadcrumbs, cream cheese, olive oil, scallions, lemon juice, and soy sauce until almost smooth. (Some texture adds to the appeal.) If necessary, add a little more olive oil to achieve the right consistency. Spray the bottom and sides of a small (2-cup) rectangular or round dish with vegetable oil spray. Scrape mixture into prepared dish and chill for several hours. (The purpose of this step is to mold the pâté into an appealing shape for serving.) Shortly before you are ready to serve, preheat the broiler. Arrange bread on a baking sheet, and broil for 1 minute on each side until lightly browned. When ready to serve, place a serving platter over the dish and, with one hand on the platter and one hand on the dish, invert them so the serving platter is on the bottom. Tap pâté onto the platter. Garnish with parsley (if using), and serve surrounded by toast triangles.

Quick Tuna Dip

This recipe adds interest to one of those soup-mix dips!

Serves 4

1 (6-oz.) can white tuna packed in water, drained

1 cup sour cream

1 (.53-oz.) pkg. vegetable soup mix

1 TB. fresh lemon juice

Salt to taste

Pinch black pepper

Tortilla or other hefty chips for serving

Mix tuna, sour cream, soup mix, lemon juice, salt, and pepper in a serving bowl, and chill for an hour or so to allow the flavors to meld. Serve with tortilla or other hefty chips, as tuna adds heft that might crack weaker platforms.

Variation: Use canned (skinless, boneless) salmon in place of tuna.

Savoir Starter

No time to "chill"? With soup-mix recipes, put the mix into a microwave-safe serving bowl, add 2 tablespoons water, mix, and microwave on high for 15 to 20 seconds. Then add the rest of your dip ingredients, mix, and serve. This quick heat softens the ingredients and accelerates the flavor spreading.

The Least You Need to Know

♦ Fish brings a baseline of flavor that makes appetizers unique and appealing.

♦ Highly flavorful fish such as sardines and anchovies present an opportunity for delicious and flavor-packed hors d'oeuvres.

♦ Salmon, in its many forms, can become the basis for many dips, spreads, canapés, and other classy appetizers.

♦ Keep an open mind about tuna. With its mild flavor, tuna blends well with many other ingredients, forming a delicious and inexpensive backbone to several appetizers.

Chapter **8**

It's Okay to Be a Shellfish Person

In This Chapter

- Ode to a crab
- This shrimp is a big deal
- Mollusk mania
- Do call this clam a dip

Shellfish is a general term for a water creature that has an exoskeleton, or shell, rather than bones, and this chapter includes delicacies using crabs, shrimp, clams, oysters, and more. Although these creatures are not all from the same species, shellfish form the "backbone" of many delicious seafood recipes.

Shellfish bring a whole new dimension to seafood recipes. Recipes involving crab, for example, produce a rich, buttery flavor; shrimp has a succulent crispness; and clams supply a meaty heartiness; but they all have that distinctive seafood tang. Here are some of my favorite recipes.

Who Are You Calling a Shrimp?

Shrimp is perhaps one of the most used seafood ingredients. There are dozens of sites on the web maintained by shrimp fans devoted exclusively to shrimp recipes. What a job …

Shrimp Spread

The whole shrimp studding this savory spread make for a tasty yet attractive appetizer.

Serves 4

½ cup (4-oz.) cream cheese or light cream cheese, softened

½ cup (4 oz.) mayonnaise

2 scallions, dark green parts removed, cut into ½-inch pieces, plus 1 scallion for garnish (optional)

1 TB. chopped fresh dill or 1 tsp. dried dill

2 tsp. fresh lemon juice

½ tsp. dried thyme

Dash hot pepper sauce (such as Tabasco)

1 (6-oz.) can tiny cocktail shrimp, drained

Melba toast or sturdy wheat crackers for serving

Gourmet Glossary
On shrimp packaging, you'll often see a reference to the **count**. This refers to the size of the shrimp according to how many compose a pound. Most of the recipes in this chapter call for 51 to 70 count (51 to 70 make up a pound), which are perfect for an appetizer.

In a food processor fitted with a metal blade, process cream cheese, mayonnaise, scallions, dill, lemon juice, thyme, and hot pepper sauce until almost smooth. Scrape spread into a serving bowl, and stir in shrimp. Sprinkle with scallion pieces for garnish (if using), and serve with melba toast or sturdy wheat crackers.

Shrimp with Sweet Pineapple Onion Relish

This is one exception to the "no sweets with seafood" rule.

Serves 6

1 (8-oz.) can pineapple chunks in juice, drained

⅓ cup honey

1 TB. fresh lemon juice

¼ cup chopped sweet onion (about ½ medium)

½ lb. (51 to 70 count, or about 30) cooked shrimp, peeled and deveined with tail off

In a food processor fitted with a metal blade, pulse pineapple, honey, lemon juice, and chopped onion to relish consistency. Scrape relish into a serving bowl, place the bowl on a plate or platter, and surround with shrimp. Serve using shrimp as dippers.

 **Savoir Starter**

When it comes to mincing onion, I find that I save time by using either a grater (using the large-hole section) for small quantities such as half an onion, or a food processor fitted with the larger piece wheel when I have larger quantities to mince. Otherwise, the mincing itself could take 5 minutes.

Jicama, Shrimp, and Cream Cheese Bites

The crunchy texture of *jicama* works magic in this recipe.

Serves 6

½ lb. (51 to 70 count or about 30) cooked shrimp, peeled and deveined with tail off

1 TB. fresh lime juice

½ cup (4 oz.) cream cheese or light cream cheese, softened

8 oz. jicama, peeled and cut into 1 by 2-inch pieces about ½-inch thick

2 TB. chopped fresh chives

Freshly ground black pepper

Lime wedges for garnish

Place shrimp into a mixing bowl, add lime juice, and toss to coat. Spread about 1½ teaspoon cream cheese on each piece of jicama, top each with 1 shrimp, and arrange on a serving plate. Sprinkle with chives, season with a few twists of black pepper, garnish with lime wedges, and serve.

Gourmet Glossary

Jicama is a juicy, crunchy, sweet-ish Central American vegetable that is eaten both raw and cooked. It is available in many large grocery stores as well as from specialty vendors. If you can't find it, use sliced water chestnuts instead.

Shrimp "Bouquet" with White Cocktail Sauce

This is shrimp cocktail you've had before, but with a twist. The bamboo skewers are a lot of fun. Pretend to offer a flower to your guests as they arrive.

Serves 6 to 8

¼ cup (4 oz.) sour cream

¼ cup (4 oz.) mayonnaise

2 TB. prepared horseradish

1 TB. fresh lemon juice

1 tsp. dried dill

1 lb. (51 to 70 count, or about 30) cooked shrimp, peeled and deveined with tail on

Combine sour cream, mayonnaise, horseradish, lemon juice, and dill in a small serving bowl and mix thoroughly. Place 1 shrimp on the end of a bamboo skewer; repeat with remaining shrimp, using 1 per skewer. Place finished skewers into a tall, slender glass or vase so they form a "bouquet." Place it and the bowl of cocktail sauce on a serving tray, and prepare to wow your guests.

Shrimp Macadamia Rafts

Here is another "this-is-too-easy-to-be-this-good" recipe.

Serves 6 to 8

½ cup (4 oz.) cream cheese or light cream cheese, softened

1½ TB. freshly grated ginger

1 (6-oz.) box plain wheat crackers

1 lb. (51 to 70 count or about 30) cooked shrimp, peeled and deveined with tail off

⅔ cup macadamia nuts (about 18)

Lime wedges

Kosher salt to taste

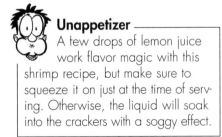

Unappetizer
A few drops of lemon juice work flavor magic with this shrimp recipe, but make sure to squeeze it on just at the time of serving. Otherwise, the liquid will soak into the crackers with a soggy effect.

Combine cream cheese and ginger in a small bowl and mix thoroughly. Spread about 1½ teaspoon cream cheese mixture on a cracker using the back of a spoon, top each with 1 shrimp, and nestle 1 macadamia nut inside curled shrimp. Arrange on a platter, drizzle with a few drops of lime juice, sprinkle with salt, and serve.

Hors D'oeuvre History _____

Fresh ginger—straight from the ginger root—is an unforgettable, piquant, savory-sweet seasoning with a better flavor than the powdered stuff in the spice rack. Buy a piece of ginger root, peel it, and keep it in the freezer in a freezerproof bag or container. When you need some, simply grate off what you need and pop the rest back in the deep freeze for next time.

It's Good to Be Crabby!

Rich, buttery crab is a taste treat. It's also a bit of an indulgence that some grocery stores now offer at a quite affordable price.

Crab Spread

Rich and hearty, this is a spread your guests will love, so you better make a little extra.

Serves 6 to 8

1 (6-oz.) can crabmeat

1 cup (8-oz.) cream cheese or light cream cheese, softened

2 scallions, dark green parts removed, cut into ½-inch pieces

1 TB. Madeira (or other sweet dessert-style wine)

1 TB. fresh lemon juice

½ tsp. dried dill

¼ tsp. freshly ground black pepper

Dash hot pepper sauce (such as Tabasco)

Wheat crackers for serving

In a food processor fitted with a metal blade, process crabmeat, cream cheese, scallions, Madeira, lemon juice, dill, black pepper, and hot pepper sauce until smooth. Scrape into a serving bowl, and serve with wheat crackers.

Variation: Mix with a spoon instead of a food processor for a chunky spread.

Savoir Starter _____

For a fun alternative in serving spreads, use them as a filling in small sandwiches. For example, prepare bread or toast triangles, and use crab spread as filling, along with a piece of arugula or watercress. What a sandwich!

Hot Crab Dip

You will find this warm, satisfying, and just slightly out of the ordinary.

Serves 6 to 8

2 (6-oz.) cans crabmeat

1 cup sour cream

½ cup (4 oz.) cream cheese or light cream cheese, softened

½ cup shredded Parmesan cheese

2 tsp. fresh lemon juice

¼ tsp. garlic salt

Dash hot pepper sauce (such as Tabasco)

Chopped scallion for garnish (optional)

Tortilla chips for serving

Combine crabmeat, sour cream, cream cheese, Parmesan cheese, lemon juice, garlic salt, and hot pepper sauce in a microwave-safe bowl and mix thoroughly. Microwave on high for 2 minutes or until bubbling, remove from oven, and stir. Top with sliced scallion pieces (if using), and serve with tortilla chips.

Crab and Romano Spread

This spread is simple but savory.

Serves 4

1 (6-oz.) can crabmeat

½ cup (4-oz.) cream cheese or light cream cheese, softened

½ cup (4 oz.) mayonnaise

½ cup shredded Romano cheese

2 tsp. fresh lemon juice

Pita crisps or pieces of fresh, crusty bread for serving

In a food processor fitted with a metal blade, process crabmeat, cream cheese, mayonnaise, Romano cheese, and lemon juice until smooth. Scrape the spread into a serving bowl, and serve with pita crisps or small pieces of fresh bread.

Three-Layer Spicy Crab Spread

Super cook Betty Frankenfield inspired this recipe. Isn't "simple" the kind of secret this book is all about?

Serves 4 to 6

1 cup (8 oz.) cream cheese or light cream cheese, softened

1 (6-oz.) can crabmeat

½ cup (4 oz.) chili sauce

4 pieces of white or wheat bread, crusts removed, cut on the diagonal to form triangles

Place cream cheese in a shallow serving dish, and spread to an even depth. Pour crabmeat over cream cheese, and spread into a uniform layer. Pour chili sauce over all, spreading again to a uniform depth. Shortly before you are ready to serve, preheat the broiler. Arrange bread on a baking sheet, and broil for 1 minute on each side until lightly browned. Serve with a knife to spread over crisp toast.

I'll Give You Fifty Clams for a Good Recipe ...

A delicious, unique seafood ingredient that adds instant flavor and texture to appetizers, clams are worth a try.

Savory Clam Dip

A hearty, flavorful dip to enjoy at the yacht club. Well, imagine the yacht club part …

Serves 6 to 8

1 (6½-oz.) can clams (minced or whole), drained

1 cup sour cream

1 cup (8-oz.) cream cheese or light cream cheese, softened

3 scallions, dark green parts removed, cut into ½-inch pieces, plus an additional chopped scallion for garnish (optional)

1 tsp. fresh lemon juice

1 tsp. steak sauce (such as A1) or Worcestershire sauce

Tortilla or sturdy ridged chips for serving

In a food processor fitted with a metal blade, pulse clams, sour cream, cream cheese, 3 scallions, lemon juice, and steak sauce to an almost-smooth consistency. Scrape dip into a serving bowl, and garnish with scallions (if using). If you have the time to make this and chill it for later in the day, do so, as the extra time will improve the flavors. Serve with tortilla or sturdy ridged potato chips.

Teriyaki Clam Dip

Teriyaki is a terrific seasoning for seafood, and nowhere is that more evident than in Teriyaki Clam Dip.

Serves 4 to 6

1 (6½-oz.) can chopped clams (juice *reserved*)

½ cup (4 oz.) cream cheese or light cream cheese, softened

½ cup (4 oz.) sour cream

1 TB. teriyaki sauce

Chopped scallions for garnish (optional)

Tortilla or sturdy ridged potato chips for serving

Gourmet Glossary
To **reserve** is to hold a specified ingredient for another use. In this case, the clam juice is reserved in case it is needed for processing.

In a food processor fitted with a metal blade, pulse clams, cream cheese, sour cream, and teriyaki sauce to an almost-smooth consistency. If necessary, add a little reserved clam juice to assist with processing and soften the dip. Scrape dip into a serving bowl, and garnish with scallions (if using). If you have the time, chill it for later in the day to allow the flavors to meld. Serve with tortilla or sturdy ridged potato chips.

Variations: Use salmon in place of clams and nonfat plain yogurt instead of sour cream.

Bacon Clam Spread

This has great clam and bacon flavor with the sharpness of the horseradish.

Serves 6 to 8

1 (6½-oz.) can chopped or minced clams, drained

½ cup sour cream

1 cup (8 oz.) cream cheese or light cream cheese, softened

½ cup shredded Parmesan cheese

1 TB. prepared horseradish

1 tsp. fresh lime juice

1 (3-oz.) jar real bacon bits, 1 TB. reserved for garnish

1 (6-oz.) pkg. pita crisps

In a food processor, process clams, sour cream, cream cheese, Parmesan cheese, horseradish, and lime juice. Scrape spread into a serving bowl, and stir in bacon bits. Sprinkle reserved bacon bits over the top, and serve surrounded by pita crisps or another hefty grain-based vehicle.

 **Savoir Starter** _____

Canned clams come packed in flavorful juice. If you choose to use this liquid in your recipe, know that it augments flavor but also adds to the liquid. To compensate for this additional liquid, use a little extra of the more solid ingredients such as cream cheese and Parmesan cheese.

Caviar for Celebrations

Caviar comes in several levels of quality and expense. When caviar is the focus, such as in caviar and toast, serve only the high-quality product, such as Beluga or Ossetra (Russian caviar) at a quantity of about 2 ounces for 4 to 6 people.

To minimize the handling of this precious substance (and avoid breaking the delicate eggs), serve it right out of its container nestled in a bed of ice. When caviar is a component of a recipe, such as caviar spread, less-expensive caviar is fine.

Caviar and Crisp Toast

From James Bond to state dinners, caviar has the cachet. This is one of the simplest recipes in this book—more a matter of presentation than preparation.

Serves 4 to 6

Crushed ice

2 oz. high-quality caviar

½ cup sour cream

½ cup chopped hard-cooked eggs

¼ cup finely chopped fresh chives or scallions

¼ cup finely chopped sweet onion (such as Vidalia)

8 pieces toasted white bread, crusts removed, cut on the diagonal from corner to corner to form triangles

Fill a large bowl with crushed ice, open caviar, and nestle the container in ice. Surround the bowl with sour cream, eggs, chives, and onion, each in a separate, smaller bowl, and set out a plate of buttered toast triangles. Serve caviar with a tiny spoon. If you have them, the traditional mother-of-pearl caviar spoons are a nice touch and will mark you as a caviar connoisseur. (A baby spoon will also do—if you have that kind of humor.)

Three-Layer Caviar Spread

Although you can use olive oil, the butter lends a welcome richness to this caviar dish.

Serves 4 to 6

2 TB. unsalted butter or olive oil

2 tsp. chopped garlic

1 cup (8 oz.) cream cheese or light cream cheese, softened

4 oz. black caviar

Scallion pieces to garnish

Baguette

Heat butter in an 8- to 10-inch skillet over medium heat. Add garlic and cook for 1 minute, stirring until garlic pieces begin to brown and crisp. Remove the skillet from heat. Place cream cheese in a serving bowl, pour garlic butter over it, and mix thoroughly. When it is blended, smooth so the surface is flat. Carefully spread caviar over the top with the back of a spoon, garnish with scallions, and serve with pieces of crusty baguette.

More Mollusk Munchies

Scallops and oysters are two other delicious ingredients that put the "shell" in shellfish. Here are some of my favorites.

Sautéed Scallops with Warm Lemon-Dill Dipping Sauce

Buttery, rich scallops cook quickly and are terrific candidates for a fast appetizer.

Serves 4 to 6

Scallops:

⅓ cup butter

1 lb. fresh sea scallops

2 TB. chopped fresh parsley

Dipping sauce:

½ tsp. dried dill

1½ TB. fresh lemon juice

½ cup sour cream

 Unappetizer _____

Cook scallops just until they turn white in the center. Scallops are perfect for appetizers because they cook so quickly; if they cook too long, they get tough. Nobody wants an ornery scallop.

Heat butter in a large (12-inch) skillet over medium-high heat. Add scallops and cook for about 1 minute per side or until flesh just turns white. Remove scallops with a slotted spoon to a serving plate, and sprinkle with parsley.

Add dill and lemon juice to the same skillet, stir, and turn off the heat. Then stir in sour cream until butter, lemon juice, and dill are thoroughly mixed. Scrape this sauce into a serving bowl, and serve with scallops, giving guests toothpicks to pick up each scallop and dip it into the dipping sauce.

Oysters on the Half-Shell

This classic is less a recipe than a time-honored method. Lemon juice and perhaps a tiny dash of hot pepper are all you need.

Serves 4 to 6

24 fresh oysters

Lemon wedges

Sprig parsley for garnish (optional)

Hot pepper sauce (such as Tabasco)

Savoir Starter

Oysters, as with all seafood, are best obtained fresh from a reliable vendor and consumed as soon as possible. For oysters on the half-shell, Atlantic oysters are generally the most popular (often Atlantic oysters are named, such as "Cape Cod" or "Bluepoint"). There are also Pacific oysters and delicious oysters from France and other maritime countries.

Use either an oyster knife or, with care, a paring knife, to "shuck" the oyster by cutting it—starting at the hinge and working the blade around until the muscle holding the shells together is cut. Drain juice. Place shucked oyster into one half of the shell, and arrange these shells on a serving platter. Place lemon wedges into a small bowl, and top with sprig of parsley (if using). Position this bowl in the center of the oyster platter along with a bottle of hot pepper sauce. To eat, squeeze a drop of lemon juice and, if desired, a tiny drop of hot sauce onto oyster, and slide it into your mouth.

Scallops and Bacon

The crisp bacon and creamy scallops are a dream combination.

Serves 6

1 lb. fresh sea scallops

½ lb. bacon slices, cut in half to make 1 by 4-inch pieces

Preheat the broiler. Wrap each scallop in a piece of bacon and fasten with a toothpick. Place bacon-wrapped scallops on a baking sheet, and broil for 2 minutes per side or until bacon begins to crisp and scallops are cooked. Serve with small plates and plenty of napkins!

Creamy Seafood Dip

This is the place for imitation crabmeat (actually fish). Real crabmeat and canned salmon will also work.

Serves 6 to 8

½ lb. imitation crabmeat

1 cup sour cream

½ cup (4 oz.) mayonnaise

2 scallions, dark green leaves removed, cut into ½-inch pieces

1 TB. fresh lemon juice

1 tsp. dried dill

Dash hot pepper sauce (such as Tabasco)

Belgian endive leaves and/or pita crisps for serving

In a food processor or blender, process imitation crabmeat, sour cream, mayonnaise, scallions, lemon juice, dill, and hot pepper sauce to a slightly coarse consistency. (I like to leave a bit of texture.) Serve in a bowl surrounded by Belgian endive leaves or pita crisps.

The Least You Need to Know

- Shellfish, with its mild yet distinctive seafood flavors, is the base for many tasty seafood appetizers.
- Shrimp recipes are easy and appealing, even for people who think they don't like seafood.
- Scallops are so quick-cooking that they enable you to make delicious 5-minute cooked dishes.
- Many shellfish are an essential part of dips and spreads.
- To quickly assess the shrimp you need for a recipe, look for the "count" (number of shrimp per pound) on the package. The 51 to 70 count are the appropriate size for many appetizer recipes.

Chapter 9

The Deli Is Not Just for Lunch: Meat-Based Appetizers

In This Chapter

- ◆ Meat: It's all about flavor
- ◆ Cooked, smoked, and cured meats are the name of the game
- ◆ Wheels, wraps, and other tasty morsels
- ◆ Simple combinations sure to please

Imagine having to roast a chicken before you could prepare these appetizers. Talk about a 5-minute nonstarter. The reason the meat-based appetizers in this chapter are possible at all is because of the work already done by your deli, from cooking to rough prep (those thin slices). The result for us is a terrific flavor foundation ... in short order.

Thinly sliced meats (and other deli fare, for that matter) enable a range of quick and savory appetizers. We'll start here for inspiration, although there are many other sources of prepared meats to review after we visit the deli. The starting points include roast chicken or turkey, roast beef, meatballs, and ham. Here are some of my favorite recipes that were born in the deli.

Starters to Squawk About

Chicken appetizers come in wondrous variety because of the many forms available—from the deli: sliced chicken and chicken loaf; from a can: chunk chicken meat; from the fridge: chicken leftovers (really). They will all work as an appetizer base.

Savoir Starter _____

If the sliced deli meats you're using in "roll-up" recipes are on the large side, I suggest cutting them in half. You'll leave enough meat to securely wrap your filling but not so much as to smother it. Because sliced deli meats come in different sizes, you can decide whether or not to use an entire piece for rolling.

Chicken, Mozzarella, and Roasted Pepper Bites

These are sort of like a gourmet deli sandwich, rolled up and bite-size.

Serves 6

1 lb. thin slices deli roast chicken (or turkey), cut in half

1 (8-oz.) pkg. fresh mozzarella balls, cut into ¼-inch-thick pieces

½ cup roasted red peppers, sliced into ½-inch-wide pieces

Salt and black pepper to taste

Place a slice of chicken on a work surface. Arrange mozzarella pieces on it in a line about 1 inch in from the longest edge of chicken slice. Top mozzarella with pepper slices. Working from that edge, roll chicken over mozzarella and peppers to form a cylinder. Insert toothpicks at ½-inch intervals along the length of the roll. Using a sharp knife, cut through the roll at the midpoint between each toothpick. Repeat with remaining chicken, mozzarella, and peppers. Arrange on a serving plate, season to taste with salt and pepper, and serve.

Variation: Use sun-dried tomatoes instead of roasted red peppers.

Buffalo Chicken Dip

Okay, so this tastes like the chicken wings you had in college. That's the point.

Serves 8 to 10

1 (16½-oz.) can chicken, drained

1 cup chunky blue cheese salad dressing

1 cup hot sauce for wings

Bagel or pita crisps for serving

Place chicken into a serving bowl, and break up larger chunks. Pour in dressing and hot sauce, and toss to combine. Serve with a sturdy grain-based dipper like bagel or pita crisps.

Variation: Heat in the microwave for 2 minutes or until heated to desired temperature.

Canapé Chicken I (for Deli Chicken)

Deli chicken never looked so good. Make extra, as these will disappear.

Serves 6

½ cup (4 oz.) cream cheese or light cream cheese, softened

1 cup shredded Parmesan or Romano cheese

1 tsp. Italian seasoning

½ tsp. salt

4 pieces white or wheat bread, crusts removed, cut into 4 triangles per slice

1 lb. thinly sliced deli roast chicken (or turkey), cut into pieces roughly corresponding to the shape of bread triangles

2 TB. finely chopped fresh parsley for garnish

Preheat the broiler. Combine cream cheese, Parmesan cheese, Italian seasoning, and salt in a bowl. Arrange bread on a baking sheet, and place a piece of chicken on each triangle. Top each with about 1 tablespoon Parmesan mixture. Broil for about 2 minutes or until bread has begun to brown around the edges and cream cheese begins to bubble. Remove from oven, and arrange on a serving tray. Sprinkle a pinch of parsley on each and serve.

Variation: To save even more time, use large wheat crackers instead of toast triangles.

Canapé Chicken II (for Canned Chicken)

You'll find this amazingly quick for a hot appetizer.

Serves 6

1 (16½-oz.) can chicken

½ cup mayonnaise

1 tsp. Italian seasoning

½ tsp. salt

4 pieces white or wheat bread, crusts removed, cut into 4 triangles per slice

1 cup shredded Parmesan or Romano cheese

2 TB. finely chopped fresh parsley for garnish

Savoir Starter

Minced onion can be prepared fresh, but if you're pressed for time, try dried minced onion from your grocery store spice section. Just use half the amount of dried as fresh, and give it some time in your dip to spread the flavor.

Preheat the broiler. Place chicken into a mixing bowl, and break up larger chunks. Add mayonnaise, Italian seasoning, and salt, and toss to combine. Spoon about 2 tablespoons chicken mixture onto each bread triangle, and top with 1 heaping teaspoon shredded Parmesan cheese. Arrange on a baking sheet, and broil for about 2 minutes or until bread has begun to brown around the edges; cheese will only slightly melt. Remove and arrange on a serving tray. Sprinkle a pinch of parsley on each and serve.

Curried Chicken Dip

This dish makes the most of simple ingredients for fast flavor.

Serves 6 to 8

1 (16½-oz.) can chicken

1 cup (8-oz.) cream cheese or light cream cheese, softened

1 cup (8 oz.) plain yogurt

2 TB. minced onion

1 TB. *garam masala* (available in Asian and Indian markets and some grocery stores)

2 tsp. fresh lime juice

1 tsp. curry powder

Bagel or pita crisps for serving

Gourmet Glossary

Garam masala is a famous Indian seasoning mixture, rich with cinnamon, pepper, nutmeg, cardamom, and other spices.

Place chicken into a serving bowl, and break up larger chunks. Add cream cheese, yogurt, onion, garam masala, lime juice, and curry powder and mix thoroughly. Chill for an hour or two to allow the flavors to meld. Serve with a sturdy grain-based dipper like bagel or pita crisps.

Variation: Stir in peanuts or mango chutney for added texture and flavor.

Pineapple, Scallion, and Chicken Spread

Serves 6

1 (16½-oz.) can chicken

1 cup (8 oz.) cream cheese or light cream cheese, softened

1 (8-oz.) can pineapple chunks, drained

2 scallions, dark green parts removed, finely chopped

1 tsp. fresh lime juice

½ tsp. salt

Bagel or pita crisps for serving

Place chicken into a mixing bowl, and break up larger chunks. Add cream cheese, pineapple, scallions, lime juice, and salt and mix thoroughly. Chill for an hour or two to allow the flavors to meld. Serve with a sturdy grain-based dipper like bagel or pita crisps.

Avocado Chicken Dip

The ripe, buttery flavor of avocado shines through this party favorite.

Serves 6

1 (16½-oz.) can chicken

1 ripe avocado

½ cup sour cream or plain yogurt

3 scallions, dark green leaves removed, chopped into ½-inch-pieces

½ tsp. hot pepper sauce (such as Tabasco)

Tortilla chips for serving

In a blender or food processor fitted with a metal blade, process chicken, avocado, sour cream, scallions, and hot pepper sauce until almost smooth. Scrape into a serving bowl, and serve with tortilla chips.

Savoir Starter _____

Do you have a favorite dip but want a new approach? Try using chunks of chicken (from a can or even cubes of cooked chicken breast) on a toothpick as the vehicle of choice. One terrific pair is chicken with the Creamy Blue Dip from Chapter 4.

Where's the Beef?

Beef is not just for dinner. Its rich flavors and textures also make for delicious appetizers.

Roast Beef and Horseradish Cream Bites

Hearty roast beef paired with piquant flavors make this a rich, satisfying hors d'oeuvre. The horseradish is the flavor throttle; vary the proportion according to your desire for flavor.

Serves 6 to 8

½ cup (4 oz.) cream cheese or light cream cheese, softened

¼ cup prepared horseradish

½ lb. thin slices roast beef, cut in half

Salt and black pepper to taste

Combine cream cheese and horseradish in a small bowl and mix thoroughly. Place a slice of roast beef on a work surface. Spoon about 1 tablespoon horseradish cream onto roast beef in a line about 1 inch in from the longest edge of the slice. Working from that edge, roll roast beef over horseradish cream to form a cylinder. Insert toothpicks at ½-inch intervals along the length of the roll. Using a sharp knife, cut through the roll at the midpoint between each toothpick. Repeat with remaining roast beef and horseradish cream. Arrange roast beef bites on a serving plate, season to taste with salt and pepper, and serve.

Variation: Use your favorite sliced ham in place of the roast beef.

Savoir Starter

Horseradish is a sharp, spicy root that forms the flavor base in many condiments, from cocktail sauce to sharp mustards. It is a natural match with roast beef. The form generally found in grocery stores is prepared horseradish, which contains vinegar and oil, among other things. If you come across pure horseradish, use it much more sparingly than the prepared version, as it could put your taste buds into shock. Creamy horseradish, on the other hand, is milder than prepared horseradish. In this case, use more in your recipe.

Meatballs with Spicy-Sweet Dipping Sauce

You can let people think you made these, when really they came from the deli. Heating the honey in the microwave makes it easier to mix.

Serves 4 to 6

⅓ cup soy sauce

⅓ cup honey, heated for 15 seconds in the microwave

2 TB. sesame oil (available in the ethnic or Asian food section of most grocery stores)

1 scallion, dark green leaves removed, finely sliced, for garnish

1 lb. precooked meatballs (choose deli meatballs that are about 1 inch in diameter)

Combine soy sauce, warm honey, and sesame oil in a small (about 1-cup) serving bowl. Sprinkle sliced scallions on top. Heat meatballs in the microwave until warm (about 3 minutes, depending on the power of your microwave). Place the bowl of dipping sauce in the center of a serving platter, and arrange meatballs around it. Skewer each meatball with a toothpick and serve.

Variation: Use hoisin sauce in place of soy sauce, or use ⅔ cup duck sauce in place of both honey and soy sauce. Duck sauce, as a glance at the ingredients will show, is already quite sweet.

Hors D'oeuvre History

Popular Asian-style sauces, such as soy, hoisin, and duck sauce, provide seasoning and flavor mixes that are unusual to our Western palates. Part of the appeal is the ability of these ingredients to marry savory seasonings with sweet ones. (Think apricots in duck sauce, for example.)

Roast Beef and Endive Bites

Adapted from notable cook Anne-Marie Kott, this recipe brings a welcome heartiness to the starter lineup.

Serves 4 to 6

2 heads Belgian endive

½ lb. thin slices rare roast beef, cut into 1 by 2-inch pieces

2 TB. capers, drained

3 sprigs (about 2 TB.) chopped fresh dill

¼ cup prepared horseradish

¼ cup Russian dressing

Arrange endive leaves on a serving platter. Top each with a piece of roast beef, and sprinkle with capers and dill. Serve with small bowls of horseradish and Russian dressing.

Savoir Starter _____

Regarding texture, do you like your spread smooth or chunky? Let your own taste be the guide. My taste generally runs to "the more texture the better." I imagine it as "farmhouse texture," complete with stone terrace, grape arbor, and sun setting over the valley. There is nothing wrong with a little imagination to season your starter …

This Ham Is on a Roll: Ham-Based Starters

Ham is one of my favorite meats, there's almost always some in our fridge. Knowing it's there opens up new possibilities …. Meet the ubiquitous sandwich ingredient in new and exciting forms!

Smoked Ham and Asparagus

Here we have an easy classic.

Serves 4

¼ cup (2 oz.) cream cheese or light cream cheese, softened

2 TB. Dijon-style mustard

½ lb. thin slices smoked ham, cut in half

1 (15-oz.) can asparagus spears (whole spears, not pieces), drained

Combine cream cheese and mustard in a small bowl and mix thoroughly. Place a piece of ham on a work surface. Place a piece of asparagus on top, about 1 inch in from the longest edge. Spread asparagus with cream cheese mixture. Working from that edge, roll ham over asparagus to form a cylinder. Repeat with remaining ham, asparagus, and cream cheese mixture. Arrange pieces on a serving plate and serve.

Variation: Use rare roast beef in place of the ham. If you've got the time, fresh asparagus, blanched for 1 minute in boiling water, is delicious instead of the canned version.

Ham and Olive Bites

I like honey ham as a counterpoint to the savory olives, but any ham will work.

Serves 4

½ lb. thin slices ham, cut in half

1 (6½-oz.) can pitted Kalamata olives, drained

¼ cup whole-grain mustard

Place a piece of ham on a work surface. Arrange olives on top, in a line about 1 inch in from the longest edge. Spread with a thin coating of mustard. Working from that edge, roll ham over olives to form a cylinder. Insert toothpicks at ½-inch intervals along the length of the roll. If you can, pierce the center of each olive with the toothpicks. Using a sharp knife, cut through the roll at the midpoint between each toothpick. Repeat with remaining ham, olives, and mustard. Arrange on a serving platter and serve.

Unappetizer _____
 Stuffed olives can be used in this delicious ham appetizer, but if you use them, taste test one olive with your mustard first to see if you're starting a seasoning battle that your palate might lose. If that's the case, omit the mustard.

Variation: Use other black pitted olives (the flavor will not be quite as pronounced, but still very good) or Spanish stuffed olives.

Ham Roll-Ups and Variations

With each of these, the basic method is the same—just vary the ingredients. What's your favorite?

Serves 4

½ lb. thin slices ham, cut in half

20 baby spinach leaves

1 (8-oz.) pkg. fresh mozzarella balls, cut into ¼-inch-thick pieces

⅓ cup *pine nuts* (good as is, but even better toasted)

1 TB. balsamic vinegar

Place a piece of ham on a work surface. Arrange spinach leaves on top, in a line about 1 inch in from the longest edge. Top with mozzarella pieces and pine nuts. Working from that edge, roll ham over spinach, mozzarella, and pine nuts to form a cylinder. Insert toothpicks at ½-inch intervals along the length of the roll. Using a sharp knife, cut through the roll at the midpoint between each toothpick. Repeat with remaining ham, mozzarella, and pine nuts. Arrange on a serving platter, drizzle with balsamic vinegar, and serve.

Gourmet Glossary

Pine nuts really do come from pine trees, although probably not the kind in your backyard. They are a rich (read: high-fat), flavorful, and, yes, a bit pine-y nut that is a traditional component of pesto. They can add a wonderful hearty crunch to many other recipes as well.

Variations:

◆ Replace mozzarella with ½ cup feta cheese mixed with ¼ cup softened cream cheese.

◆ Replace mozzarella with ricotta, and sprinkle the finished bites with garlic salt instead of balsamic vinegar (my wife's favorite).

◆ Replace mozzarella with ½ cup blue cheese mixed with ¼ cup softened cream cheese, and use thin apple slices in place of pine nuts. (This is a very different, albeit delicious, taste.)

Ham and Pineapple

This is a time-honored and tasty pairing.

Serves 4

1 (8-oz.) can pineapple chunks, drained

½ lb. thin slices ham, cut into 1 by 4-inch pieces

⅔ cup duck sauce

Wrap each pineapple chunk in a piece of ham and fasten with a toothpick. Arrange on a serving platter, and serve with a small bowl of duck sauce for dipping.

Savoir Starter

The toothpick serves two purposes in these recipes. The first is to give your guest a handle with which to lift each bite; but the other, just as important, is to bind the ingredients together so they don't fall apart. To this end, make sure you insert the toothpick all the way through the rolled meat so it comes out the other side and holds the end piece to keep it from coming loose.

Endive with Herbed Sausage and Apricot Preserves

This hearty sweet and savory spread is unlike so many of the creamy spreads. I know—it's not ham, but it is in the family.

Serves 4

½ lb. cooked spicy sausage meat

1 cup apricot preserves

1 scallion, dark green leaves removed, cut into ½-inch pieces

Belgian endive leaves for serving

In a food processor fitted with a metal blade, process sausage, preserves, and scallion pieces until spreadable but still chunky. Scrape spread into a serving bowl, and place the bowl on a platter surrounded by Belgian endive leaves.

Ham and Apple Spread (Adapted)

A hearty, savory-sweet spread that somehow seems perfect for fall or winter—I suppose that's what makes this a comfort food …

Serves 4

½ lb. ham (deli, canned, or even leftover)

1 Granny Smith apple, cored, sliced into sections

½ cup (4 oz.) cream cheese or light cream cheese, softened

¼ tsp. cinnamon

Belgian endive leaves and/or wheat crackers for serving

In a food processor fitted with a metal blade, process ham, apple, cream cheese, and cinnamon until spreadable but still chunky. Scrape spread into a serving bowl, and serve with Belgian endive leaves or wheat crackers.

Unappetizer

Recipes calling for fresh fruit are best consumed quickly, as the fruit, once cut, will immediately begin to oxidize (turn brown) and lose its flavor. This natural process can be slowed through the addition of acid (technically referred to as "acidulation") by rubbing the slices of fruit with a lemon half. Your taste buds won't notice the difference, but the appearance is improved.

Ham-Wrapped Dates

These are oh so simple, yet you've got to give them a try.

Serves 4

½ cup (4 oz.) cream cheese or light cream cheese, softened

⅓ lb. dried, pitted dates (about 20), sliced in half lengthwise

½ lb. thin slices ham, cut into 1 by 4-inch pieces

Spread about 1 teaspoon cream cheese on a date, wrap ham around it, and fasten with a toothpick. Arrange on a serving platter and serve.

The Least You Need to Know

- Many meat-based appetizers offer savory flavors and satisfying heft—perfect for those hungry guests.
- The 5-minute time limit means that we must focus on already-cooked, smoked, or cured meats. That might sound like a limit, but a visit to the deli will show you just how many possibilities there really are.
- Don't be afraid of simple recipes. By choosing a few main ingredients (ham and asparagus, for example) with careful attention to quality and matching, the resulting flavors can be every bit as magnetic as a recipe taking many more steps and much more time.

Part 2

A 5-Minute World Tour

The cuisine of each part of the world is unique—from seasoning to base ingredients and methods used. In a simple but compelling sense, this learning is the opportunity that exotic appetizers can bring.

We'll visit Mexico (and slightly north of that border) for tortillas, tostadas, and quesadillas, to name a few. We'll sail through the Straits of Gibraltar to explore the cuisine of the Mediterranean with appetizers featuring olives, figs, and other wholesome ingredients. We'll travel to France to sample pâté and mushrooms and to Italy for prosciutto. We'll fly to the orient to sample cumin and mint as well as curry spices in combinations that will make your taste buds dance. And we'll discover a peanut sauce like you've never tasted before.

10

South(west) of the Border

In This Chapter

- ◆ Sunny Southwest seasoning
- ◆ The magic of lime juice
- ◆ That's a (tortilla) wrap!
- ◆ Yes, you can cook these in 5 minutes

When it comes to appetizers, we owe a huge flavor debt to Southwestern and Mexican cuisine. The word for many of these dishes is *antojitos*, which translates as "whimsies," or "little cravings." What a perfect name for an appetizer!

Southwest Building Blocks

The following are just a few of the building blocks at our disposal for the recipes in this chapter.

Popular Ingredients and Seasonings

Base Ingredients	Seasonings
"Mexican"-style cheese (Monterey Jack cheese and others)	*Chili powder*
Guacamole	Cumin
Salsa	Hot chili peppers
Corn	Cilantro
Lime	Oregano
Fresh fruits (avocado to jicama)	Basil
Fresh tomatoes and tomatillos	Paprika
Sliced black olives	
Refried beans	
Ground beef (or other meats)	
Seafood (all kinds)	

These components are independently delicious. Together they create a symphony of Southwestern flavor.

Gourmet Glossary

Chili powder is a justly famous seasoning blend that includes chili peppers, cumin, oregano, and, in some cases, garlic. Proportions vary between different versions, but they all offer a warm rich flavor that offers, at least in the imagination, a culinary trip south of the border.

Dips and Savory Spreads

In this section, I've included some of my favorite dips and spreads. Some are authentic, as might be served in Acapulco; others use seasonings that evoke cuisine south of the border but might take a bit more license with other ingredients.

My Favorite Salsa

I've made many different versions of salsa, but this one adapted from Fanny Farmer is my favorite. This classic is always better when made with fresh tomatoes. Make the individual tomato pieces small enough to be scooped with tortilla chips.

Serves 4 to 6

2 large (about 8 oz. each) tomatoes, chopped into ¼-inch-square pieces

½ cup sweet onion (such as Vidalia), chopped into ¼-inch-square pieces or smaller

1 (4½-oz.) can green chilies, drained and chopped

¼ cup chopped fresh cilantro

2 TB. red wine vinegar

3 TB. fresh lime juice

1 tsp. kosher salt

½ tsp. dried oregano

¼ tsp. hot pepper sauce (such as Tabasco)

Tortilla chips for serving (optional)

Combine tomatoes, onion, chilies, cilantro, vinegar, lime juice, salt, oregano, and hot pepper sauce in a serving bowl and mix thoroughly. Fresh salsa is best eaten soon after it's made, but it will survive in the fridge for a day or two. Serve with tortilla chips or as a topping on other Mexican-style dishes.

Salsa Verde

The texture of Salsa Verde is like fresh salsa; the flavor is quite different because of the unique, piquant *tomatillo* flavor.

Serves 4 to 6

½ lb. tomatillos, papery peel removed and flesh chopped into ¼-inch-dice or smaller

½ cup sweet onion (such as Vidalia), chopped into ¼-inch dice or smaller

½ can (about 2 oz.) green chilies, drained and chopped

¼ cup chopped fresh cilantro

1 TB. fresh lime juice

1 tsp. kosher salt

Tortilla chips for serving

Combine tomatillos, onion, chilies, cilantro, lime juice, and salt in a serving bowl and mix thoroughly. Serve with tortilla chips or as a topping on other Mexican-style dishes.

Gourmet Glossary

The **tomatillo,** available in specialty and large grocery stores, looks like a green tomato with a papery skin, but it is actually a closer botanical relative of the gooseberry. It is a small, round fruit with a distinctive spicy flavor. Tomatillos are a traditional component of many south-of-the-border dishes.

Guacamole

For many fans of Mexican-style foods, avocados are the perfect fruit. By that logic, this elegant, flavorful dip is, therefore, the perfect food. The sour cream adds decadent texture, but it can be omitted to somewhat reduce the fat content.

Serves 6

2 ripe avocados

½ cup sour cream (optional)

½ can (about 2 oz.) green chilies, drained and chopped

3 TB. fresh lemon juice

1 TB. olive oil

1 tsp. chopped garlic

½ tsp. kosher salt

Dash hot pepper sauce (such as Tabasco)

Tortilla chips for serving

Cut avocados in half, and remove the pits by embedding the blade (not the tip) of a sharp knife into each. Turn the knife slowly to release the pit. Scoop the flesh from the peel. Combine avocado, sour cream, chilies, lemon juice, olive oil, garlic, salt, and hot pepper sauce in a serving bowl, and mix thoroughly until smooth but slightly chunky. Serve with tortilla chips and a frozen margarita (margarita optional but nice).

Kissin' Cousins

These next few dips explore variations on the Southwest theme. They are all cousins, but each has a different personality.

Mexican Tuna Dip

This one is savory and hearty.

Serves 6

1 cup (8 oz.) cream cheese or light cream cheese, softened

1 cup chunky medium to hot salsa

1 cup (4 oz.) shredded Monterey Jack or Mexican-style cheese

1 (6-oz.) can chunk white tuna in water, drained

1 tsp. chili powder

½ cup sliced black olives

Spread cream cheese evenly over the bottom of a microwave-safe serving dish. Pour salsa over cream cheese and spread evenly. Combine shredded cheese, tuna, and chili powder in a bowl and mix thoroughly; then spread tuna mixture over salsa. Scatter black olives over tuna mixture, and microwave for 3 minutes or until dip just begins to bubble. Serve with tortilla chips.

Four-Layer Bean Dip

This flavorful dip makes good use of Mexican seasonings. For a low-fat version, seek out canned refried beans made without lard. This big batch will keep a small army (uh, party) satisfied.

Serves 10 to 12

1 (15-oz.) can plain refried beans

1 (1¼-oz.) pkg. taco seasoning mix

1 (16-oz.) pkg. guacamole (store-bought for speed)

2 cups sour cream

1 cup tomato salsa (your favorite)

2 cups (8-oz.) shredded Mexican-style cheese

Tortilla chips for serving

Combine refried beans and taco seasoning in a bowl and mix thoroughly. Spread this mixture evenly over the bottom of a pie plate or similar-size serving dish. Spread guacamole over refried beans. Mix sour cream and salsa, and spread over guacamole. Sprinkle shredded cheese over sour cream. Serve with tortilla chips.

Mexican Chili Dip

As easy as this is to make, the problem with this dip is that it's also very easy to see it disappear. This is middle-ground spicy; to vary the intensity of the heat, increase or reduce the amount of chili powder and hot sauce.

Serves 6

1 cup (8 oz.) cream cheese, softened

1 cup (4 oz.) shredded Mexican-style or Monterey Jack cheese

½ cup chunky medium salsa

1 TB. fresh lime juice

1 TB. chili powder

1 tsp. kosher salt

Dash hot pepper sauce (such as Tabasco)

Tortilla chips for serving

Combine sour cream, cheese, salsa, lime juice, chili powder, salt, and hot pepper sauce and mix thoroughly. Microwave for 2 minutes or until warm, stir to evenly distribute the temperature, and serve with tortilla chips.

Warm Mexican Bean Dip

This quick dip is also hearty.

Serves 8 to 10

1 (16-oz.) can spicy refried beans

2 cups (16 oz.) sour cream, ¼ cup reserved for garnish

1 cup tomato salsa (your favorite)

Tortilla chips for serving

Unappetizer

Many brands of canned refried beans contain lard, an ingredient that might add to taste but one that many people would rather not eat. To avoid lard, seek out fat-free or vegetarian beans.

Scrape refried beans into a microwave-safe serving bowl, and microwave on high for 1 minute. This not only heats the beans but also makes stubborn solid refried beans easier to break up. Add 2 cups sour cream and salsa, microwave for another minute, and mix thoroughly. Top with remaining ¼ cup sour cream, and serve with the bowl surrounded by tortilla chips.

Tortilla Starters

When we talk about the most famous grain platform of Southwest and Mexican cuisine, we think of the tortilla, a round flatbread that is Mexico's daily fare. Tortillas can be made of corn or wheat and come in several forms, including the following:

- **Soft tortillas.** The basis for the other tortilla products, soft tortillas are available in grocery stores in 5- to 12-inch sizes.
- **Taco shells.** Tacos are tortillas wrapped around various kinds of food. Crispy taco shells come ready to fill.
- **Tortilla chips.** Fried tortilla wedges, tortilla chips are crispy and irresistible—who can eat only one?

These recipes use tortillas as the vehicle of choice.

Quesadilla-Based Recipes

A quesadilla is, in a simplistic sense, a south-of-the-border grilled cheese sandwich. That description, of course, doesn't do it justice. Although my kids might stick to flavorless American cheese, a quesadilla should have the highest-quality ingredients, flavorful cheeses, and a universe of fillings and seasonings. The classic quesadilla differs from a taco in that it is folded (although contemporary cooks often use two tortillas).

What you see here are just a few of my favorites, but experiment with the list of ingredients from the beginning of this chapter (and others) and discover your own favorites. The basic method is the same; it's the ingredients that change.

Chili, Chicken, and Lime Quesadillas with Sour Cream

This accelerated method packs a lot of flavor between those crisp tortilla wedges. Be careful serving this as an appetizer; people will be tempted to camp out at your appetizer table and treat it as a meal.

Serves 6 to 8

3 TB. olive oil

6 (6-inch) flour tortillas

2 cups (8 oz.) shredded Monterey Jack or Mexican-style cheese, separated into ⅔ cup per tortilla

½ lb. thin slices deli chicken or ⅔ of a 12-oz. can (8 oz.) chicken, drained

1 TB. fresh lime juice

½ tsp. chili powder

Sour cream for garnish

Chopped fresh chives for garnish

Heat oil in a 10-inch skillet over medium-high heat. Working quickly, set 1 tortilla in the skillet, top it with about ⅓ cup cheese, ⅓ chicken, and another ⅓ cup cheese. Drizzle with 1 teaspoon lime juice, sprinkle with a pinch of chili powder, and top with another tortilla. Cook for about 1 minute, flip with a spatula, and cook for another 30 seconds or so until cheese inside is melted sufficiently to bind quesadilla together. Remove quesadilla to a serving plate, and slice pie-style into six (or eight) wedges and keep warm. Repeat with remaining tortillas and filling ingredients. Serve with sour cream and a spoon for spreading. A sprinkling of fresh chopped chives would complete the picture.

Savoir Starter

I've suggested the pan-frying method for quesadillas, but broiling is also an option. Simply brush a bit of oil (or use butter or margarine) on each side of the tortilla and broil on the high rack for about 1 minute per side.

Pineapple, Ham, and Mozzarella Quesadillas

This is a slightly unusual set of ingredients for a quesadilla, but poetic license can be a good thing.

Serves 6 to 8

3 TB. olive oil

6 (6-inch) flour tortillas

2 cups (8 oz.) shredded mozzarella cheese, separated into ⅔ cup per tortilla

½ lb. thin slices deli ham

1 (8-oz.) can crushed pineapple, drained

½ tsp. salt

Heat oil in a 10-inch skillet over medium-high heat. Working quickly, set 1 tortilla in the skillet, top it with about ⅓ cup mozzarella, ⅓ ham, ⅓ crushed pineapple, and another ⅓ cup cheese. Sprinkle with a pinch of salt, and top with another tortilla. Cook for about 1 minute, flip with a spatula, and cook for another 30 seconds or so until cheese inside is melted sufficiently to bind quesadilla together. Remove to a serving plate, slice pie-style into six (or eight) wedges, and keep warm. Repeat with remaining tortillas and filling ingredients and serve.

Quesadillas with Roasted Red Pepper, Goat's Milk Cheese, and Parmesan

This mixes cultural metaphors for a unique but delicious flavor treat.

Serves 6 to 8

3 TB. olive oil

6 (6-inch) flour tortillas

1 (8-oz.) pkg. fresh goat's milk cheese

1 (10- to 12-oz.) jar roasted red peppers, drained and cut into 1-inch pieces

1 cup shredded Parmesan cheese, separated into ⅓ cup per tortilla

½ tsp. salt

Heat oil in a 10-inch skillet over medium-high heat. Arrange 3 tortillas on a work surface, and spread each with ⅓ goat's milk cheese. Working quickly, set 1 tortilla topped with cheese into skillet (cheese side up), and scatter about ⅓ roasted peppers over it, ⅓ cup Parmesan, and a pinch of salt; top with another tortilla. Cook for about a minute, flip with a spatula, and cook for another 30 seconds or until cheese inside is melted sufficiently to bind quesadilla together. Remove to a serving plate, slice pie-style into six (or eight) wedges, and keep warm. Repeat with remaining tortillas and filling ingredients and serve.

Tostada-Based Recipes

Tostadas—classically speaking, fried tortillas laid flat and topped with a "filling"—can be even quicker than quesadillas for the 5-minute-appetizer specialist, as they can be broiled rather than pan-fried. Because the ingredients are open to the (heating) elements, no flipping is required.

Use many of the same ingredients with a bit more of an eye toward arrangement, as the "filling" is on display with each slice. Also, note that the cheese does not completely cover the tortilla (unlike a pizza, where the cheese is intended to completely coat the bread).

Shrimp and Salsa Tostadas

Delicious shrimp and savory salsa—what a combination.

Serves 6 to 8

4 (6-inch) flour tortillas

2 cups (8 oz.) shredded Monterey Jack or Mexican-style cheese, separated into ½ cup per tortilla

1 cup tomato salsa (your favorite), drained of excess liquid if very juicy

2 (6-oz.) cans tiny cocktail shrimp, drained

½ tsp. chili powder

Sour cream (optional)

 **Unappetizer**
Avoid the temptation to add extra ingredients with a lot of moisture, like salsa. Use just enough to add texture and flavor. Too much ends up creating soggy tortillas and messy drips.

Preheat the broiler. Arrange tortillas on a baking sheet or two, depending on size of tray. Top each with ½ cup cheese, ¼ cup salsa, and ¼ shrimp, and spread evenly. (The tortilla will not be completely covered, but that's okay.) Sprinkle with chili powder, and broil for 2 to 3 minutes or until cheese begins to melt. Remove to a serving plate, slice pie-style into six wedges, and serve with sour cream as an additional accoutrement.

Bacon and Swiss Tostada

Unconventional and delicious, this is ready in minutes.

Serves 4 to 6

2 (12-inch) soft flour tortillas

1 (8-oz.) pkg. shredded Swiss cheese

¼ cup real bacon bits

 **Unappetizer**
Watch closely any food that's broiling. The problem is not going over 5 minutes; it's the danger of overcooking in only 1 minute.

Preheat the broiler. Place tortillas on a baking sheet, and sprinkle with ½ Swiss cheese and ½ bacon bits. Broil for 2 minutes or until cheese is melted and starting to bubble. Slice on a cutting board, and serve pizza-style.

Tostada with Fresh Mozzarella and Roasted Peppers

Here we have half-art, half-appetizer. The green tortilla contrasts nicely with the glistening red, white, and black of the pepper, mozzarella, and olives. Spinach tortillas are wheat tortillas that include spinach when they are made.

Serves 4 to 6

2 (12-inch) spinach tortillas

8 fresh mozzarella balls (in brine), drained and cut in half

16 roasted red pepper pieces, about 1 inch square

8 pitted Kalamata olives, sliced in half length-wise

3 TB. shredded Parmesan cheese

1 TB. olive oil

Kosher salt to taste

Preheat the broiler. Place tortillas on a baking sheet. Arrange 8 mozzarella ball halves equally spaced around the perimeter of each tortilla. Then, working inward from mozzarella halves, place pieces of pepper and olive so the result resembles spokes in a wheel. Sprinkle each tortilla with Parmesan cheese, dress with a swirl of oil, and broil for about 2 minutes or until tortilla begins to crisp. Sprinkle with salt. Slice, pizza style, making your cuts in between mozzarella/pepper/olive rows. Separate the pieces to form a sort of decorative wreath and serve.

Variation: Use oil-packed, sun-dried tomato pieces in place of roasted pepper and dress with oil from the tomatoes.

Tortilla and Scallion Tostada

A touch of sour cream makes this a magical bite.

Serves 4 to 6

2 (12-inch) soft flour tortillas

2 cups (8 oz.) shredded Monterey Jack or Mexican-style cheese

4 scallions, washed, dark green parts removed, and thinly sliced

1 tsp. chili powder

1 cup sour cream

Preheat the broiler. Place tortillas on a baking sheet, and sprinkle with ½ cheese, ½ scallion pieces, and ½ teaspoon chili powder. Broil for 2 minutes until cheese is melted and just starts to bubble. Slice on a cutting board, and serve pizza style with sour cream for a topping.

That's a (Tortilla) Wrap!

Don't forget your microwave. This is a variation on "flautas," a tortilla-wrapped, fried morsel.

Cheese, Garlic, and Spinach Wraps

Simple, once again, is good.

Serves 4 to 6

4 (8-inch) flour tortillas

2 cups (about 4 oz.) baby spinach leaves

2 cups (8 oz.) shredded Monterey Jack or Mexican-style cheese

½ tsp. garlic salt

1 cup sour cream for dipping

Place tortilla on a work surface. Arrange spinach leaves in a line about 1 inch in from the side closest to you. Top with ½ cup shredded cheese and a pinch garlic salt. Starting from the side closest to the filling, roll tortilla into a cylinder. If necessary, hold it in place with a toothpick. Repeat with other tortillas and filling ingredients, place all on a microwave-safe plate, and heat for 1 minute or until cheese begins to melt. Cut each in half, and arrange pieces on a serving plate like the spokes on a wheel, surrounding a bowl of sour cream for dipping.

The Cheese, Garlic, and Spinach Wraps is just one star in the constellation. If you like it, try wraps with any of the following:

- ◆ Shrimp and rosemary
- ◆ Chili (powder) and lime
- ◆ Olives and feta
- ◆ Sautéed onions and mozzarella
- ◆ Bean sprouts and mozzarella

Other Favorites

Here are several other Southwest-style dishes to tantalize your guests.

Fresh Jicama

In Mexico, our friends Joaquin and Melissa serve slices of jicama as a snack for their kids. I admit I ate half of what they set out. Crunchy and succulent, these fresh-tasting vegetables are a palate-cleansing counterpoint to richer appetizers. (The appeal is in the novelty—obviously not tied to prep time!) When you are peeling jicama, take off both the thin skin and the fibrous layer just under it.

Serves 4 to 6

1 lb. jicama, peeled and sliced into ½ by ½ by 4-inch sticks

Juice of 1 lime

4 thin slices lime, for garnish

Arrange jicama sticks around the edge of a platter facing outward like the spokes of a wheel. Drizzle with lime juice, decorate at four points with lime slices, and serve.

Variation: Serve seasoned with a pinch of chili powder or salt.

Quick-Grilled Shrimp with Chili and Lime

Succulent shrimp is served with a hint of spice and the fresh, cool flavor of lime.

Serves 4 to 6

½ lb. (31 to 40 count, about 18) cooked shrimp, peeled and deveined with tail off

3 TB. fresh lime juice

1 tsp. chili powder

2 TB. olive oil

1 tsp. chopped garlic

Place shrimp into a mixing bowl, pour in 2 tablespoons lime juice, and toss shrimp to coat. Sprinkle shrimp with chili powder and toss again. Heat olive oil and garlic in a 12-inch skillet over medium-high heat; add shrimp and sauté for 2 minutes, turning once. Remove warm shrimp to a serving plate, insert a toothpick in each, *drizzle* with remaining 1 tablespoon lime juice, and serve.

Gourmet Glossary

To **drizzle** is to lightly sprinkle drops of a liquid over food. Drizzling is often the finishing touch to a dish.

Nachos

The definition of nachos seems to change from house to house. Here's one of my favorite versions, but keep that list of potential toppings in mind to create your own favorite!

Serves 4

1 (16-oz.) can nonfat refried beans

Canola oil, if needed

8 oz. salted white corn tortilla chips (not flavored)

4 cups (16 oz.) shredded Monterey Jack or Mexican-style cheese

Pinch of chili powder

½ cup tomato salsa or to taste

½ cup sour cream or to taste

Scrape refried beans into a microwave-safe bowl, and heat for 1½ minutes or until hot. Stir to loosen beans. If necessary, add a little canola oil to make beans more spreadable.

While beans are heating, arrange chips in a double, loose layer on a microwave-safe serving platter.

Spoon refried beans over chips. Sprinkle cheese over refried beans, and microwave for 2 minutes or until cheese is melted. Sprinkle with a bit of chili powder, and top nachos to taste with salsa and sour cream.

The Least You Need to Know

- Southwestern and Mexican ingredients are a rich source of inspiration for fast appetizers.
- Tortillas enable tasty, quick recipes with just a touch of the unusual.
- Southwestern and Mexican appetizers are some of the few kinds of hors d'oeuvres that can actually be cooked and served hot in only 5 minutes.
- Fresh ingredients and careful use of fragrant seasonings make these appetizers sure winners.

Chapter 11

Mediterranean Breezes

In This Chapter

- ◆ Seasonings that bring to mind the seaside in the Old Country
- ◆ Perfect matches of fruits and meats
- ◆ Garlic in the spotlight
- ◆ Simple, elegant, and ultra-quick "bites"

These simple dishes, full of natural ingredients, make me think of a farm-house meal somewhere in the Mediterranean countryside. I take a bite, close my eyes, and I'm there.

We've all read those articles about the "Mediterranean Diet." I won't make the health claims here, but in this chapter, you'll find those ingredients and flavors that bring the fabled diet to life: olive oil, nuts, fresh vegetables, and, of course, garlic.

Button Mushroom and Black Olive Skewers with Lemon Garlic Dressing

This is a fragrant, savory dish featuring fresh mushrooms.

Serves 6 to 8

2 (6-oz.) cans pitted large ripe olives, drained

1 (8-oz.) pkg. button mushrooms

2 TB. extra-virgin olive oil

1 TB. fresh lemon juice

1 tsp. chopped garlic

1 tsp. chopped fresh rosemary

Salt and freshly ground black pepper to taste

> **Unappetizer**
> As we bask in Mediter-ranean breezes and recipes, garlic crops up almost everywhere. If you're a garlic lover like me, that's a good thing, but it's not a bad idea to make sure your guests like garlic, too!

Combine olives and mushrooms in a mixing bowl. In a measuring cup, combine olive oil, lemon juice, garlic, and rosemary and mix thoroughly. Pour over olives and mushrooms, then assemble olive and mushroom bites on toothpicks, with 1 olive and 1 mushroom on each toothpick. Arrange these bites on a plate, sprinkle with salt and black pepper and serve.

Mediterranean Olive Medley

Many people who have spent time in southern Europe are passionate about olives. They come in different sizes and colors, each representative of the variety and method of preparation. Here's an opportunity for an informal olive tasting.

Serves 4 to 6 (if you serve all 4 types)

⅓ lb. Kalamata olives

⅓ lb. Mission olives

⅓ lb. Spanish olives

⅓ lb. Nicoise olives

2 TB. extra-virgin olive oil

Crusty bread for serving

Arrange Kalamata, Mission, Spanish, and Nicoise olives in a single layer on a plate or shallow pan, such as a quiche pan. Drizzle olives with olive oil, and serve with crusty bread.

Hors D'oeuvre History

Olives are perhaps one of the first appetizers ever; the oldest of world literature features this wonderful tiny fruit. To assemble a platter of mixed varieties is to offer delicious variations on a theme. The curing process almost always includes salt, so you won't need to season olives. A drizzle of olive oil, on the other hand, gives them an appetizing shine. You'll find a greater variety of olives that still have their pits at your deli, so simply make a separate empty bowl available for them.

Olive Tapenade

A tapenade is a rich spread traditionally made with capers, anchovies, and olives. This flavorful and distinctive olive-based version echoes the flavor of the Mediterranean.

Serves 4 to 6

1 cup pitted black olives

1 cup pitted green olives

½ cup roasted red pepper pieces

¼ cup olive oil

1 tsp. chopped garlic

1 tsp. fresh lemon juice

Wheat crackers or sliced crusty bread for serving

In a food processor fitted with a metal blade, process black and green olives, red pepper, olive oil, garlic, and lemon juice until you have a chunky paste. Scrape tapenade into a serving bowl, and serve surrounded by wheat crackers or slices of crusty bread.

Hors D'oeuvre History

Canned, pitted olives in the grocery store, although tasty, are not on the same distinctive flavor level as specifically named (usually still with pits) olives from particular regions of the world. When you prepare a dish that is all about olives, stick to the best. When olives are a supporting component of a recipe, there to provide color, texture, and some flavor, head for the can of pitted olives.

Magic Garlic Mayonnaise Aioli

Traditionally a sauce for main courses, aioli can also be used as a dip or garnish—or all of the above.

Serves 4 to 6

1 cup mayonnaise

1 TB. chopped garlic

1 TB. high-quality olive oil

2 tsp. fresh lemon juice

Toast points or sliced mushrooms for serving

Savoir Starter

I've found that I save quite a bit of time by using chopped garlic. The flavor is not quite as good, but convenience wins out.

Combine mayonnaise, garlic, olive oil, and lemon juice in a serving bowl and mix thoroughly. Serve with toasted bread pieces or with pieces of sliced mushroom.

Greek Cucumber Dip (*Tsatsiki*)

This classic Greek dip is refreshing and delicious.

Serves 4 to 6

1 cup plain yogurt

½ cucumber, peeled and finely chopped

1 TB. crushed garlic

1 TB. olive oil

2 tsp. fresh lemon juice

½ tsp. freshly ground black pepper

½ tsp. salt

Pita wedges for serving

Combine yogurt, cucumber, garlic, olive oil, lemon juice, pepper, and salt in a bowl and mix thoroughly. Serve with pita wedges.

Unappetizer

When preparing dishes that include fresh vegetables from cucumbers to spinach, make them just prior to serving to preserve texture and flavor. Wilted vegetables are very unappetizing.

Sun-Dried Tomato Spread

This creamy, rich spread is a real crowd pleaser.

Serves 6

1 cup (8 oz.) cream cheese or light cream cheese, softened

⅔ cup sun-dried tomatoes, drained and cut into ½-inch pieces (to aid processing)

⅓ cup sour cream

⅓ cup pitted Kalamata olives

2 scallions, coarsely chopped

1 scallion, thinly sliced for garnish

Pita wedges for serving

In a food processor fitted with a metal blade, process cream cheese, tomatoes, sour cream, olives, and 2 coarsely chopped scallions, pulsing to achieve a chunky-creamy consistency. Scrape spread into a serving bowl, top with 1 thinly sliced scallion, and serve with pita wedges.

Fig and Goat's Milk Cheese Bites

This fruit and cheese combination falls into the category of "simple combinations, sublime results." Although I have experimented with garnishes from chives and parsley to dried herbs, the simple combination of goat's milk cheese with fig was the winner for me.

Serves 4

6 dried figs, sliced in half lengthwise

4 oz. fresh goat's milk cheese

Spread each fig half with about 1 teaspoon goat's milk cheese, and arrange on a serving plate.

Grapes with Walnut Goat's Milk Cheese

What a great bite of flavor! The forest of toothpicks is an impressive sight.

Serves 4 to 6

½ cup (4 oz.) fresh goat's milk cheese

½ cup (4 oz.) sour cream

4 oz. chopped walnuts

1 lb. red seedless grapes

Combine goat's milk cheese, sour cream, and walnuts in a serving bowl and mix thoroughly. Place the bowl on a serving platter, and surround with grapes on toothpicks. Have your guests use a spreading knife to place a small dab of goat's milk cheese-walnut mixture on a grape and pop it in.

Marinated Chicken and Fig Spears

The savory flavor of marinated chicken with the sweetness of a bite of fig is a memorable flavor sensation.

Serves 6

1 (12-oz.) can chicken, drained and cut into ¾-inch-square chunks

½ cup Greek-style or Italian dressing

5 ripe figs, sliced in quarters lengthwise

1 to 2 TB. chopped fresh chives for garnish

Gourmet Glossary

Skewers are thin wooden or metal sticks, usually about 8 inches long, that are perfect for assembling kebabs, dipping things into hot liquid, or serving single-bite food items with a bit of panache.

Place chicken in a bowl, pour dressing over it, and turn to coat. Spear 1 piece chicken and 1 fig quarter on a *skewer* or toothpick. Repeat with remaining chicken and figs, using 1 piece of each per skewer. Place skewers on a serving platter, arranging them so the food is at one side of the plate and the handles are on the other. Sprinkle with chopped chives and serve.

Pepperoni and Olive Bites

You want flavor? You will certainly find it here.

Serves 6 to 8

18 to 24 pitted Kalamata or medium black olives

18 to 24 thin pepperoni slices

1 TB. olive oil

Wrap each olive with 1 pepperoni slice and fasten with a toothpick. Pepperoni will not completely surround olive. Arrange olive side up on a serving platter, drizzled with olive oil.

Savoir Starter _____

When I'm in a pinch for a quick appetizer, the first thing I check the fridge for is sliced pepperoni. Pepperoni stuffed with roasted red pepper, goat's milk cheese, olives, tomatoes, or, well, just about anything will serve. I also find Pepperoni and Olive Bites useful when I feel the need to have "just one extra" appetizer to set out, as the base ingredients tend to be lurking in the fridge already and it only takes a minute to put together.

Quick Lamb Spread with Feta and Garlic

For a taste of the mountains surrounding the Mediterranean, try this hearty appetizer.

Serves 4 to 6

½ lb. ground lamb

1 TB. olive oil

1 TB. minced onion

2 tsp. chopped garlic

½ tsp. chopped fresh rosemary

½ cup (4 oz.) plain yogurt

¼ lb. crumbled feta cheese

Sprig parsley for garnish

4 small (6-inch) flat breads, such as pita, each cut into 4 wedges

Salt and freshly ground black pepper to taste

Cook lamb, oil, onion, garlic, and rosemary in a small skillet over high heat for about 3 minutes, stirring often until lamb is completely cooked and no longer pink. Remove from the heat, and mix in yogurt and feta cheese. Scrape lamb mixture into a heatproof serving bowl, top with sprig of parsley, and surround with pita wedges. Serve with salt and pepper. Use a spreading knife to spread a couple tablespoons lamb on a piece of pita.

Garlic Shrimp Sauté

Garlic and shrimp are a perfect match. Using cooked shrimp accelerates preparation.

Serves 4

3 TB. olive oil

1 TB. chopped garlic

½ lb. (51 to 70 count, or about 30) cooked shrimp, peeled and deveined with tail on

½ tsp. kosher salt

2 TB. shredded Parmesan cheese for garnish (optional)

Heat oil and garlic in a 10- to 12-inch skillet over medium-high heat. Add shrimp and heat thoroughly, stirring, for 1 to 2 minutes or until shrimp is firm and completely pink/coral in color. Remove shrimp to a serving plate, sprinkle with salt and Parmesan cheese (if using), insert toothpicks and serve.

Savoir Starter

Although cooked shrimp gets you moving faster, raw shrimp (the peeled and deveined kind) can also be used after it's quickly cooked. Simply cook in butter or oil over medium heat for 3 to 4 minutes, turning to cook each side, until the shrimp turns opaque.

Spinach-Wrapped Bacon and Parmesan Bites

The fresh taste of baby spinach leaves lends a welcome freshness and springtime feel to this simple dish. Pick spinach leaves that are large enough to completely surround the filling to avoid spillage.

Serves 4

⅓ lb. (about 6 oz.) cream cheese or light cream cheese, softened

⅓ cup shredded Parmesan cheese

3 TB. real bacon bits

18 to 24 baby spinach leaves (use the larger ones)

1 TB. extra-virgin olive oil

Kosher salt to taste

Combine cream cheese, Parmesan cheese, and bacon pieces in a small bowl and mix thoroughly. Place about 2 teaspoons cheese mixture onto each spinach leaf, wrap leaf around cheese, and fasten with a toothpick. Arrange on a serving plate, drizzle with olive oil, sprinkle with salt and serve.

The Least You Need to Know

- ◆ Mediterranean-style dishes make use of simple ingredients carefully paired together to achieve flavor excitement.
- ◆ Many Mediterranean-style dishes are perfect for garlic lovers.
- ◆ Italian and Mediterranean-style recipes are both elegant and extremely quick to make.
- ◆ The highest-quality fresh and preserved fruits, vegetables, and seafood make these appetizers not only tasty but healthful, too.

Chapter 12

Vive la France

In This Chapter

- ◆ The taste sensations of foie gras and pâté
- ◆ Appetizers featuring rich French cheeses
- ◆ Simple, speedy, and classy recipes
- ◆ The secret to real "French onion" flavor

Many books have been written about the rich world of French cuisine, and I won't claim to cover anything but a small part of this tradition. This chapter offers appetizer versions of some of my favorite representative ingredients and combinations, including rich cheeses, fruits, and savory pâtés and terrines.

Roquefort Chicken Spread

This hearty spread gets its distinctive flavor from Roquefort, that famous blue sheep's milk cheese.

Serves 4

¼ lb. (4 oz.) Roquefort cheese

1 cup (8 oz.) cream cheese or light cream cheese, softened

1 (12-oz.) can chicken, white meat

2 TB. minced onion

2 TB. chopped walnuts for garnish

Sliced crusty bread for serving

Combine Roquefort cheese, cream cheese, chicken, and onion in a serving bowl and mix thoroughly, breaking up the larger pieces of chicken. Chill for an hour to allow the flavors to meld, top with chopped walnuts, and serve with slices of crusty bread.

Quick Grilled Chevre on Toast Points

This is too good to be this quick.

Serves 4

8 slices of white or wheat bread, crusts removed, cut into 4 triangles per slice

8 oz. fresh chevre (goat's milk cheese)

¼ tsp. garlic salt

¼ tsp. paprika

Preheat the broiler. Arrange bread on a baking sheet, and broil for about 1 minute on each side until lightly browned. Remove from the oven and spread each toast point with about 2 teaspoons chevre, sprinkle with garlic salt and paprika, and broil for an additional minute until chevre begins to melt and bubble. Arrange on a serving tray and serve.

Chevre and Apricot Bites

This is another fruit and cheese pair to remember.

Serves 4

12 dried apricots, sliced in half lengthwise   4 oz. fresh chevre (goat's milk cheese)

Spread each dried apricot with about 1 teaspoon chevre, and arrange on a serving plate.

Roquefort and Pear Bites

Blue cheese and pears is yet another combination that is worth a trip to taste. Fortunately, a flight to France isn't needed, because these are incredibly easy to make. Allow the Roquefort to sit out for an hour to bring out its flavors; then slice the pears and assemble this plate in a few minutes.

Serves 4 to 6

3 ripe Anjou pears   ¼ cup sliced almonds, toasted, for garnish

½ lb. Roquefort cheese

Cut 2 pears lengthwise into 8 to 10 slices each, removing seeds and core. Arrange slices in a nesting pattern around the perimeter of a circular serving platter or tray, then add another circle inside that if there's room. Place a small slice (about 2 teaspoons, if you can visualize) of Roquefort on each pear slice, and top with a pinch of almonds. In the center of the plate, place remaining whole pear. If pear slices will be sitting out for a while, rub them with the cut half of a lemon to prevent browning.

Variation: Use a different blue cheese. The flavor won't be identical, but it will be similar.

Pâtés and Terrines

These thick, sliceable, and spreadable dishes, typically made from ground meats, spices, and fat, can be found throughout France—each carrying the character of its region of production through the unique ingredients. We have several choices when it comes to pâté—from using store-bought versions for a lightning-fast start to making a quick version of our own.

Terrine with Toast

This quick presentation of store-bought ingredients is several steps above cheese and crackers.

Serves 4

8 slices white or wheat bread, crusts removed, cut into 4 triangles per slice

¾ lb. (12 oz.) *terrine de campagne* (or pâté, available at many delis and specialty food stores)

Sprigs fresh parsley for garnish

> **Gourmet Glossary**
>
> A **terrine** is actually the container that contains pâté, but the term also refers to the pâté itself. **Terrine de campagne** is generally a "country style" or chunky pâté, usually composed of ground meats, fish, or poultry, lots of seasoning, and, of course, fat.

Preheat the broiler. Arrange bread on a baking sheet and broil for about 1 minute on each side or until lightly browned. Remove from oven and the tray, and spread toast points with about 1 tablespoon terrine de campagne each. Arrange on a serving tray, garnish with parsley, and serve. You might serve terrine whole, spreading just a few toast points, and leave the remainder surrounding terrine so guests can serve themselves.

Variation: Use high-quality crisp wheat crackers instead of toast points.

Chicken Pâté

This quick spread makes use of cooked ingredients for one version of the famous French dish.

Serves 6

1 (12½-oz.) can chicken (white meat)

½ cup plain breadcrumbs

½ cup mayonnaise

2 TB. olive oil, plus more if needed

4 scallions, dark green parts removed, cut into ½-inch sections

1 TB. fresh lemon juice

2 tsp. Worcestershire sauce

¼ tsp. hot pepper sauce (such as Tabasco)

8 slices white or wheat sandwich bread, crusts removed, cut on the diagonal to form triangles

In a food processor fitted with a metal blade, process chicken, breadcrumbs, mayonnaise, olive oil, scallions, lemon juice, Worcestershire sauce, and hot pepper sauce until smooth. If necessary, add a little more olive oil to achieve a smooth consistency. Scrape mixture into a serving bowl and chill. Just before you are ready to serve, preheat the broiler. Arrange bread on a baking sheet, and broil for 1 minute per side until lightly browned. Serve pâté with toast triangles.

 Savoir Starter

For the complete "pâté effect," grease a small loaf or rectangular baking pan and chill your homemade pâté in it. To serve, invert the pan to place the pâté loaf at the center of your serving platter and surround it with toast triangles.

Pork Sausage Pâté

Texture and flavor ... we certainly have that here.

Serves 6

½ lb. cooked pork sausage, cut into ½-inch pieces

½ cup plain breadcrumbs

½ cup (4 oz.) cream cheese or light cream cheese, softened

3 TB. butter, softened

4 scallions, dark green parts removed, cut into ½-inch sections

2 tsp. Worcestershire sauce

½ tsp. salt

½ tsp. freshly ground black pepper

Olive oil for processing

8 slices white or wheat sandwich bread, crusts removed, cut on the diagonal to form triangles

In a food processor fitted with a metal blade, process sausage, breadcrumbs, cream cheese, butter, scallions, Worcestershire sauce, salt, and pepper until smooth. If necessary, add a little olive oil to aid with processing. Scrape mixture into a serving bowl and chill. Just before you are ready to serve, preheat the broiler. Arrange bread on a baking sheet, and broil for 1 minute per side until lightly browned. Serve pâté with toast triangles.

Foie Gras

Foie gras, French for "fat liver," is made from the fattened goose liver or sometimes duck liver. On a memorable vacation years ago, I drove with my family through the Perigord region of France, where much of the country's foie gras is produced. On the roadside, we saw many signs with grinning geese and the words *Foie Gras 1 km*. Even at that time, I had a feeling that those geese probably shouldn't be smiling. When I tried foie gras for the first time, however, I was more than smiling, I was ecstatic. It was one of the most delicious foods I had ever tasted. Rich, buttery, and slightly nutty, it is a flavor institution by itself, and, as an appetizer, merely needs delicate treatment and a vehicle.

Foie Gras and Toast

An elegant dish, foie gras in small appetizer portions is one of the royal family of hors d'oeuvres.

Serves 4

7 oz. *pâté de foie gras*	5 TB. butter
4 pieces bread, crusts removed, cut into 4 triangles per slice	Sprigs fresh parsley for garnish

Preheat the broiler. Place chilled pâté de foie gras on a serving plate or platter. Arrange bread on a baking sheet, and broil for about 1 minute on each side until lightly browned. Remove from oven and spread about 1 teaspoon butter on each piece, arrange around foie gras, garnish with parsley, and serve with a knife for spreading.

Gourmet Glossary

Foie gras is the actual goose liver. **Pâté de foie gras** is a pâté that contains mostly goose liver, but also contains other ingredients such as herbs, pork fat, cream, and brandy. For our purposes, prepared (store-bought) pâté de foie gras is the place to start, as it's ready to go with no additional prep. You can find it in gourmet stores and some supermarkets.

Warm Herbed Cheese (Boursin) with Endive

A simple, creamy, flavorful spread for those special guests. There's the irony of using Italian seasoning in a nominally French recipe, but those herbs are found in the South of France as well!

Serves 4

1 cup (8 oz.) cream cheese or light cream cheese, softened

3 TB. butter, softened

1 TB. chopped garlic

2 tsp. Italian seasoning

½ tsp. kosher salt

½ tsp. freshly ground black pepper

Belgian endive leaves or sliced crusty bread for serving

Combine cream cheese, butter, garlic, Italian seasoning, salt, and pepper in a microwave-safe serving bowl and mix thoroughly. Microwave on high heat for 90 seconds or until warm. Stir again and serve with Belgian endive leaves or crusty bread.

Cognac Cream Shrimp

Creamy and just slightly sweet, this shrimp dish is very unusual.

Serves 4 to 6

1 TB. butter

1 tsp. chopped garlic

½ lb. (31 to 40 count, or about 18) cooked shrimp, peeled and deveined with tail on

1½ TB. cognac

¼ cup heavy cream

½ tsp. salt

¼ tsp. freshly ground black pepper

Heat butter and garlic in a 12-inch skillet over medium-high heat for about 30 seconds or until garlic begins to soften; add shrimp and sauté for 1 minute, stirring, until shrimp is pink. Add cognac and heat for an additional minute. Remove warm shrimp to a serving platter, and using the same skillet, increase heat to high, add cream, heat for about 30 seconds, until bubbling. Remove from heat. Drizzle shrimp with cognac cream, sprinkle with salt and pepper, insert a toothpick in each and serve.

Fromage Miele (Honey Cheese)

This is a sweet, rich, fruity cheese spread just perfect for the appetizer lover with a sweet tooth. If you have the time, toast the walnuts; that's even better. (To toast nuts, simply spread them on a baking sheet and slide them under a preheated broiler for 2 to 3 minutes, watching closely to avoid burning.)

Serves 4 to 6

1 cup (8 oz.) cream cheese or light cream cheese, softened

3 TB. honey

3 TB. apricot preserves

2 TB. chopped walnuts for garnish

Crusty sweet bread or crisp apple slices for serving

Gourmet Glossary
Portuguese-style sweet **bread** is a thick, sweetened loaf available in many grocery stores. It's great with Fromage Miele, but it's also delicious as toast or made into French toast.

Combine cream cheese, honey, and preserves and mix thoroughly. Scrape spread into a serving bowl, sprinkle with chopped walnuts, and serve with crusty sweet bread (such as *Portuguese-style sweet bread*) and crisp apple slices.

Variation: Substitute your favorite all-fruit mixture, such as blackberry, raspberry, or even rhubarb, for apricot preserves.

Warm Artichoke Hearts with Chevre and Garlic

This is terrific as a dinner-party hors d'oeuvre, served on small plates and eaten with a knife and fork.

Serves 4

1 TB. olive oil

1 TB. chopped garlic

4 oz. fresh chevre (goat's milk cheese)

1 (14-oz.) can artichoke hearts, drained

1 TB. white wine

Salt and freshly ground black pepper to taste

In a small (6-inch) saucepan, heat oil and garlic over medium-high heat for 1 minute, stirring occasionally and watching to make sure garlic does not burn. Meanwhile, spread about 1 teaspoon chevre on top of each artichoke heart, arrange on a microwave-safe serving plate, and microwave on high for about 30 seconds or until warm and cheese begins to soften. Remove plate from microwave. Add white wine to oil and garlic, heat, stirring for an additional 30 seconds, and drizzle oil-garlic-wine mixture over artichoke hearts. Season to taste with salt and pepper, and serve on small plates with forks.

Savoir Starter
The Warm Artichoke Hearts with Chevre and Garlic recipe is fun to eat with your fingers, but have plenty of napkins on hand.

Baby Brie and Apples

Everybody loves this classic. If the sliced apples will be out for long, rub them with the cut side of a lemon half to delay browning.

Serves 8 to 10

1 (13-oz.) wheel "baby brie," at room temperature

4 crisp Granny Smith apples (or another tart, crisp variety), cored and each cut into 8 to 10 slices

Unwrap brie and place it at the center of a serving platter. Surround with freshly sliced apples. Serve with a knife so guests can spread cheese on each slice.

Variation: Serve with fresh, crisp pear slices or wheat crackers.

Hors D'oeuvre History
Soft cheeses, like brie, come to a wonderful spreadable consistency and a richer mouthfeel when they are served at room temperature than when served straight out of the fridge (with a hard consistency). Another variation is to serve brie warm. To do this, heat the brie in the microwave for about 20 seconds. Be very careful not to overheat, as you will end up with expensive hot liquid.

French Onion Spread

The secret is in the bouillon and the toasted flavor of the garlic and the onions, which is achieved through a minute under the broiler.

Serves 4 to 6

3 TB. dried minced onion

1 TB. chopped garlic, drained of all liquid

1 cup (8 oz.) cream cheese or light cream cheese, softened

1 cup (8 oz.) sour cream

3 scallions, dark green parts removed, and cut into ½-inch pieces

1 (.15-oz.) pkg. beef bouillon powder

1 scallion, dark green parts removed, thinly sliced for garnish

Wedges of warm, crusty bread for serving

Preheat the broiler. Spread onion and garlic on a baking sheet, and broil for 1 minute or until onion is lightly browned. Watch the broiler carefully to avoid burned onion sacrifices! Transfer onion and garlic to a food processor fitted with a metal blade, add cream cheese, sour cream, 3 chopped scallions, and beef bouillon, and process until almost smooth. Scrape spread into a serving bowl, and chill for an hour or 2 to allow the flavors to meld. Garnish with remaining sliced scallion, and serve with wedges of warm crusty bread.

Champignons au Saucisson (Sausage-Stuffed Mushrooms)

These are tasty and self-contained—each in its own cap.

Serves 4 to 6

½ lb. cooked chicken sausage (available in gourmet markets and grocery stores), cut into ½ inch sections

¼ cup duck sauce

1 TB. olive oil

½ tsp. salt

¼ tsp. freshly ground black pepper

1 (8-oz.) pkg. small white mushrooms, stems removed

Preheat the broiler. In a food processor fitted with a metal blade, process sausage, duck sauce, olive oil, salt, and pepper. Fill each mushroom cap with about 1 tablespoon sausage mixture, and set on a baking sheet. Broil for 2 minutes or until filling begins to bubble. Arrange on a serving platter and serve.

Bagel-Crisp Canapés

Here's a lightning-fast recipe that combines creamy French cheese in a warm, delicious appetizer.

Serves 4

1 (6-oz.) pkg. garlic or herb bagel crisps

1 (6- to 8-oz.) wedge port, salut, or brie cheese, sliced into thin pieces slightly smaller than the size of the bagel crisps

3 scallions, thinly sliced

½ tsp. paprika

Preheat the broiler. Arrange bagel crisps on a baking sheet in a single layer, top each with a slice of cheese, and top cheese with a pinch of scallions. Broil for 1 minute or until cheese begins to melt. Arrange canapés on a serving platter, sprinkle with paprika and serve.

Variation: Use pita crisps or melba toast as the vehicle.

The Least You Need to Know

♦ For an appetizer that is rich, flavorful, and often just slightly out of the ordinary, try French-inspired appetizers.

♦ Although preparing conventional pâté is a time-consuming process, a fast, similar-tasting alternative is possible using readily available ingredients.

♦ From a land famous for its wonderful cheeses, several French-style appetizers highlight rich cheese flavors.

♦ Several elegant appetizers, such as pâté de foie gras and terrine (pâté) can be made with prepared ingredients, enabling a lightning-fast hors d'oeuvre.

13

Antipasti: Italian-Style Appetizers

In This Chapter

- ◆ Prosciutto—the hors d'oeuvre hero
- ◆ The delights of bread and garlic
- ◆ More magic combinations: simple pairs that work wonders on the palate
- ◆ Appetizers featuring olives, figs, and fresh fruits

Italian cuisine is one of the world's most popular culinary concepts. Although *Italian* means different things to different people, there are a number of common ingredients I've utilized here, including frequent use of high-quality cheeses and meats (think prosciutto), fresh Italian bread, garlic, and the generous use of extra-virgin olive oil.

Tastes of the Italian Countryside

Italian food is all about making the most of the gifts of the earth: fruits and vegetables, meats and cheeses, and, of course, bread and wine. Treated simply and with respect, these dishes are elegant, simple, fast, and delicious.

Hors D'oeuvre History

For many people, wine is an important element in the enjoyment of Italian food. The choices can be simple and fun; simply remember to look for a wine that comes from the region where the dish originates. In this chapter, many of these appetizers will pair beautifully with a dry Italian red such as a Chianti or a white such as a Pinot Grigio.

Quick-Broiled Garlic and Herb Bread

Garlic bread is one of those foods that inspires emotion. Everybody loves it! This crispy version is just a bit of a twist on the original. The smell of these pieces, toasting under the broiler, will get everyone salivating.

Serves 8

⅓ cup olive oil

1½ TB. chopped garlic

1½ TB. prepared *pesto*

1 baguette or slender loaf of crusty bread, cut into ½-inch slices

Warm pizza sauce for serving (optional)

Gourmet Glossary

Pesto is a thick spread or sauce made with basil, garlic, olive oil, and pine nuts. (Other new versions call for different herbs or sun-dried tomatoes.) Rich and flavorful, pesto can be homemade or purchased in a grocery store, and it can be used on anything from appetizers to pasta and other main dishes.

Preheat the broiler. Combine olive oil, garlic, and pesto in a bowl, and whisk until thoroughly blended. Arrange bread on a baking sheet in a single layer, and brush each piece with some garlic-oil mixture. Broil for 1 to 2 minutes or until bread begins to brown. Flip bread, brush other side, and broil for an additional minute. Serve alone or with a bowl of warm pizza sauce for dipping.

Quick Cannellini Dip

Cannellini beans bring a rich texture to spreads without dairy products.

Serves 4 to 6

1 (8-oz.) can cannellini beans (white kidney beans), drained

⅓ cup shredded Parmesan cheese

¼ cup olive oil

1½ TB. chopped garlic

½ tsp. salt

½ tsp. dried oregano

Sliced crusty bread or toast for serving

In a food processor fitted with a metal blade, process beans, Parmesan cheese, olive oil, garlic, salt, and oregano just enough to pulverize beans but leave plenty of chunky texture. Scrape dip into a serving bowl, and serve surrounded by crusty pieces of bread or toast.

Olive Spread

This is a flavorful and delicious spread for bruschetta.

Serves 4 to 6

1 (6-oz.) can pitted ripe black olives, drained

¼ cup olive oil

1 (2½-oz.) pkg. pine nuts

1 TB. chopped garlic

1½ tsp. Italian seasoning

⅓ cup shredded Parmesan cheese

Sliced crusty bread or toast for serving

In a food processor fitted with a metal blade, process olives, olive oil, pine nuts, garlic, Italian seasoning, and Parmesan cheese just enough to pulverize olives but leave plenty of chunky texture. Scrape spread into a serving bowl, and serve surrounded by crusty pieces of bread or toast.

Quick-Sautéed Tortellini with Dipping Sauce

If your deli knew it was making this appetizer so easy for you, it would probably start charging more. Note that this recipe makes use of prepared pasta. Pasta that requires cooking will push you over the 5-minute mark.

Serves 4 to 6

¼ cup olive oil

1 TB. chopped garlic

1 lb. (16 oz.) prepared fresh tortellini (from the deli)

1 (15-oz.) can pizza sauce

3 TB. Parmesan cheese

Salt to taste

Heat olive oil and garlic in a large (12-inch or larger) skillet over medium heat. Add tortellini in a single layer, and heat for 2 to 3 minutes, turning once. Meanwhile, heat pizza sauce in a microwave-safe serving bowl for 2 minutes or until warm. Stir sauce and sprinkle with 1 tablespoon Parmesan cheese. Transfer pasta to a serving plate, sprinkle with remaining 2 tablespoons Parmesan cheese, insert toothpicks, and serve to guests, with salt if desired, inviting them to dip tortellini in the sauce.

Variation: Use fresh ravioli or other fun cooked pasta.

Mozzarella-Stuffed Plum Tomatoes

This is a recommendation from Italo, my barber and Italian food consultant.

Serves 6

12 fresh small mozzarella balls, drained

3 TB. extra-virgin olive oil

1 TB. chopped fresh basil or 1 tsp. dried basil

6 ripe plum tomatoes, sliced in half lengthwise, seeds removed

½ tsp. kosher salt

Unappetizer

Some appetizers are good candidates for advance preparation and refrigeration, but dishes with fresh tomatoes are not among them. Refrigeration causes tomatoes to lose their fresh flavor and texture.

Drizzle mozzarella balls with olive oil, sprinkle with basil, and gently turn to coat. Arrange tomatoes on a serving platter in a single layer, hollow side up, and place 1 mozzarella ball into each tomato, reserving oil used from marinating cheese. When platter is assembled, drizzle with oil, sprinkle with salt and serve.

Olivada with Toast Points

This one's a hearty, savory party favorite.

Serves 4

1 (6-oz.) can pitted ripe black olives, drained

¼ cup olive oil

1 tsp. fresh lemon juice

¾ tsp. freshly ground black pepper

4 slices white or wheat sandwich bread, crusts removed, cut on the diagonal to form triangles

In a food processor fitted with a metal blade, process olives, olive oil, lemon juice, and pepper until almost smooth. Scrape into a serving bowl. Arrange bread on a baking sheet in a single layer, and broil for 1 minute on each side or until lightly browned. Remove from oven, and serve spread surrounded by toast triangles.

Gourmet Glossary
Olivada is a simple combination of olives, oil, and black pepper that carries a wealth of flavor without the pretension. Yes, another perfect food—gee, there are a lot of those in this book!

Pinzimonio with Extra-Virgin Olive Oil

How many vegetables fit in one appetizer? You're about to find out. This is best for a sit-down appetizer where the occasional drip of oil will be forgiven.

Serves 6

4 scallions, white parts sliced in quarters lengthwise, leaves reserved

1 sweet yellow pepper, seeded, pith removed, and cut into long, thin strips

1 sweet green pepper, seeded, pith removed, cut into long, thin strips

2 long carrots, cut into long, thin strips

2 celery sticks, cut into long, thin strips

6 long arugula or cress leaves

1½ cups olive oil

½ cup balsamic vinegar

Salt and freshly ground black pepper to taste

Place 1 scallion leaf on a work surface and place a strip of yellow pepper in the center of it at a 90-degree angle to scallion. Repeat with 1 strip each of green pepper, carrot, celery, carrot, arugula, and white scallion. Tie each bundle together loosely by bringing the two ends of scallion leaf together. Repeat with remaining vegetables. Place bundles on separate appetizer plates for each guest. Combine olive oil and balsamic vinegar and mix thoroughly. Pour equal portions of dressing into 6 small bowls (the size of dipping sauce bowls), and place 1 bowl on each plate beside vegetable bundle. Have your guests take up the bundle of vegetables, dip it into dressing, season it to taste with salt and pepper, and enjoy fresh vegetables the way they were meant to be tasted.

> **Gourmet Glossary** _____
>
> **Pinzimonio** is an Italian vegetable dish in which combinations of sliced vegetables are served with olive oil, vinegar, salt, and pepper. There's nothing magical about pinzimonio. After all, it's only a time-honored way to serve fresh vegetables. On the other hand, maybe this is exactly what *is* magical about pinzimonio. There is no prescription for the vegetables. I've suggested vegetables I like, but feel free to use your own.

Roasted Red Pepper and Olive Spread

Roasted red peppers add a creamy sweetness to this hearty spread.

Serves 4 to 6

1 cup (8 oz.) cream cheese or light cream cheese, softened

⅔ cup roasted red peppers

1 (2¼-oz.) can sliced black olives, drained

2 scallions, dark green parts removed, cut into ½-inch pieces

1 scallion, dark green parts removed, thinly sliced for garnish

Crisp wheat crackers for serving

> **Savoir Starter** _____
> To add a bit of zing to your Roasted Red Pepper and Olive Spread, add a dash of hot pepper sauce.

In a food processor fitted with a metal blade, process cream cheese, peppers, olives, and 2 chopped scallions, pulsing to achieve a chunky-creamy consistency. Scrape spread into a serving bowl, top with remaining thinly sliced scallion, and serve with crisp wheat crackers.

White Pizza with Olives and Fresh Mozzarella

Want an elegant appetizer version of America's favorite food? Look no farther.

Serves 4

1 (10-oz.) prepared thin pizza crust

1 cup (4 oz.) shredded mozzarella cheese

10 fresh mozzarella balls, cut in half

10 pitted Kalamata olives, sliced in half lengthwise

1 TB. olive oil

½ tsp. dried basil

¼ tsp. garlic salt

Preheat the broiler. Place pizza crust on a baking sheet, and sprinkle with shredded mozzarella. Scatter fresh mozzarella balls and olive halves on top, drizzle with olive oil, sprinkle with basil and garlic salt, and broil for about 3 minutes or until shredded mozzarella begins to melt. Slice into slender pieces and serve. *Voilà!* Er, I mean *presto!*

Hors D'oeuvre History

Pizza is not just for the main meal, but is also an appetizer opportunity for fun and flavor, made possible in short order by using prepared pizza crusts. For appetizer pizza, stick with thin crusts. The thicker crusts just don't heat fast enough. Sure, some of the same themes from its larger cousin are fine with appetizers (pepperoni, pepper, onion, sausage, and so on), but with appetizers, where the intent is focused flavors, there's also room to take chances. Think of sliced Kalamata olives with fresh mozzarella, garlic, shrimp, even anchovies. These are a few of my favorites, but (you've heard this tune before) use them as inspiration and feel free to experiment to find your own top 10 list.

Crostini with Apple and Fontina

The simple combination of apple with this delicious cheese, as well as crisp toast, makes for a tasty starter.

Serves 4 to 6

6 slices white or wheat sandwich bread, crusts removed, cut on the diagonal to form triangles

3 Granny Smith or similarly tart apples

½ lb. Italian Fontina d'Aosta cheese, sliced into ¼-inch-thick pieces, slightly smaller than the bread slices to be used

Preheat the broiler. Arrange bread on a baking sheet in a single layer, and broil for 1 minute on each side or until lightly browned. Remove from oven. Cut 2 apples lengthwise into 8 to 10 slices each, removing core and seeds. Place a piece of cheese and an apple slice on each toast triangle. Arrange toasts on a platter surrounding remaining whole apple to set the mood.

Shrimp and Asiago Crostini

Succulent shrimp and sharp, flavorful cheese make a tasty combination.

Serves 6 to 8

6 slices white or wheat sandwich bread, crusts removed, cut on the diagonal to form triangles

½ cup (4 oz.) cream cheese or light cream cheese, softened

1 lb. (31 to 40 count, about 18) cooked shrimp, peeled and deveined with tail on

4 oz. Asiago cheese, cut into ½-inch cubes

1 TB. chopped fresh chives

Lemon wedges to garnish

Preheat the broiler. Arrange bread on a baking sheet in a single layer, and broil for 1 minute on each side or until lightly browned. Remove from oven. Spread about 1 teaspoon cream cheese on each toast triangle, top each with 1 shrimp, and place 1 Asiago chunk inside curled shrimp. Arrange these toasts on a platter, sprinkle with chopped chives, and serve with lemon wedges.

Toasted Prosciutto and Provolone

This is sort of related to a grilled cheese—in the same way that both a jet and a car are "passenger vehicles."

Serves 6

⅓ cup olive oil

1 baguette or slender loaf crusty bread, cut into ½-inch slices

8 oz. thin slices prosciutto, cut into 2-inch-square pieces, or roughly corresponding to the size of bread slices

4 oz. provolone cheese, thinly sliced and cut in pieces roughly corresponding to the size of the bread slices

Preheat the broiler. Brush a bit of olive oil on both sides of each piece of bread, and arrange bread on a baking sheet in a single layer. Broil on the high rack for 1 minute per side until lightly browned. Remove from oven, arrange bread on a serving tray, top each piece with 1 piece prosciutto and 1 piece provolone, and serve.

Variation: Broil the completed toast-prosciutto-provolone combination for an additional minute to melt the cheese.

Gourmet Glossary
Prosciutto—dry, salt-cured ham—is salty, rich, and evocative of Italy. It is popular in many simple dishes in which its unique flavor is allowed to shine.

Antipasto

This classic appetizer plate provides a hearty start to any gathering. This is only one possible assortment, as many other prepared meats and vegetables can be included.

Serves 6 to 8

⅓ lb. thin slices prosciutto

⅓ lb. thin slices *capicolla*

⅓ lb. fresh mozzarella balls, sliced in half

⅓ lb. marinated mushrooms

⅓ lb. prepared marinated olives

Sliced Italian bread

Arrange prosciutto, capicolla, mozzarella, mushrooms, and olives on a large platter in a decorative pattern, and provide a serving fork. The Italian bread can be served alongside in a basket. Guests, each armed with a small plate, may select their preferred assortment.

Gourmet Glossary
Capicolla is seasoned, aged pork shoulder—a traditional component of antipasto dishes.

Prosciutto d'Italo

My barber is an enthusiastic cook and a native of Italy. This is his idea of an appetizer, simple and delicious. Who am I to argue?

Serves 4 to 6

½ lb. prosciutto, cut into slices ½-inch thick (This will be a special request from your deli.)

½ lb. Pecorino-Romano cheese, cut into small chunks ½-inch thick

Sliced Italian bread

Arrange prosciutto on a platter with pieces of Pecorino-Romano. Serve with wedges of crusty bread and a glass of Italian red wine to complete the picture.

Figs and Prosciutto with Variations

Here's another delicious combination of two ingredients. By themselves they are on the unusual side, but together they inspire visions of the Tuscan countryside. Thanks to Aileen Zogby for the inspiration for this one.

Serves 4

4 ripe figs, sliced in half lengthwise

½ cup (about 2 oz.) diced prosciutto

Preheat the broiler. Arrange figs, cut side up, on a baking sheet, sprinkle about ½ tablespoon prosciutto, and broil for a minute or 2. Arrange fig pieces on a plate and serve.

Variations: A common version of this dish is to entirely wrap thin strips of prosciutto around figs before broiling. A sprinkling of Parmesan, Romano, or even feta cheese (small pieces) along with the prosciutto is a nice addition. Finally, a drizzle of balsamic vinegar is a nice flavor addition.

Cantaloupe and Prosciutto Bites

This famous combination pairs sweet and salty and dry and juicy, to great effect. Try one—you'll be addicted.

Serves 6

½ medium ripe cantaloupe (about 1½ lb.), scooped into ½-inch balls using the smaller side of a melon scoop

8 oz. thin slices prosciutto, cut into 1 by 4-inch pieces

Wrap each melon ball in a prosciutto strip, and fasten with a toothpick.

> **Savoir Starter** _____
> For fun presentation, arrange Cantaloupe and Prosciutto Bites by placing the scooped shell of the cantaloupe on a plate, cut side up, and pile as many melon balls into that half as you can. Spread the rest around the base. What an inviting sight!

Cantaloupe, Muskmelon, and Prosciutto Kebabs

For summertime appetizers, there's nothing like melon. For a touch of class, there's nothing like a bit of dry-cured prosciutto—one of the fancier versions of ham.

Serves 6 to 8

12 oz. thin slices prosciutto, cut lengthwise into strips about ¾-inch wide

½ medium ripe cantaloupe (about 1½ lb.), scooped into ½-inch balls using the smaller side of a melon scoop

¼ ripe muskmelon (about 1½ lb.), scooped into ½-inch balls using the smaller side of a melon scoop

1 tsp. fresh lemon juice

Using bamboo skewers, pierce one end of a strip of prosciutto and then pierce a cantaloupe piece, wrapping prosciutto around cantaloupe and piercing it again on the skewer. Then skewer a piece of muskmelon and wrap that with prosciutto, so alternating cantaloupe and muskmelon balls are separated by an undulating S of prosciutto. Repeat with remaining prosciutto and melon, and arrange in parallel on a serving plate. Drizzle with lemon juice and serve.

> **Hors D'oeuvre History** _____
> As with many of the simple appetizers in this section, the appeal is as much visual as it is flavorful. If you communicate "fun" through your presentation, your guests will join in!

Mushrooms Stuffed with Prosciutto and Parmesan

Rich mushroom, salty ham, sharp cheese … *ah!*

Serves 6

1 (8-oz.) pkg. medium white mushrooms, stems removed

1 cup (about 4 oz.) diced prosciutto

½ cup (about 2 oz.) shredded Parmesan cheese

2 TB. olive oil

Salt and freshly ground black pepper to taste

Preheat the broiler. Arrange mushrooms hollow side up on a baking sheet. Fill each with about 2 teaspoons prosciutto and 1 teaspoon Parmesan cheese. Broil for 2 minutes, remove, and arrange on a serving plate. Drizzle with olive oil, season to taste with salt and pepper and serve.

Variations: Bacon pieces may be substituted for the prosciutto and goat's milk cheese for Parmesan (resulting in a different, but delicious, variation).

The Least You Need to Know

- Appetizers inspired by Italian ingredients tend to emphasize delicious cheeses, preserved meats, and a multitude of fruits and vegetables.
- One of the heroes of the Italian appetizer family is prosciutto—the famous, elegant cured ham.
- Judicious use of fragrant garlic is one of the hallmarks of many Italian starters.
- Many of these appetizers also feature terrific ingredients in simple, quick-to-prepare combinations that create flavor sensations.
- Extra-virgin olive oil works a flavor and appearance-enhancing magic on many Italian-style dishes.

A Wok on the Wild Side: Asian-Inspired Appetizers

In This Chapter

◆ Seasonings from the Far East

◆ Exciting combinations from India

◆ Ginger, teriyaki, soy, and peanuts

◆ Fast cooking with the wok

We all have flavors we know and love, but tasty appetizers do not all have to be familiar friends. Indeed, new taste combinations add interest and fun. The first time I enjoyed a truly good curry dish, the combination of spicy curry and cool mint was such an eye-opening experience I remember it to this day.

In this chapter, you'll find some of my favorite appetizers that pay homage to the ingredients and seasoning combinations from Asia.

Far Eastern Influence

Fresh vegetables and fruits; sauces redolent with soy, ginger, and garlic; and seafood and poultry are prepared in delicious combinations on the other side of the world. Here you'll find several delicious appetizers in the spirit of the Far East.

Mango and Scallion Bites with Dipping Sauce

The mango pieces are disproportionately large in this recipe because of the pungency of the scallions. However, I think you'll find that the flavor strikes the right balance.

Serves 4

1 ripe mango, peeled, pitted, and flesh cut into about ¾-inch cubes

3 scallions, dark green parts removed, cut into ¼-inch pieces

½ cup duck sauce

1 tsp. peeled, grated fresh ginger

Savoir Starter

Duck sauce, that ubiquitous sauce found in Chinese restaurants, is a terrific multipurpose sweet dipping sauce. Although recipes vary, common components include apricots, garlic, and vinegar.

Using toothpicks, pierce a piece of mango, a piece of scallion, another mango piece, and another scallion piece. Repeat with remaining mango and scallion, and arrange in a single layer on a serving platter with a bowl of duck sauce next to the plate. Sprinkle bites with ginger and serve, inviting your guests to dip before enjoying.

Teriyaki Portobello Wedges in Baby Spinach

Rich, meaty portobello mushroom pieces pair perfectly with teriyaki. Wrapped in fresh spinach, these bites are a gift for your taste buds.

Serves 6

2 TB. olive oil

1 (6-oz.) pkg. sliced portobello mushrooms, cut into 1-inch pieces

2 TB. *teriyaki* sauce

Baby spinach leaves corresponding to the number of portobello pieces (about 25)

Heat olive oil in a wok or 10-inch skillet over medium-high heat. Place portobello pieces in the skillet, and cook, stirring, for 2 minutes. Remove the skillet from heat, drizzle mushroom pieces with teriyaki sauce, and wrap each mushroom piece in a spinach leaf, fastening it with a toothpick. Arrange spinach and mushroom bites on a serving platter and serve.

Savoir Starter
Teriyaki works beautifully with vegetables, seafood, and most meats.

Savoir Starter
Although not quite as decorative, quick-cooked teriyaki mushrooms can also be served without the spinach—each speared with a toothpick on a serving platter. Sprinkle the finished platter with 1 tablespoon sesame seeds for visual appeal.

Teriyaki Shrimp, Pineapple, and Baby Spinach Bites

Lightning fast, this is also very tasty.

Serves 8

½ lb. (31 to 40 count, about 18) cooked shrimp, peeled and deveined with tail on

1 (8-oz.) can pineapple chunks in juice, drained

18 large (about 1 by 2½-inch) baby spinach leaves

1 to 2 TB. teriyaki sauce

Wrap 1 shrimp and 1 pineapple chunk in a spinach leaf with the tail sticking out (kind of cute and also allows diners to avoid biting the tail), and fasten with a toothpick. Repeat with remaining ingredients. Arrange bites on a serving platter, drizzle with teriyaki sauce and serve.

Variation: Use "tail-off" shrimp for convenience rather than visual appeal.

Water Chestnuts and Bacon

The crunch of the water chestnuts and the salty crisp of bacon make for a simple, memorable bite.

Serves 4 to 6

1 (8-oz.) can whole *water chestnuts*, drained

¼ lb. bacon, cut into 1 by 4-inch strips

1 tsp. peeled, grated fresh ginger

 **Gourmet Glossary**
Water chestnuts, which are actually a tuber and not a chestnut, are a popular element in many types of Asian-style cooking. The flesh is white, crunchy, and juicy, and it holds its texture whether cool or hot.

Preheat the broiler. Wrap each water chestnut with a piece of bacon, and fasten with a toothpick. Place bacon-wrapped water chestnut bites on a baking sheet, sprinkle a few grains ginger on each, and broil on the top rack for about 3 minutes or until bacon is crispy, turning once. Arrange on a serving plate and serve.

Pineapple Shrimp Skewers

If you like the combination of shrimp and pineapple, try this warm version.

Serves 4 to 6

3 TB. canola oil

½ lb. (31 to 40 count, about 18) cooked shrimp, tail on

1 (8-oz.) can pineapple chunks in juice, drained

1 TB. sesame seeds

½ tsp. *chili oil*

Salt to taste

Heat canola oil in a wok or 10-inch skillet over medium-high heat. Add shrimp, heating for 1 minute, stirring. Add pineapple chunks, and heat for 1 additional minute. Pierce 1 pineapple chunk and 1 shrimp on a bamboo skewer. Repeat with remaining shrimp and pineapple pieces. Arrange skewers on a serving plate, with shrimp at the center and the handles extending out in a circle like the spokes on a wheel. Sprinkle shrimp with sesame seeds, drizzle with chili oil, season with salt to taste and serve.

Gourmet Glossary

Chili oil is a fiery-hot pepper-infused oil popular in many Asian dishes. It is available in most grocery and specialty food stores. It's not a bad accompaniment to non-Asian heat-loving dishes, either.

Savoir Starter

When spearing pineapple and shrimp, it's a good idea to spear the pineapple first, as it tends to slide on the skewer. The shrimp will then prevent it from sliding off.

If you want to save your guests a bit of time looking for a place to chuck those tails, look for "tail-off" shrimp. Otherwise, you might consider breaking off the tails prior to skewering.

Hoisin Chicken Dip

The many fans of hoisin sauce will love this creamy dip.

Serves 6 to 8

1 (16½-oz.) can chicken, drained, pieces broken up

1 cup (8-oz.) cream cheese or light cream cheese, softened

½ cup (4 oz.) mayonnaise

¼ cup hoisin sauce

3 TB. onion flakes

2 scallions, dark green leaves removed, finely chopped, for garnish

Combine chicken, cream cheese, mayonnaise, hoisin sauce, and onion flakes in a bowl and mix thoroughly. Scrape dip into a serving bowl, top with chopped scallions, and serve surrounded by sturdy dippers such as pita or tortilla chips.

Gyoza

Buy these premade in either the frozen food section of your grocery store or fresh from an Asian specialty food store.

Serves 4

¼ cup canola oil

1 lb. (about 16) prepared *gyoza*, thawed

2 TB. soy sauce

Heat canola oil in a skillet over medium heat, and cook gyoza according to package instructions. Remove from heat and place 3 to 4 dumplings on each of 4 appetizer plates. Drizzle with soy sauce, and serve with chopsticks (or forks).

Gourmet Glossary _____
Gyoza are small (usually 1½- to 2-inch-long) dumplings filled with chicken, seafood, or vegetables. Also known as *pot stickers*, they are traditionally served with soy sauce for dipping.

Sushi Platter

Take advantage of the sushi recommendation of your local grocer or Asian foods store. Here is one popular assortment.

Serves 4

4 pieces tuna sushi

4 pieces salmon sushi

4 pieces cucumber sushi

2 TB. wasabi (Japanese horseradish) paste

2 TB. pickled ginger slices

4 TB. soy sauce, divided equally between 4 small bowls or cups

Place 1 piece tuna sushi, 1 piece salmon sushi, and 1 piece cucumber sushi on each of 4 appetizer plates. Spoon small portions of wasabi and ginger slices on each plate, and place a small bowl of soy sauce on each. Each guest may use chopsticks (or his fingers) to flavor sushi with his favorite combination of seasonings.

Unappetizer

Several high-octane seasonings such as wasabi, hot peppers, or curry powder should be used in moderation until you're comfortable with your heat tolerance.

Hors D'oeuvre History

As a student living in Japan, I learned to love sushi, a delicious appetizer. I've tried sushi topped with all kinds of raw fish (tuna and salmon are my favorites), squid, octopus, and other sea creatures. Although the term *sushi* specifically refers to the sticky rice part of the dish, we usually picture sushi as rice topped with seafood. Sushi is increasingly popular in North America; large, well-equipped grocery stores now carry it, as do specialty stores. I'm not going to try to convince you that a full sushi dish can be prepared in 5 minutes, but if I can convince you to take advantage of these premade morsels, you'll add a fantastic new set of flavors to your appetizer arsenal.

Ginger Shrimp Sticks

Fresh ginger and shrimp is another one of those "perfect pairs." Try these on for size.

Serves 4

3 TB. olive oil

1 tsp. chopped garlic

½ lb. (31 to 40 count, about 18) cooked shrimp, peeled and deveined with tail on

1 TB. soy sauce

1 tsp. peeled, grated fresh ginger

Heat olive oil and garlic in a 10- to 12-inch skillet over medium-high heat for about 30 seconds. Add shrimp and heat thoroughly, stirring, for 1 to 2 minutes. Add soy sauce, and heat for an additional 30 seconds, stirring. Remove shrimp to a serving plate, sprinkle with ginger, insert toothpicks and serve.

Teriyaki Shrimp on Belgian Endive Leaves

A delicious combination of flavors and textures, serve these warm.

Serves 4

3 TB. olive oil

1 tsp. chopped garlic

¼ cup sliced almonds

2 scallions, dark green leaves removed, finely chopped

½ lb. (31 to 40 count, about 18) cooked shrimp, peeled and deveined with tail removed

2 TB. teriyaki sauce

3 TB. plain breadcrumbs

2 heads Belgian endive, large leaves separated and arranged on a serving plate

Heat olive oil, garlic, almonds, and scallions in a wok or 10- to 12-inch skillet over medium-high heat for 1 minute. Add shrimp and heat thoroughly, stirring, for 1 to 2 minutes. Turn off the heat and stir in teriyaki sauce and breadcrumbs. Using a soupspoon, scoop 1 shrimp with some almonds, scallions, and juice to each Belgian endive leaf and serve.

Variation: Use crisp romaine lettuce leaves in place of the endive leaves.

Teriyaki Dip

If you like more flavor after you've assembled this dip, stir in another tablespoon of teriyaki.

Serves 4

½ cup (4 oz.) cream cheese or light cream cheese, softened

½ cup sour cream

1 TB. teriyaki sauce

2 scallions, dark green leaves removed, finely chopped

3 TB. sesame seeds

Potato chips or sesame crackers for serving

In a serving bowl, combine cream cheese, sour cream, teriyaki sauce, scallions, and 2 tablespoons sesame seeds until blended but with plenty of texture. If possible, chill for an hour or more. To serve, garnish with remaining 1 tablespoon sesame seeds and serve with potato chips or sesame crackers.

Variations: Use nonfat plain yogurt instead of sour cream, and cottage cheese instead of cream cheese.

Coconut Shrimp

For those of you with a sweet tooth, these little morsels have your name all over them.

Serves 4

½ lb. (31 to 40 count, about 18) cooked shrimp, peeled and deveined with tail on

½ cup duck sauce

¾ cup shredded coconut

Place shrimp in a bowl, pour duck sauce over it, and turn shrimp to coat. Place coconut into another bowl. Spear 1 shrimp with a toothpick, and dredge in coconut, coating all sides. Repeat with remaining shrimp. Arrange coated shrimp on a serving platter, each with its own toothpick, and serve.

Sweet-and-Sour Scallop Skewers

This recipe is perfect for countertop grills (like the George Foreman Grill). Don't forget to soak your bamboo skewers in water to make them safe for grilling. Just remove from water and drain before using.

Serves 4

½ lb. sea scallops, rinsed

2 TB. prepared sweet-and-sour sauce or hoisin sauce

1 (8-oz.) can whole water chestnuts, drained

1 TB. sesame seeds

Salt to taste

½ tsp. chili oil

Savoir Starter

If you have those large scallop shells (available in many grocery and seafood stores), these are terrific to use as an individual "plate." Lay the end of one scallop skewer on each shell on a serving platter, and let the guest take the shell, too.

Preheat the grill. Place scallops in a bowl, add 1 tablespoon sweet-and-sour sauce and stir gently. Using bamboo skewers that have been soaked in water and drained, spear a scallop and then a water chestnut, leaving them close to the end of the skewer. Place the skewers, handle sticking out, on the grill, and cook for 2 minutes or until scallops are firm, opaque, and thoroughly cooked. Remove skewers and arrange on a serving platter with scallops at the center and the handles extending out in a circle like the spokes on a wheel. Sprinkle with sesame seeds and salt, drizzle with chili oil and serve.

Celery and Banana Chips with Peanut Sauce

This is peanut butter like you've never seen it before.

Serves 4 to 6 (can easily be doubled)

1 cup dried banana chips (available in the fruit section of many grocery stores)

2 stalks celery, cut into ½ by 3-inch sticks

½ cup all-natural peanut butter

2 TB. canola oil

2 TB. honey

1 TB. soy sauce

1 tsp. chopped garlic

1 tsp. peeled, finely shredded fresh ginger

Dash hot sauce (such as Tabasco)

Arrange banana chips and celery on a serving plate, leaving space for a bowl for peanut sauce. Combine peanut butter, canola oil, honey, soy sauce, garlic, ginger, and hot sauce, and mash and stir until thoroughly mixed. Place on the platter and serve.

Indian Delicacies

Berinder Singh, a terrific cook, and a native of India, was kind enough to test a number of recipes for this book. Here are three of the winners.

Tandoori Chicken Bites

Chicken breasts cook quickly, enabling this savory appetizer.

Serves 4

2 TB. canola oil

½ lb. chicken breast cut into pieces about ¾-inch square

½ tsp. ground ginger

½ tsp. ground garlic

¼ tsp. tandoori *masala* or garam masala (found in larger grocery and Indian food stores)

Salt to taste

Freshly ground black pepper to taste

1 tsp. fresh lemon juice

Heat canola oil in a wok or 12-inch skillet over medium-high heat. Cook chicken pieces, ginger, garlic, tandoori masala, and salt, stirring, for about 3 minutes, until chicken is golden brown and its juices run clear. Remove chicken to a serving platter, sprinkle with black pepper and lemon juice, and serve with toothpicks.

Gourmet Glossary

A **masala** is an Indian spice blend. Garam masala is available in many large grocery stores; tandoori masala is available often in specialty food shops. Both include coriander, cinnamon, nutmeg, and ginger, as well as other delicious spices.

Spicy Mint Chutney

Warm seasonings and cool mint are a delicious counterpoint for each other in this simple dish.

Serves 4

½ cup fresh mint leaves

½ (4½-oz.) can (about 2 oz.) green chilies, drained and chopped

2 tsp. chopped garlic

½ tsp. granulated sugar

¼ tsp. red chili powder

Salt to taste

2 tsp. fresh lemon juice

In a food processor fitted with a metal blade, process mint, chilies, garlic, sugar, chili powder, and salt to the consistency of a coarse paste. Scrape chutney into a small serving bowl, add lemon juice, and mix to combine. Serve this with Tandoori Chicken Bites (see previous recipe) or as a savory spread for pieces of tomato, cucumber, or bread.

Cucumber Crunch

This simple but refreshing treatment of the common cucumber will tantalize your taste buds.

Serves 4

1 (7-inch) cucumber, striped and cut into ½-inch wide pieces

½ tsp. plus ¼ tsp. salt (for rendering water and for flavoring)

½ tsp. crushed red pepper

1 tsp. olive oil

½ tsp. fresh lemon juice

3 pieces white or wheat sandwich bread, crusts removed, cut on the diagonal to form triangles

In a food processor fitted with a grater attachment, process cucumber, sprinkle with ½ teaspoon salt, and let sit for 2 minutes. After 2 minutes, salt will cause cucumber to render its liquid. Strain by pouring cucumber onto several layers of paper towels, cover with several more pieces and press. A lot of liquid will come out.

In a serving bowl, thoroughly mix cucumber, remaining ¼ teaspoon salt, crushed red pepper, olive oil, and lemon juice. Just before you are ready to serve, heat the broiler. Arrange bread on a baking sheet in a single layer, and broil for 1 minute on each side or until lightly browned. Spread cucumber mix over toast points and serve.

The Least You Need to Know

◆ Asian-influenced appetizers include several unique seasonings such as soy, teriyaki, and hoisin sauces; Asian spice blends; as well as ingredients somewhat new to our palates such as coconut.

◆ Part of the appeal of appetizers from India and the Far East is the unique combination of otherwise familiar seasonings, such as sweet-and-sour and fruits with savory ingredients. These combinations add interest and fun.

◆ Because it's designed for cooking small bits of food quickly over high heat, a wok enables fast preparation of dishes that otherwise might not be possible within our 5-minute time goal.

Other Must-Visit Stops on the "World Tour"

In This Chapter

◆ Seasonings from the Middle East

◆ Exciting combinations from Latin America

◆ Cardamom and cinnamon, walnuts and yogurt

◆ Fresh and dried fruits to the rescue

This chapter relays some of the flavors of several other regions of the world, from the Middle East to Latin America. These cuisines reflect a very different genesis of seasoning and base ingredients.

From the eastern Mediterranean, we sample appetizers made from dried fruits, walnuts, herbs, and creamy feta cheese. From the Middle East, delicacies including pita bread, yogurt, cumin, and spices. From South America, fresh fruits and seafood. These rich and flavorful foods evoke images of a lifestyle wholly different from our own. As with many of the cuisines of the world, these foods are part of a culture and, as such, an opportunity to explore.

Toasted Grilled Pita with Parmesan

These are a slightly softer cousin of the popular crisps you can buy at the grocery store, but, of course, they are much better served hot from the oven.

Serves 4

2 *pita breads*, sliced into 8 wedges each

2 TB. olive oil

2 TB. shredded Parmesan cheese

Coarse salt to taste

Sprig fresh parsley for garnish (optional)

Preheat the broiler. Arrange pita wedges on a baking sheet in a single layer, drizzle with olive oil, and sprinkle a pinch of Parmesan cheese on each piece. Broil for about 1 minute or until pita begins to brown and crisp. Remove from the broiler and arrange on a serving platter, season to taste with coarse salt, place a parsley sprig in the center of the platter (if using) and serve.

Gourmet Glossary

Pita bread, also known as Syrian bread, is a flat, hollow wheat bread from the Middle East that can be used for sandwiches or sliced pizza style. Pita bread is terrific soft with dips and baked or broiled as a vehicle for other ingredients.

Hummus

Here is a fast, tasty Middle Eastern dish that is good for you as well.

Serves 4 to 6

1 (15-oz.) can chickpeas, drained

¼ cup tahini (sesame paste, available in most grocery stores and Middle Eastern markets)

2 TB. olive oil

1 TB. chopped garlic

Juice of 1 lemon

1 tsp. salt

4 fresh pieces of pita bread, sliced pizza style into 8 wedges

Cucumber sticks, baby carrots, and olives for serving

In a food processor fitted with a metal blade, process the chickpeas, tahini, oil, garlic, lemon juice, and salt until *hummus* is creamy. If the mixture is too thick, add a little more olive oil.

Scrape hummus into a bowl, set on a large platter; arrange pita wedges, cucumber sticks, baby carrots, and olives around the platter and serve.

Gourmet Glossary

Hummus is a thick spread made of puréed chickpeas (garbanzo beans), lemon juice, olive oil, garlic, and often tahini (sesame seed paste).

Endive with Hummus and Arugula

Arugula brings a sharp freshness to this vegetable dish.

Serves 4

1 cup (8 oz.) hummus (homemade or store-bought)

2 cups chopped fresh arugula

3 heads Belgian endive, leaves separated

2 TB. shelled pistachios

Combine hummus and arugula in a bowl and mix thoroughly. Spread about 1 tablespoon hummus on the stem end of a Belgian endive leaf, and arrange leaves on a serving plate. Sprinkle a few pistachios on each and serve.

Savoir Starter

In just about every recipe that calls for nuts—such as pistachios, sliced almonds, or chopped walnuts—the dish will taste even better if the nuts are toasted. (It's easy—just roast for 3 minutes under the broiler.)

Grilled Hummus Triangles

These crispy treats are a flavor sensation tailor-made for the garlic lover.

Serves 6 to 8

1 cup (8 oz.) hummus (homemade or store-bought)

1 TB. chopped garlic

3 pita breads, sliced into 8 wedges each

2 TB. shredded Parmesan cheese

2 TB. olive oil

Savoir Starter

If you find hummus with roasted garlic at the grocery, use that and save yourself the step of stirring additional garlic into your hummus.

Preheat the broiler. Combine hummus and garlic in a small bowl and mix thoroughly. Spread about 1 teaspoon hummus on each piece of pita bread. Sprinkle each with a pinch of Parmesan cheese. Arrange pita pieces on a baking sheet in a single layer, and broil for about 1 minute until pita begins to brown and cheese begins to glisten. Remove from the broiler, arrange on a serving plate, decorate with a very thin swirl of olive oil around the plate that touches each piece of hummus and serve.

Pita Crisps with Warm Mango Salsa

Okay, so this is mixing cultural metaphors. It's still darn good.

Serves 4 to 6

2 pita breads, sliced into 8 wedges each

4 oz. fresh goat's milk cheese

¾ (6-oz.) jar mango salsa

¼ tsp. freshly ground black pepper

Preheat the broiler. Arrange pita wedges on a baking sheet in a single layer, and broil for 1 minute per side. Remove from broiler, spread about 1½ teaspoons goat's milk cheese on each in a thin layer, and broil for about 30 seconds until cheese begins to melt. Remove from broiler, and spread about 2 teaspoons mango salsa on each pita wedge. Arrange wedges on a serving platter, sprinkle with black pepper and serve.

Savoir Starter

Don't forget that the speed with which something broils is directly related to how close the food is to the heating element. On the lower rack, a piece of pita will take about 1 week to toast (just kidding, but it *is* slow). On the high rack, about 1 minute. Corollary: The closer to the heating element, the closer the attention you must give to what you're broiling … I know, I've said that before.

Couscous Goat's Milk Cheese Spread

This intriguing, easy spread is minutes away.

Serves 4 to 6

1 cup prepared couscous

½ cup (4 oz.) goat's milk cheese, softened

½ cup plain yogurt or sour cream

½ cup slivered pecans or almonds, toasted

¼ cup finely chopped fresh chives, plus 1 additional tablespoon for garnish

Pita wedges or Belgian endive leaves for serving

Combine couscous, goat's milk cheese, yogurt, almonds, and chives in a serving bowl and, if possible, chill for 1 hour or more. Sprinkle with chopped chives and serve with pita wedges or, for a bit of fun, Belgian endive leaves.

Cumin-Mint Dip

How can a dip be fiery and cool at the same time? Try this combination and find out ...

Serves 4 to 6

1 cup (8 oz.) plain yogurt

½ cup (4 oz.) cream cheese, softened

¾ cup fresh mint leaves

1 TB. fresh lemon juice

2 tsp. ground cumin

½ tsp. salt

Dash hot pepper sauce (such as Tabasco)

Pita bread wedges for serving

In a food processor fitted with a metal blade, process yogurt, cream cheese, mint, lemon juice, cumin, salt, and hot pepper sauce until completely mixed. Scrape dip into a mixing bowl, and serve with pita bread wedges.

Baba Ghanouj

We might not be able to make this delicious baba ghanouj (pronounced *baba ga-noush*) spread in 5 minutes, but we can certainly buy it and arrange a tasty platter. This is firmly and deliciously in the "dressing up store-bought" category.

Serves 4

1 (8-oz.) pkg. baba ghanouj (available at most grocery stores and Middle Eastern markets)

2 pita breads, sliced into 8 wedges each

1 English-style cucumber, striped and cut lengthwise into 4-inch-slices

½ cup Kalamata olives

Scrape baba ghanouj into a serving bowl, and place the bowl on a platter. Surround it with fresh pita wedges and cucumber slices. Sprinkle olives around the platter to complete the picture and serve.

Gourmet Glossary

Baba ghanouj is a spread comprised of eggplant, lemon juice, garlic, olive oil, and tahini. I recommend that you buy it; it requires eggplant that is thoroughly cooked—an accomplishment I haven't figured out how to do in 5 minutes. Common methods include grilling or broiling an eggplant, turning it frequently, for between 45 minutes to an hour, until the insides are completely soft and can be mixed with the other ingredients. Some recipes also call for baking the eggplant, usually for about 45 minutes in a 375° to 400°F oven.

Feta Spread

The creamy saltiness of feta is a great partner to sun-dried tomatoes and pistachios.

Serves 6

½ lb. (8 oz.) crumbled feta cheese

½ cup (4 oz.) plain yogurt

½ cup sun-dried tomatoes (oil-packed), drained and cut into ½-inch pieces

½ cup shelled salted pistachios

¼ cup chopped fresh chives

Pita crisps or sturdy sesame crackers for serving

In a blender or food processor fitted with a metal blade, process feta, yogurt, sun-dried tomatoes, all but 1 tablespoon pistachios, and chives until thoroughly combined but still chunky. Scrape spread into a serving bowl and chill, if possible, for several hours. Garnish with reserved 1 tablespoon pistachios and serve with pita crisps or sturdy sesame crackers.

Fattoush

This traditional "bread salad" makes for an interesting sit-down-meal appetizer, as it's best eaten from a plate with a fork.

Serves 4

3 pieces wheat bread, sliced into ½-inch cubes

1 cucumber, striped and cut into ½-inch cubes

1 red pepper, seeded, pith removed, and cut into ½-inch pieces

2 cups shredded sturdy lettuce, such as romaine or iceberg

15 to 18 grape tomatoes, halved lengthwise

4 scallions, dark green leaves removed, cut into ¼-inch pieces

¼ cup chopped fresh mint leaves

¼ cup chopped fresh parsley

2 tsp. chopped garlic

Juice of 1 lemon

½ cup olive oil

Salt to taste

Preheat the broiler. Arrange bread on a baking sheet in a single layer and broil for 2 minutes or until bread cubes crisp. Combine cucumber, red pepper, lettuce, tomatoes, scallions, mint, parsley, and garlic in a bowl, and toss to mix. Pour lemon juice and olive oil over the salad, and toss again to mix. Add salt to taste, and serve on individual plates for each guest.

Variation: To save even more time, use unseasoned (or lightly seasoned) croutons or melba toasts in place of the bread.

Turkish Yogurt and Walnut Dip

Talk about flavor! This recipe, adapted from *Cooking Light* magazine, is a real winner.

Serves 4 to 6

1 cup plain yogurt	Salt to taste
1 tsp. chopped garlic	Pinch freshly ground black pepper
3 TB. chopped walnuts	Pita bread wedges for serving
Dash hot pepper sauce (such as Tabasco)	

Combine yogurt, garlic, walnuts, hot pepper sauce, salt, and black pepper in a bowl and mix thoroughly. If possible, allow a half-hour for flavors to blend, stir, and serve with pieces of pita bread.

Chicken, Goat's Milk Cheese, and Walnut Spread

The richness of walnuts sets off beautifully against the creamy saltiness of the goat cheese.

Serves 6 to 8

1 (12-oz.) can chicken, drained, large pieces broken	½ cup finely chopped cucumber (about ½ cucumber)
1 cup (8 oz.) fresh goat's milk cheese	2 tsp. garlic
½ cup plain yogurt	¼ tsp. freshly ground black pepper
½ cup chopped walnuts	Olive oil
	Pita wedges for serving

In a blender or food processor fitted with a metal blade, process chicken, goat's milk cheese, yogurt, walnuts, cucumber, garlic, and black pepper using a thin stream of olive oil if necessary to produce a coarse paste. Scrape spread into a serving bowl, and serve with pita wedges.

Spiced Date Spread

An intensely flavored sweet and rich fruit spread.

Serves 4 to 6

¼ lb. pitted dates

½ cup (4 oz.) goat's milk cheese, softened

1 tsp. lemon juice

¼ tsp. ground cinnamon

Apple wedges or sesame crackers for serving

In a blender or food processor fitted with a metal blade, process dates, goat's milk cheese, lemon juice, and cinnamon until reduced to a thick paste. Scrape spread into a small serving bowl, and serve with pieces of crisp apple or sesame crackers.

Spiced Goat's Milk Cheese and Grape Crackers

The espresso powder adds a surprising richness.

Serves 4

8 oz. goat's milk cheese, softened

½ cup toasted walnuts, chopped

¼ tsp. espresso powder (available in the coffee section of large grocery stores)

Plain wheat crackers for serving

15 green or red grapes, sliced in half lengthwise

Combine goat's milk cheese, walnuts, and espresso powder in a serving bowl and mix thoroughly. For best spreading texture, serve at room temperature, with about 1½ teaspoons goat's milk-cheese-mixture spread on a wheat cracker, topped with a half-grape, with crackers arranged on a plate.

Cumin Chicken with Sliced Apples

This is another tasty pairing, where the cumin-spiced chicken balances deliciously with crisp apples.

Serves 4

1 (12-oz.) can chicken, drained

1 cup (4 oz.) plain yogurt

2 TB. minced onion flakes

½ tsp. ground cumin

¼ tsp. ground cinnamon

½ tsp. salt

Dash hot pepper sauce (such as Tabasco)

Apple slices or crisp wheat crackers for serving

Combine chicken, yogurt, onion flakes, cumin, cinnamon, salt, and hot pepper sauce in a serving bowl, mix thoroughly, and chill for 1 hour. Serve with apple slices or crisp wheat crackers. If the apple slices will be set out in advance, minimize browning by rubbing them with the cut side of a half lemon.

Sun-Dried Tomato and Chive Relish with Pita Chips

This serves up a savory, piquant flavor.

Serves 4

1 cup sun-dried tomatoes (oil-packed), drained and finely chopped

¼ cup minced sweet onion, fresh if possible, or 2 TB. dried onion

2 TB. olive oil or oil from sun-dried tomatoes

2 TB. finely chopped fresh chives

½ tsp. salt

Dash hot pepper sauce (such as Tabasco)

Pita crisps for serving

Combine tomatoes, onion, oil, chives, salt, and hot pepper sauce in a serving bowl, mix thoroughly, and chill for at least 1 hour to allow flavors to meld. Serve with crisp pita chips.

Variation: Mix this relish with 1 cup (8 ounces) cream cheese if you like a slightly milder, creamier spread.

Scallops al Pil Pil

Popular in South America, this is a quick and savory dish of scallops seared at high heat with garlic and hot peppers. I've found that the most appealing presentation is with a dinner party— each guest served several scallops on a small plate with parsley and lemon wedges.

Serves 4

3 TB. olive oil

2 tsp. chopped garlic

2 TB. white wine

½ tsp. crushed red pepper

½ lb. sea scallops

Lemon wedges

4 sprigs fresh parsley

Heat olive oil in a wok or 10-inch skillet over high heat. Cook garlic, wine, and crushed red pepper for 30 seconds. Add scallops and cook, stirring, for 2 to 3 minutes until scallops are firm and opaque. Distribute equal portions of scallops to small plates, and serve with lemon edges. Garnish each plate with a sprig of parsley. Invite your guests to drizzle their scallops with lemon juice.

Savoir Starter

You can use cooked shrimp in place of scallops, but because you're now only interested in heating, as opposed to cooking, only heat the shrimp for about 1 minute. This, as a result, is an even quicker recipe.

Coconut Shell Salsa

You don't have to use the coconut shell, but if you have one hanging around from the last time you ate a coconut, it does add to the fun.

Serves 4 to 6

1 (12-oz.) jar prepared sweet fruit salsa, such as mango salsa

1 (8-oz.) can pineapple chunks, cut in half

1 maraschino cherry, for garnish

Tortilla chips for serving

Mix salsa and pineapple chunks, and mound into a carefully balanced coconut shell or a small bowl. Top salsa with cherry, and serve surrounded by tortilla chips and luau music.

Spicy Chicken-Pineapple Dip

An appetizer for the sweet tooth. Well, maybe the sweet-and-sour tooth …

Serves 6

1 (12-oz.) can chicken, drained

1 (8-oz.) can pineapple chunks

½ cup honey

2 TB. minced onion flakes

½ tsp. salt

½ tsp. red pepper flakes

Belgian endive leaves or crisp wheat crackers for serving

Combine chicken, pineapple, honey, onion flakes, salt, and red pepper flakes in a serving bowl, mix thoroughly, and chill for 1 hour. Serve with Belgian endive leaves or crisp wheat crackers.

The Least You Need to Know

◆ Herbs and spices, as well as main ingredients, are used in all sorts of different combinations across the globe. These exciting combinations can be used in appetizers to create original and interesting dishes.

◆ Foods inspired by cultures from South America to the Middle East use ingredients native to those regions. To use them is not only to create taste treats, but to learn a bit about a culture as well.

◆ Pitas are versatile, delicious appetizer vehicles you can use for many dishes— Middle Eastern or not.

◆ Dried fruits such as dates and figs and rich seasonings from cardamom to chili pepper can create taste sensations in appetizers.

Part  3 Vegetable- and Fruit-Focused Appetizers

A huge range of relatively healthful ingredients exists that can make appetizers every bit as compelling as the rich flavors and textures that accompany fat (think butter, cheese, cream, and some meats). I'm not promising no fat at all, but with the right use of familiar (and some new) ingredients and seasonings, dishes can be prepared that no one will believe are low fat.

The first approach is to find lower-fat alternatives to the high-fat originals; that's the low- or nonfat sour cream and so on. The second is to explore ingredients and methods that don't even pretend to use alternatives but are delicious by themselves. This part is all about finding those secrets and making them into delicious reality.

Chapter 16

Fun and Flavor with Fruits of the Earth

In This Chapter

- ◆ "Healthy appetizer" does not have to be a contradiction in terms
- ◆ Freshness for flavor
- ◆ Seasoning secrets
- ◆ Healthy alternatives

This chapter, indeed this part of the book, might come as a surprise. After all, many of us have only seen appetizers overflowing with fats and oils. For every one of these dishes, however, there is a healthier alternative, whether through using low-fat versions of normally fat-loaded ingredients or simply creating an appetizer using naturally healthy stuff.

Tips for Low-Fat Cooking

To set the stage, "healthy" must take into account …

- **The core dish:** The main ingredients and seasoning.
- **The vehicles and accoutrements:** A nonfat dip is of limited value if you eat it with bacon.
- **The method of preparation:** If a recipe calls for cooking, does that method introduce additional fat or calories?

Here are a few appetizer-related tips from the National Institutes of Health, with examples of how to reduce fat as a component in dishes you prepare. I hope you'll note that these approaches are featured prominently in many of the recipes in this book and especially in Part 3.

- Use nonfat or lower-fat spreads, such as jelly or jam, fruit spread, apple butter, nonfat or reduced-calorie mayonnaise, nonfat margarine, or mustard.

Hors D'oeuvre History

Studies have shown that people who consume foods that include olive oil (high in monoun-saturated fats) rather than foods high in saturated fats have lower rates of heart disease.

- Use high-fat foods only sometimes; choose more low-fat and nonfat foods.
- Use a little lemon juice, dried herbs, thinly sliced green onions, or a little salsa as a nonfat topping for vegetables or salads.
- Use small amounts of high-fat toppings. For example, use only 1 teaspoon butter or mayonnaise; 1 tablespoon sour cream; 1 tablespoon regular salad dressing.

- Switch to 1 percent or skim milk and other nonfat or lower-fat dairy products (low-fat or nonfat yogurt or nonfat or reduced-fat sour cream).
- Cut back on cheese by using small (1-ounce) amounts on sandwiches and in cooking or use lower-fat and fat-free cheeses (part-skim mozzarella, 1 percent cottage cheese, or nonfat hard cheese).
- Choose small portions of lean meat, fish, and poultry; use low-fat cooking methods (baking, poaching, or broiling); trim off all fat from meat, and remove skin from poultry.
- Choose lower-fat luncheon meats such as sliced turkey or chicken breast, lean ham, and lean sliced beef.

Source: "Action Guide for Healthy Eating" from the Federal Consumer Information Center (The full text can be found in Appendix B and at the Federal Consumer Information Center website at www.pueblo.gsa.gov/cic_text/food/guideeat/Actiongd.html.)

Victory with Vegetable Victuals

Dishes that make use of fresh vegetables offer several benefits, including terrific taste with a minimum of preparation, high nutrition, and that tantalizing fresh appearance. For the cook who wants terrific flavor in a hurry, no cooking is good cooking.

Flower Bed Canapés

Easy and fun, the canapés and cream cheese bring texture and act as a frame around the fresh flavors of the flowers.

Serves 4 to 6

½ cup (4 oz.) light cream cheese, softened

4 slices white or wheat sandwich bread, crusts removed, cut into 4 triangles per slice

16 fresh edible flowers about 1½ inches across (such as nasturtiums or edible chrysanthemums), or 32 smaller edible flowers (such as signet marigolds)

Salt to taste (optional)

Spread about ½ tablespoon cream cheese on each bread triangle, top with an edible flower or two if the flowers are small, and sprinkle with salt (if using). Arrange canapés on a festive platter and serve.

Hors D'oeuvre History

Each growing season, I reserve part of my garden for edible flowers such as nasturtiums, signet marigolds, and Shungiku (Japanese single chrysanthemums). These flowers offer color and distinctive flavor. And the marigolds really do taste like they smell. They also add fun and interest to salads, appetizers, and even main dishes.

Crisp Snow Peas with Dill Dip

Crunchy and cool, this is the perfect dish to enjoy in the late spring when the peas are in season.

Serves 4 to 6

¾ cup low-fat sour cream

½ cup low-fat mayonnaise

3 scallions, dark green leaves removed and finely chopped

1 tsp. dried dill

1 tsp. fresh lemon juice

½ tsp. salt

1 lb. fresh snow peas, washed and stems removed

Mix sour cream, mayonnaise, scallions, dill, lemon juice, and salt in a serving bowl. If possible, chill dip for several hours to allow the flavors to meld. Serve surrounded by snow peas as dippers.

> **Unappetizer**
> Crisp Snow Peas with Dill Dip is a terrific recipe for in-season, crisp fresh snow peas. When they are out of season, consider another crisp vegetable such as snap beans, blanched asparagus, or baby carrots. Droopy pea pods just don't set the stage for a tasty appetizer.

Sun-Dried Tomato Spread

This spread is creamy, hearty, and flavorful. If you want, you can add some of the oil from the sun-dried tomatoes in place of the olive oil.

Serves 4 to 6

1 (15-oz.) can chickpeas (garbanzo beans), drained

1 cup sun-dried tomatoes (oil-packed), oil reserved

¾ cup plain nonfat yogurt

¼ cup olive oil, plus more if needed

½ tsp. salt

Baked tortilla chips for serving

In a blender or food processor fitted with a metal blade, process chickpeas, tomatoes, yogurt, olive oil or reserved oil from sun-dried tomatoes, and salt until spread achieves the consistency of a thick paste. If necessary, add a little more olive oil to achieve the right consistency. Scrape spread into a serving bowl, and serve with baked tortilla chips.

Double Dips

This presents tasty fruits and vegetables in a simple and fun way.

Serves 6

1 (12-oz.) jar light blue cheese dressing

1 pint (about 24) grape tomatoes

1 pint (about 24) green grapes

Pour dressing into a serving bowl, and place the bowl in the center of a large platter. (A circular platter will match the shape of the pattern you're about to create.) Spear one tomato on one end of a bamboo skewer and one grape on the other end. Place this skewer just to one side of the bowl of dressing so the center of the skewer touches the bowl. Skewer remaining tomatoes and grapes, setting them down in an alternating pattern (grape alternating with tomato) around the side of the bowl so the end result is a circle of fruit around the dip. Have guests help themselves to a spear and dip one end, then the other. Accompany the platter with a narrow glass or vase for the used skewers.

Garden Tomato Pyramid

For a tomato lover, this is nirvana. Each variety of tomato has a slightly different taste and texture. This sit-down recipe requires a knife and fork.

Serves 6

1 large red tomato, such as a beefsteak, cut into ¼-inch slices

2 medium yellow tomatoes, cut into ¼-inch slices

3 plum (Roma) tomatoes, cut into ¼-inch slices

6 grape tomatoes, halved

¼ cup low-fat vinaigrette dressing

2 tsp. dried basil

Salt and freshly ground black pepper to taste

Crusty bread for serving

Place a slice of red tomato on each of 6 appetizer plates. Follow it by a slice of yellow tomato, plum tomato, and grape tomato half. Drizzle each plate with vinaigrette; sprinkle with basil, salt, and pepper; and serve with a knife and fork and a piece of crusty bread to mop up savory tomato juices.

Sweet Pepper-Tomato Bites

This treat gives a flavor burst from sweet peppers and tomatoes. Grape tomatoes are easier to work with in this colorful melange, but chunks of larger tomatoes can be used.

Serves 6 to 8

½ pint (about 12) grape tomatoes, halved

2 large yellow sweet peppers, pith and seeds removed, and cut into ¾-inch squares

¼ cup low-fat or light Italian dressing (your favorite)

1 TB. chopped fresh basil leaves or 1 tsp. dried

Salt to taste

Slide each grape tomato half onto a toothpick and follow with a pepper square. Arrange bites on a platter, drizzle with Italian dressing, sprinkle with basil and salt and serve.

Savoir Starter _____

In my opinion, tomato-reliant recipes are for the late summer. During this part of the season, fresh farmstand—or even better, garden tomatoes—are available in spades. These tomatoes bring sweet, juicy flavor infinitely better than any fruit imported from far away.

Grape Tomato "Bouquet" with Dill Dip

This bouquet is fun and tasty.

Serves 6

2 cups nonfat plain yogurt

2 TB. chopped dried onion

1½ TB. dried dill weed

½ tsp. garlic salt

1 pint (about 24) grape tomatoes

Combine yogurt, onion, dill, and garlic salt in a serving bowl, mix thoroughly, and chill for 1 hour or more. Serve tomatoes with dip, each tomato speared on the end of a bamboo skewer and arranged like flowers in a vase or tall, slender glass.

Roasted Pepper-Garlic Bruschetta

These crusty, flavorful toasts will disappear faster than you can make them.

Serves 4 to 6

¼ cup olive oil

2 TB. chopped garlic

4 slices white or wheat sandwich bread, crusts removed, cut into 4 triangles per slice

1 cup (8 oz.) roasted red peppers, cut into pieces about 1-inch square

1 tsp. kosher salt

2 TB. finely chopped fresh parsley for garnish

Preheat the broiler. Combine olive oil and garlic in a bowl and mix thoroughly. Arrange bread on a baking sheet, brush each piece with some garlic-oil mixture, and broil until lightly browned.

Remove bread from oven, and arrange on a serving tray. Top each triangle with a piece of red pepper, sprinkle with salt and a pinch of parsley, and serve.

White Bean Salad Spread

This makes a tasty, healthy spread.

Serves 4 to 6

1 (15-oz.) can cannellini beans, drained

1 cup fresh basil leaves

¼ cup chopped sweet onion (such as Vidalia)

1 TB. red wine vinegar

1 TB. olive oil (plus more if needed)

½ tsp. kosher salt

Fresh vegetables or crusty wheat bread for serving

In a blender or food processor fitted with a metal blade, process beans, basil, onion, vinegar, olive oil, and salt to the consistency of a thick, chunky paste. If necessary, add a little more olive oil to achieve the right consistency. Scrape spread into a serving bowl, and serve with fresh vegetables or crusty wheat bread.

Savoir Starter

In some recipes where I've called for olive oil to assist processing, other high-moisture ingredients such as nonfat yogurt will also do the trick—but use it only where the inherent yogurt flavor will not conflict with the rest of the ingredients.

Nuts About ... Nuts (and Fruit)

For the quick cook, pecans, almonds, and walnuts are available chopped (sliced or slivered in the case of almonds) and ready to go at your grocery store. They are all terrific toasted and make fine accompaniments to cheeses, for example:

◆ Pecans are a rich, buttery nut native to North America. Their flavor is a terrific addition to appetizers at least partially because of their high (unsaturated) fat content.

◆ Almonds bring a milder, sweeter flavor and combine nicely with creamy and sweet food items. (Think of cannolis!)

◆ Walnuts, grown worldwide, bring a similarly rich, slightly woody (in a good way) flavor.

Chickpea and Pecan Spread

This savory, rich spread disappears fast. Toast the nuts before preparing the spread for even better flavor.

Serves 4 to 6

1 (15-oz.) can chickpeas (garbanzo beans), drained

½ cup chopped pecans or almonds

1 TB. chopped garlic

½ tsp. salt

¼ cup olive oil, plus more if needed

Baby carrots or pita wedges for serving

Place chickpeas, pecans, garlic, and salt in a food processor. Turn on the processor, and add olive oil in a thin stream, processing until spread achieves the consistency of a thick chunky paste. If necessary, add a little more olive oil to achieve the right consistency. Scrape spread into a bowl, and serve with baby carrots or pita wedges.

Pear and Walnut Wraps

The juicy sweetness of a ripe pear, along with hearty nuts, is another of those perfect pairs (pun intended).

Serves 6

2 ripe pears, core and seeds removed, and each cut into 8 to 10 (¼-inch) slices

½ lb. sliced deli turkey, cut into 2 by 3-inch pieces

½ cup toasted walnut halves

1 TB. aged balsamic vinegar

Place 1 pear slice on a piece of sliced turkey, and top with 1 walnut half and a few drops balsamic vinegar. Wrap turkey around pear and walnut, and fasten with a toothpick, inserting it through turkey but avoiding walnut, as that is a difficult nut to pierce. Arrange on a plate and serve.

If pear slices will be out for long, minimize browning by rubbing the slices with the cut end of a lemon half.

> **Unappetizer**
> Most recipes that call for fruits and vegetables taste their best when these ingredients are as fresh as possible. Because of this necessity, making these appetizers in advance (with a few "need to chill" exceptions) is not a great idea.

Water Chestnut and Pecan Relish

The crisp freshness of water chestnuts paired with the toasted crunch of pecans is a compelling combination.

Serves 4

1 cup water chestnuts

1 cup chopped pecans, toasted

¼ cup chopped fresh parsley

1 TB. fresh lemon juice

1 tsp. granulated sugar

¼ tsp. salt

Belgian endive leaves for serving

In a food processor fitted with a shredding blade, process the water chestnuts until chunky.

Combine pecans, water chestnuts, parsley, lemon juice, sugar, and salt in a bowl and mix thoroughly. Scrape relish into a serving bowl, and let guests spread it on Belgian endive leaves.

The Least You Need to Know

- ◆ The abundance of flavor in fruits and vegetables enable terrific quick hors d'oeuvres.
- ◆ Most fruits and vegetables are naturally low in fat, while also being great sources of nutrition.
- ◆ Fresh fruits and vegetables add fun and interest—essential characteristics of appetizers that set the tone for a festive gathering.
- ◆ When the flavor is inherent in the base ingredients (fruits and vegetables), you've got less work to do to assemble a tasty starter.

Chapter 17

Carrot Shtick: Vegetable-Intensive Appetizers

In This Chapter

◆ Hors d'oeuvres that make the most of vegetable flavors
◆ Tricks for quick prep
◆ Blanching to win friends and influence people
◆ Super tomatoes

This chapter is all about vegetables from artichokes to zucchini. There's a wealth of flavor to be found in the garden. From sweet summer tomatoes, still warm from the sun, to crisp carrots and cool cucumbers, vegetables offer a range of flavors and textures that work magic even without our efforts at preparation. Our job is to put a frame around this delicious picture while keeping the focus on the vegetable star. These recipes explore several ways to present vegetables raw, crunchy, and tasty, and others that benefit from quick cooking.

Fast Spinach and Artichoke Dip

This variation on the traditional uses the microwave to accelerate preparation.

Serves 6 to 8

2 cups fresh baby spinach leaves

1 (14-oz.) can artichokes, drained

1 cup (about 3 oz.) shredded Parmesan cheese

½ cup (4 oz.) light cream cheese, softened

½ cup low-fat mayonnaise

½ cup nonfat plain yogurt

¼ cup shredded mozzarella cheese

½ tsp. chopped garlic

Dash hot pepper sauce (such as Tabasco)

Tortilla chips or wheat crackers for serving

In a food processor fitted with a metal blade, process spinach, artichokes, Parmesan cheese, cream cheese, mayonnaise, yogurt, mozzarella cheese, garlic, and hot pepper sauce until thoroughly combined but still very chunky. Scrape mixture into a microwave-safe serving dish, and microwave on high for 2 minutes or until bubbling. Stir and serve with tortilla chips or wheat crackers.

Onion Shell

This is not so much a recipe as a suggestion for a fun method of serving.

1 very large onion

Slice onion crosswise so you see the rings when you make the cut, about halfway down from the top. Reserve the top half for another use. Slice off bottom of onion just above the root line so the bottom of those same rings is exposed. With some onions, pressure on the center of the cut bottom will cause the middle of the onion to pop out of the top, leaving a hollow shell. With others, a little "convincing" with a knife is in order. Working on the top (widest diameter) of the onion half, insert the blade of the knife between layers, starting three or four layers in from the outside shell, and pry the middle of the onion out. You can even cut out some of it, allowing the remainder to be pushed out from the bottom.

Remove as many inside layers as you need to leave room for your dip or spread. Set onion on a platter or plate (and don't move it afterward—remember there is a hole in the bottom), fill it with your dip, and serve surrounded by your selected vehicles.

Cucumber-Dill Dip

Refreshing and cool, this dip is perfect for summer parties.

Serves 6 to 8

½ English-style cucumber

½ cup plain yogurt

½ cup light cream cheese, softened

2 tsp. chopped garlic

1½ tsp. dried dill

1 tsp. fresh lemon juice

Double dash hot pepper sauce (such as Tabasco)

Baby carrots, zucchini slices, cucumber strips, celery sticks, and tortilla chips for serving

In a food processor fitted with a shredding attachment, shred the cucumber. (You can also use a hand grater.) Combine cucumber, yogurt, cream cheese, garlic, dill, lemon juice, and hot pepper sauce in a serving bowl or a mixing bowl and mix thoroughly. If you want, pour this dip into an onion shell (recipe follows). Surround with baby carrots, zucchini slices, cucumber strips, or celery sticks, or tortilla chips.

Hors D'oeuvre History

If there is a continuum between art and science in culinary arts, preparing a recipe is surely somewhere in the middle. I was reminded of this as I wrote the words *double dash* when testing this recipe. Very few things are carved-in-stone sacred (the science part), but there are general rules to ensure what you make is edible. One of those rules is to "replace like with like." Replacing cream cheese with sour cream in a recipe, for example, is probably fine. You'll change the texture somewhat, but the two ingredients are otherwise similar in taste, mouthfeel, and appearance. Replacing cream cheese with sardines, on the other hand … well, you get the idea.

A "double dash" doesn't change the nature of a recipe (over a single dash); it's merely a matter of degree. Feel free to change amounts according to your taste. If in doubt, start with less, then add more, as you're not going to be able to remove that extra dash after the fact.

Marinated Balsamic Baby Carrots

A couple minutes sets this recipe in motion and then time in the fridge does the rest of the work. These carrots get even better over a day or so.

Serves 4 to 6

1 (16-oz.) pkg. baby carrots, carrots sliced in half lengthwise

⅓ cup balsamic vinegar

3 TB. olive oil

1½ tsp. salt

1 TB. Italian seasoning

Savoir Starter

After serving your Marinated Balsamic Baby Carrots, save the remaining balsamic vinegar mixture. It makes a quite passable salad dressing or marinade for chicken breasts.

Place carrots into a bowl with a lid (or a zip-type plastic bag). Pour balsamic vinegar and olive oil over carrots, and sprinkle with salt and Italian seasoning. Cover securely, shake to completely coat carrots, and chill for several hours. To serve, use a slotted spoon to remove the carrots to a small serving bowl and serve (with napkins).

Grilled Artichoke Pieces with Goat's Milk Cheese Caps

Although a bit messy, these taste so good they are worth the napkins.

Serves 4

3 TB. olive oil

1 TB. chopped garlic

½ tsp. dried oregano

1 (9-oz.) pkg. frozen artichoke hearts, thawed

4 oz. fresh goat's milk cheese

Heat olive oil, garlic, and oregano in a 12-inch skillet over medium heat. Add artichoke hearts and sauté, stirring occasionally, for about 2 minutes per side. Transfer artichokes to a serving plate, reserving cooking liquid. Top each artichoke heart with about 2 teaspoons goat's milk cheese. Drizzle the platter with reserved garlic and oil, and serve with toothpicks.

Mushroom Caps with Sun-Dried Tomato– Goat's Milk Cheese Spread

Fresh white mushroom caps are the key to that crisp mushroom texture.

Serves 4 to 6

1 (8-oz.) pkg. fresh goat's milk cheese, softened

½ cup sun-dried tomatoes (oil-packed), drained and finely chopped

½ tsp. garlic salt

1 (8-oz.) pkg. white button mushrooms, stems removed

2 TB. chopped fresh chives

Combine goat's milk cheese, tomatoes, and garlic salt in a bowl and mix thoroughly. Spoon about 1 tablespoon goat's milk cheese mixture into each mushroom cap. Arrange caps cheese side up on a platter, sprinkle with chives and serve.

Portobello Pizza Slices

These are made in a skillet for quick cooking.

Serves 4

3 TB. olive oil

1 TB. chopped garlic

1 (6-oz.) pkg. sliced portobello mushrooms

1 cup (4 oz.) shredded mozzarella cheese

½ tsp. garlic salt

Pinch ground cayenne (optional)

Heat olive oil and garlic in a 12-inch skillet over medium heat. Add mushroom slices and sauté for about 2 minutes. Turn slices and sprinkle each with about 1 tablespoon shredded mozzarella. Cover the skillet, and cook for an additional 2 minutes or until cheese has begun to melt. Remove mushrooms to a serving platter, reserving the cooking liquid. Drizzle with reserved garlic and oil, sprinkle with garlic salt and a tiny amount of cayenne (if using), and serve with toothpicks.

Tofu Salad Spread

Thanks to Marci Goldberg, a good friend of mine and a terrific cook, for this tasty addition.

Serves 4 to 6

1 (15-oz.) pkg. firm *tofu*, drained

½ cup light mayonnaise

2 large carrots, shredded

1 TB. *miso*

Pita wedges for serving

To get as much liquid as possible out of tofu (and avoid a soupy consistency), slice tofu into thick slices, place on several thicknesses of paper towels, cover with more paper towels, and press.

Combine tofu, mayonnaise, carrots, and miso in a serving bowl and mix thoroughly. Serve with pita wedges.

Gourmet Glossary

Tofu is a cheeselike substance made from soybeans and soy milk. Flavorful and nutritious, tofu is an important component of foods across the globe, especially those from the Far East. **Miso** is fermented and flavorful soybean paste. It is a key ingredient in many Japanese dishes.

Blanched Asparagus with Tarragon Cream

Simple, once again, is good.

Serves 4 to 6

¼ cup light sour cream

¼ cup light cream cheese, softened

1 tsp. fresh lemon juice

½ tsp. dried tarragon

½ tsp. dried dill

¼ tsp. garlic salt

1 bunch (about 16 oz.) thin asparagus spears, tough stem ends removed

Combine sour cream, cream cheese, lemon juice, tarragon, dill, and garlic salt in a small bowl and mix thoroughly. If possible, make this ahead of time, and chill for 1 hour or more.

Fill a large (4-quart) saucepan halfway with water, and bring to a rolling boil. Meanwhile, prepare a bowl of ice water. Plunge asparagus spears in boiling water for 1 minute. Then, using tongs or a slotted spoon, quickly plunge asparagus into ice water for 30 seconds to halt the cooking process and set the color. Drain. Scrape tarragon cream on a small platter, and surround with blanched asparagus spears for dipping. You can prepare the asparagus at the same time as the tarragon cream, and refrigerate it until ready to serve.

Savoir Starter

If you have an electric kettle, use it to boil part of the water and accelerate this recipe even more. Although you're only "cooking" the asparagus for 1 minute, it takes time for the water to boil.

Crudité Platter

Here are some of my favorites.

Serves 6 to 8

2 carrots, peeled and sliced into ¼ by 3-inch sticks, or ½ lb. baby carrots

2 celery stalks, sliced into ¼ by 3-inch sticks, or pre-sliced celery sticks

2 sweet red peppers, seeds and pith removed, and cut into ¼-inch-wide slices

2 cups broccoli florets, cut into 1 by 2-inch pieces

1 (8-oz.) pkg. fresh button mushrooms

Salt to taste

Serve a platter of carrots, celery, red peppers, broccoli, and mushrooms alone, or place them in a circle around Cucumber-Dill Dip or one of the other vegetable-friendly dips in this book. Serve salt alongside.

Variation: If you have a bit more time, blanch broccoli pieces first using the method described for Blanched Asparagus to create a tender-crisp bite and a brilliant green color.

Gourmet Glossary

Crudités are fresh vegetables—one of the simplest appetizers of all. The key, of course, is the word *fresh*, when vegetables are at their most crisp and have the greatest flavor. To this end, make careful selections at your grocery store, and, of course, take advantage when possible of in-season vegetables.

Summer Tomato Platter

When I told friends about the topic for this book, they insisted that I include this recipe from *The Complete Idiot's Guide to 20-Minute Meals*. For a fresh tomato lover, this oh-so-simple recipe is irresistibly delicious—even romantic. Just one bite, and you're on the terrace of your Tuscan villa, looking out over the olive groves.

Serves 4 to 6

2 large fresh tomatoes, cut into ½-inch slices	Good-quality extra-virgin olive oil
Handful fresh basil leaves	Kosher salt
½ lb. fresh mozzarella cheese, sliced in ¼-inch medallions	Italian bread for serving

Arrange tomato slices in a single layer on a large platter. Place 1 basil leaf on each tomato slice, then top with a piece of mozzarella. Drizzle platter with olive oil, and sprinkle with salt.

With fresh Italian bread, this is delicious and a meal in itself.

Hors D'oeuvre History

Tomatoes, whether beefsteak or grape, are an opportunity for the creative appetizer cook. In season, larger tomatoes bring a ripe, juicy flavor and texture that just can't be beat. In fact, in the late summer, you haven't lived until you've enjoyed a thick slice of fresh tomato with mayo between two slices of wheat toast. Gorgeous!

The good news in the off season is that even though the hard, flavorless drop-shipped tomatoes should be avoided, tiny grape tomatoes are usually just fine. This wonderful little variety somehow holds on to some of that bright sunny tomato flavor—in beautiful contrast to the slush outside. For that reason, I've included a number of recipes that specifically call for that magical little fruit.

Fried Parmesan Zucchini

These delicious morsels are cooked just enough to make the outside crisp while keeping the squash crunchy inside. Small squash make for pieces that are easier to eat whole. This simple recipe can be easily scaled for larger groups.

Serves 4 to 6

¼ cup olive oil

½ cup breadcrumbs

½ cup shredded Parmesan cheese

¼ tsp. ground red pepper

1 egg, beaten

2 small (each about 1 inch in diameter and 6 inches long) zucchini, ends removed, sliced into ¼-inch-thick medallions

Salt and freshly ground black pepper to taste

Heat olive oil in a 10-inch skillet over medium heat. Mix breadcrumbs, Parmesan, and red pepper in a bowl, and place next to the bowl with beaten egg. Using a fork, dip each zucchini piece in egg, turn to coat, then dip in Parmesan-breadcrumb mix, and turn to coat. Carefully place coated zucchini into the skillet, being careful not to spatter hot oil. Cook for about 1 minute per side, remove to a serving plate, and season to taste with salt and pepper. Serve with toothpicks.

 **Unappetizer**

When grilling any vegetables, make sure you've applied plenty of oil or oil-based marinade (olive oil and so on) and watch grilling vegetables closely to make sure they don't dry out. For those of us who need to create an appetizer in a hurry, overcooking is not usually a problem, but still ....

Grilled Zucchini

A summertime favorite with a glass of dry white wine, this is also tasty as a side dish.

Serves 4 to 6

3 small zucchini, sliced lengthwise into ¼ by ½-inch pieces

⅓ cup olive oil

2 tsp. chopped garlic

2 tsp. dried basil

Salt and freshly ground black pepper to taste

Heat the grill. Put zucchini slices in a small container with a lid (or a zip-type plastic bag). Combine olive oil with garlic in another bowl, mix thoroughly, and pour over zucchini. Seal securely, and shake to coat. Sprinkle with basil, salt, and pepper. Place pieces on the grill at right angles to the grill grates to minimize the risk of a piece slipping through. Cook 2 minutes per side, brush with remaining oil mixture, and serve.

Variation: Pour oil left from coating the squash into a 12-inch skillet, heat, then cook squash.

Grape Tomatoes Stuffed with Bacon and Goat's Milk Cheese

Make these in minutes; they disappear in seconds.

Serves 4 to 6

4 oz. fresh goat's milk cheese, softened

3 TB. real bacon bits

¼ tsp. salt

¼ tsp. freshly ground black pepper

1 pint (about 24) grape or cherry tomatoes, halved

Combine goat's milk cheese, bacon bits, salt, and pepper in a small bowl and mix thoroughly. Spread about 1 teaspoon goat's milk cheese mixture on the cut side of a grape tomato, and top with another tomato half. Continue with remaining tomato halves. Arrange on a platter and serve.

Quick-Dressed Grape Tomatoes

This is another one that would be just too simple if it wasn't also just too good. We just can't argue with flavors from Mother Nature.

Serves 4 to 6

1 pint (about 24) grape or cherry tomatoes, halved

¼ cup Italian-style dressing (your favorite)

¼ cup finely crumbled feta cheese

Toss tomato halves with Italian dressing in a serving bowl, and sprinkle with feta cheese. Serve with toothpicks.

The Least You Need to Know

- Vegetable appetizers are naturally flavorful and healthy.
- Fresh, in-season vegetables have the best flavor and texture.
- Several herbs, including basil, dill, and oregano, are great matches with fresh vegetables.
- Don't forget presentation. Visual aides—from fresh flowers to skewer "bouquets"—make an appetizer fun and appealing.

Tutti-Fruity

In This Chapter

◆ Fruit flavors and unique appetizers

◆ Fantastic fruit and cream combinations

◆ Spicy-sweet magic

◆ Cheese: part of a perfect pair

Fruit appetizers bring to a recipe a quality dramatically different from vegetables. The inherent sweetness in most fruits carries through all the associated ingredients, making some new combinations possible. Many fruits, especially cut fruits, are also very delicate—they beg to be consumed immediately after preparation.

Because of their unique characteristics, fruit appetizers also require thought regarding when to serve them. For example, should you serve a sweet appetizer before a savory meal, or would such an appetizer be better on its own at a summer afternoon cocktail party? Ah, the weighty questions we must face ....

Perfect Pears

You might remember the huge variety of potential cheese assortments from Chapter 3, where the intent of the accoutrements—bread, nuts, and fruit—are to frame and emphasize the flavors of the cheese. This time around, the point is to try to find perfect pairs (pears) to highlight great fruit flavors. Brie, for example, is one of a number of mild, soft cheeses that contrast beautifully with the bright acidity and crisp texture of apples and pears.

Sautéed Balsamic Pears

You will find these meltingly soft and flavorful. When you're serving this to fruit lovers, you've got a decent shot at becoming a hero.

Serves 4 to 6

2 TB. butter

2 pears, seeds removed, and cut lengthwise into 10 to 12 slices each

2 tsp. balsamic vinegar

Gourmet Glossary

Amaretto is a popular almond liqueur. A small drizzle of it works flavor-enhancing magic on fruit.

Melt butter in a 12-inch skillet over medium heat. Arrange pear slices in the skillet in a single layer, and cook for 1 minute. Turn and cook for another minute. Transfer pears to a serving tray, drizzle with balsamic vinegar, and serve with toothpicks and plenty of napkins.

Variation: In place of balsamic vinegar, drizzle pear slices with the equivalent amount of *amaretto* or similar liqueur.

Fall Orchard Fruits with Brie

No matter where you eat these, life is suddenly a picnic under a shady oak out on the hillside.

Serves 6 to 8

1 (13-oz.) block baby brie, at room temperature

2 ripe pears, seeds removed, and cut into ¼-inch-thick slices at their widest

2 ripe apples, seeds removed, and cut into ¼-inch-thick slices at their widest

½ lb. red seedless grapes, cut into small bunches

Place brie in the center of a large platter, and surround with pears, apples, and small bunches of grapes. Serve with a sharp knife for cutting and spreading brie on slices of crisp fruit. (Although a matter of taste, the rind on brie is usually fine to eat.) Guests can also spread brie on grapes, but grapes are often simply eaten separately. If the sliced fruits will be out for long, delay browning by rubbing the slices with the cut half of a lemon.

Variation: Use another soft cheese such as St. Andre or Port Salut—or use all three!

 Savoir Starter
Take the cheese out of the refrigerator an hour or 2 before you plan to serve it, and let it come to room temperature. With a cheese like brie, this will result in a bit more flavor and a wonderful spreadable consistency that makes the fruit taste even better.

Cream Cheese Spread with Dried Mediterranean Fruits

The flavors in this rich, satisfying spread derive from the concentrated essence of dried fruits.

Serves 4 to 6

1 cup (8 oz.) light cream cheese, softened

4 pitted dates, cut into ½-inch pieces

4 dried figs, cut into ½-inch pieces

2 TB. honey

Crusty bread, toast points, fresh fig slices, or apple slices for serving

In a food processor fitted with a metal blade, process cream cheese, dates, figs, and honey until thoroughly combined but still chunky. Scrape spread into a serving bowl, and serve with pieces of crusty bread, toast points, and fig or apple slices.

Variation: Use dried apricot pieces in place of, or in addition to, the dates and/or figs.

 Savoir Starter
If the honey is too thick to mix at room temperature, 10 seconds in the microwave will loosen it up.

Dizzy Tropical Fruit

This appetizer is simple to make and very tasty. Because it is served in small bowls, it might be best as a starter at a sit-down affair. Lemon juice not only provides a nice zing, but also helps keep your dish fresh from *oxidation*.

Serves 6 to 8

½ ripe cantaloupe (about 12 oz.), carved into balls with a melon scoop

¼ ripe muskmelon (about 12 oz.), carved into balls with a melon scoop

1 banana, peeled and cut into ¼-inch rounds

1 (8-oz.) can pineapple chunks, juice reserved

2 TB. fresh lemon juice

2 TB. amaretto liqueur

Combine cantaloupe, muskmelon, banana, and pineapple chunks in a large serving bowl and mix gently. Drizzle fruit with reserved pineapple juice, lemon juice, and amaretto. Serve in small bowls with a spoon.

Gourmet Glossary

Although it's best to prepare fresh fruit dishes just before serving, sometimes that isn't possible. If you need to cut apples in advance, to avoid **oxidation**, the browning of the white flesh that happens over time and with exposure to air, rub the cut pieces with a lemon half. That will buy you some time and keep your apples from turning.

Orchard Fruit Melange

The Northern Hemisphere counterpoint to tropical fruit, orchard fruits offer clean, bright flavors with refreshing acidity (that's the "tart" flavor you get in a bite of a green apple).

Serves 6 to 8

About 1 lb. green or red seedless grapes

2 apples, peeled, cored, and chopped into grape-size pieces

2 ripe peaches, pitted and chopped into grape-size pieces

½ pint pitted cherries

½ pint blueberries

Juice of ½ lemon

Combine grapes, apples, peaches, cherries, and blueberries in a large bowl (a glass bowl is a nice touch for viewing fruit). Drizzle with lemon juice and toss gently. Serve in small bowls with a spoon.

Fruit Chaat

This fresh fruit dish is inspired by Indian cooking.

Serves 6 to 8

1 banana, peeled and cut into ½-inch rounds

1 papaya, cut into ½-inch pieces

1 apple, cut into ½-inch pieces

1 orange, peeled and separated into slices, each slice cut in thirds

2 cups watermelon, seeds removed, cut into ½-inch pieces

2 cups cantaloupe, cut into ½-inch pieces

Juice from 1 lime (about 2 TB.)

Pinch red chili powder

Salt and freshly ground black pepper to taste

Combine banana, papaya, apple, orange, watermelon, and cantaloupe in a bowl. Drizzle with lime juice, and sprinkle with chili powder, salt, and black pepper. Toss lightly and serve in small bowls with spoons.

Apricots with Herbed Cheese

Although this is simple and delicious, you do need to make sure to give the cream cheese and herbs time to meld ... or buy store-brand herbed spreadable cheese.

Serves 6 to 8

1 cup (8 oz.) cream cheese or light cream cheese, softened	½ tsp. dried oregano
	½ tsp. dried thyme
1 tsp. dried dill	24 dried apricot halves

Combine cream cheese, dill, oregano, and thyme in a bowl and mix thoroughly. Chill for 1 hour or more. Spread about 1 teaspoon cheese mixture on each piece of apricot, arrange on a serving platter and serve.

Avocado and Grapefruit Bites

Here is pure fruit in a rich, creamy-tart mouthful. This combination is just irresistible!

Serves 4 to 6

1 ripe avocado	2 TB. fresh lemon juice
1 ripe grapefruit, peeled, sectioned, pith removed, and each section cut in half	

> **Unappetizer**
>
> The reason for the "carefully" advice when cutting the avocado is the tendency of a ripe avocado to disintegrate. One way to prevent this is to make sure the avocados you use are not too ripe (the riper, the more the pieces fall apart). The other way to minimize disintegration is, well, to be careful.

Carefully cut avocado in half and remove the pit by embedding the blade (not the tip) of a sharp knife into it. Turn the knife slowly to release the pit. Remove peel and cut avocado into 1-inch pieces. Spear 1 grapefruit piece and 1 avocado piece on a toothpick. Repeat with remaining grapefruit and avocado, and arrange on a serving plate. (A half-grapefruit, cut side up, on the center of the platter might be a nice touch.) Drizzle bites with lemon juice and serve.

Bacon and Avocado Bites

The creamy richness of avocado pairs well with the crisp bacon.

Serves 4 to 6

1 ripe avocado

½ lb. bacon, strips cut in half to about 1 by 4 inches

Preheat the broiler. Soak toothpicks in water and drain. Carefully cut avocado in half and remove the pit by embedding the blade (not the tip) of a sharp knife into it. Turn the knife slowly to release the pit. Remove peel and cut into ½ by 1-inch pieces. Wrap each avocado piece with bacon, and fasten with a toothpick. Place wrapped avocado-bacon bites on a baking sheet, and broil for about 3 minutes on the high rack, turning once, until bacon is crispy. Arrange on a serving plate and serve.

Bacon-Wrapped Prunes

The rich, mellow taste of prunes is a great partner with savory bacon.

Serves 4 to 6

6 oz. (about 24) prunes

½ lb. bacon, strips cut in half to about 1 by 4 inches

Preheat the broiler. Soak toothpicks in water and drain. Wrap each prune with bacon, and fasten with a toothpick. Place prune-bacon bites on a baking sheet, and broil for about 3 minutes on the high rack, turning once, until bacon is crispy. Arrange on a serving plate and serve.

Variation: Try with other dried fruits such as figs, dates, or even apricots.

Dates Stuffed with Chutney Cheese

Decadent and elegant, this recipe is a sure crowd pleaser.

Serves 4 to 6

1 cup (8 oz.) cream cheese or light cream cheese, softened

1 (8-oz.) jar ginger-mango chutney or other mango-based chutney

16 pitted dates, sliced lengthwise

1 cup chopped pecans

Combine cream cheese and chutney in a small bowl and mix thoroughly. Stuff dates with cream cheese mixture, sprinkle with pecans, and serve.

 Savoir Starter

Years ago, when I first heard the idea of using sour cream with fruit, I thought it was a joke. But the fact is, this is a perfect pair. Try it; you'll like it. Have I said that before?

Creamy and Dreamy

Fruit and cream combinations appeal to the senses in every way, from the taste (decadent and rich, with tart fruit flavors balanced by creamy sweetness), to the smell, to the visual appeal, to our memories of such dishes from childhood. A bite of blueberries and cream is to go back in time—well, for me at least. Start your own memories with some of these recipes.

Fruit and Cream Platter

This is a dipping dish made in a fruit-and-cream heaven.

Serves 6 to 8

1 cup light sour cream

¼ cup granulated sugar

1 pint fresh strawberries

½ lb. seedless grapes

1 fresh, crisp apple, cored, seeded, and sliced lengthwise into about ½-inch-wide slices

Combine sour cream and sugar in a serving bowl and mix thoroughly. Place the bowl on a platter; surround the bowl with strawberries, grapes, and apples; and serve, inviting guests to dip fruit into cream. If apple slices will be out for a while, rub with a cut lemon half to delay browning.

Variation: Serve with just one type of fruit (grapes or strawberries are terrific), or pick another fruit to try.

Blueberry-Cream Dream

This recipe basically goes one step further than the Fruit and Cream Platter. This time the fruit is *in* the cream. Decadent? Of course!

Serves 4

½ cup light sour cream

3 TB. granulated sugar

½ lb. (about 1½ cups) fresh blueberries

Combine sour cream and sugar in a serving bowl and mix thoroughly. Gently stir in berries. Serve with coffee on the veranda as the sun sets over your land holdings.

Variation: Use raspberries, blackberries, cherries, or seedless grapes instead.

Cream Cheese with Sweet and Sugared Fruits

Bright, sweet fruit flavors make this type of spread a favorite for kids and adults.

Serves 4 to 6

1 cup (8 oz.) light cream cheese, softened

½ cup orange marmalade

Party rye slices or celery sticks for serving

Combine cream cheese and orange marmalade in a serving bowl, mix thoroughly, and serve with pieces of savory cocktail bread (such as "party rye" bread) or celery sticks.

Variation: The potential list of sweet fruits and mixtures to pair with cream cheese is limited only by your imagination. Try cherry preserves, blueberry preserves, diced ripe peaches, or crushed pineapple and honey (make sure you drain the pineapple though).

Pumpkin Mousse Dip

For a simple and rich cocktail party dish, serve this in a bowl with gingersnap dippers!

Serves 6 to 8

2 cups milk

1 cup canned pumpkin

2 (3-oz.) pkg. vanilla pudding mix

1 tsp. pumpkin pie spice, or ½ tsp. ground cinnamon, ¼ tsp. grated nutmeg, 1 pinch ground cloves, and 1 pinch ground allspice

1 cup whipped topping

Combine milk, pumpkin, pudding mix, and spice. Stir in whipped topping and serve.

Unappetizer

Banana pieces taste quite good as well with these fruit dips, although they should be prepared immediately before serving to avoid unappetizing browning. Tossing the pieces with lemon juice will help delay this effect.

Fluff Fruit Dip

For the certifiable sweet tooth, even when it comes to appetizers ... Fluff Fruit Dip.

Serves 6 to 8

1 cup (8 oz.) cream cheese or light cream cheese, softened

1 cup *marshmallow topping*

Assorted fruit for serving

Combine cream cheese and marshmallow topping in a bowl and mix thoroughly. Serve with an assortment of fruit such as strawberries, raspberries, and pear slices.

Hors D'oeuvre History _____

Remember that sweet **marshmallow topping** from your school days? Check the ingredients—no fat or cholesterol to be found. Of course, there's plenty of sugar ...

Lemon-Cranberry Fruit Dip

This tart-sweet masterpiece is worth a try.

Serves 4 to 8

1 cup (8 oz.) lemon yogurt

½ cup cranberry relish

¼ tsp. ground cinnamon

1 pinch ground cloves

1 pinch ground allspice

Sliced apples, pears, or other fruit for serving

Combine yogurt, cranberry relish, cinnamon, cloves, and allspice in a serving bowl and mix thoroughly. If possible, chill for several hours, then serve with slices of apples, pears, or other fruits.

Savoir Starter _____

The easiest way I've found to slice pears is to cut them in half lengthwise, then cut wedges around the core. If you're slicing thinly, each pear will produce 10 to 12 slices.

Raspberry Fruit Dip

Here's another creamy, fruity dip for those summer evenings on the farmhouse porch ...

Serves 6 to 8

2 cups whipped topping

1 cup (8 oz.) seedless raspberry yogurt

Assorted fruit for serving

Combine whipped topping and yogurt and mix thoroughly. Serve with an assortment of fruit such as strawberries, raspberries, and pear slices.

The Least You Need to Know

◆ Fruit-based appetizers bring a whole new spectrum of flavors to appetizers.

◆ Sugar is a natural component of most fruits, and the appetizers in this chapter make the most of this characteristic. Some of the most delicious appetizers are those that successfully pair spicy-sweet flavors.

◆ Many fruits are also naturally acidic. Creamy ingredients, from cream cheese to sour cream, often provide a refreshing balance with these flavors.

◆ Dried and packaged fruits can be used any time. Fresh fruits are best when they are local and in season.

Chapter 19

Low-Fat Appetizers

In This Chapter

- Flavor without fat
- Secrets of rich texture
- Low-fat dips and spreads
- More healthful alternatives

In this chapter, I give many recipes in which you have the option of choosing between the low- or nonfat ingredients. The quest for a low-fat diet is a matter of degree and choice, and we usually also must consider the flavor and texture that, like it or not, accompanies ingredients with some fat.

There are, relatively speaking, "good" oils and "bad" oils. Although I urge you to consider the advice of nutrition experts (which is evolving as we speak), oils that are low in saturated fats are generally considered to be better, even more healthful, than those with a higher proportion of saturated fats. Olive oil is generally considered to be relatively "healthful," and because of its wonderful flavor, I've included it as a component of recipes in this chapter as well as throughout this book.

Although this chapter focuses on appetizers low in fat, you can find similar low-fat recipes and alternatives throughout this book.

Healthful Dips and Spreads

Through careful selection of healthful foundations, this section offers flavor and texture without a lot of fat.

Herbed Cottage Cheese

This dip is flavorful and tasty.

Serves 4 to 6

2 cups low- or nonfat *cottage cheese*

3 TB. chopped fresh chives

2 tsp. dried dill

½ tsp. dried tarragon

½ tsp. garlic salt

Fresh vegetables for serving

Combine cottage cheese, 2 tablespoons chives, dill, tarragon, and garlic salt in a serving bowl, mix thoroughly, and refrigerate, if possible, for 1 hour or more. Garnish with remaining 1 tablespoon chives, and serve with fresh vegetables.

Gourmet Glossary

Cottage cheese is a fresh cow's milk cheese. Those chunks you see are the curds, which vary in size. (The container of cottage cheese will specify size, for example, "small curd" or "large curd.") With its mild flavor and creamy texture, cottage cheese in its low- and nonfat forms is a useful component of low-fat dips, spreads, and other recipes.

Roasted Pepper-Mustard Spread

This savory, piquant spread makes the most of rich roasted pepper flavors.

Serves 4 to 6

½ cup roasted red pepper pieces, finely chopped

½ cup low- or nonfat cottage cheese

2 TB. whole-grain mustard

2 scallions, dark green leaves removed, and finely chopped

½ tsp. salt

Additional chopped scallion pieces for garnish (optional)

Crisp low-fat wheat crackers or melba toast for serving

Combine red pepper, cottage cheese, mustard, scallions, and salt in a serving bowl, mix thoroughly, and refrigerate, if possible, for 1 hour or more. Scatter chopped scallion pieces over top (if using), and serve with crisp low-fat wheat crackers or melba toast.

Lemon-Pepper Dipping Sauce

This is a perfect dip for pinzimonio, the multi-vegetable appetizer I describe in Chapter 13.

Serves 4 to 6

2 TB. honey

2 TB. extra-virgin olive oil

2 tsp. fresh lemon juice

1 tsp. peeled, grated, fresh ginger

½ tsp. freshly ground black pepper

Salt to taste

Pour honey into a serving bowl, and microwave for 10 seconds. Add olive oil, lemon juice, ginger, pepper, and salt and mix thoroughly. Serve with fresh vegetable dippers, or pinzimonio.

Hors D'oeuvre History

For dippers, the suspect list will be familiar, although I've removed a few popular platforms such as potato chips and tortilla chips that, unless baked, have a lot of oil. Those to use freely include fresh vegetables, Belgian endive leaves (listed separately from vegetables because they are so perfectly shaped for dipping), pieces of crusty bread, low-fat wheat crackers, and breadsticks.

Chutney and Cottage Cheese Dip

This dip is a lower-fat, but no less flavorful, iteration of the cream cheese spreads.

Serves 4 to 6

1 cup low- or nonfat cottage cheese

1 (9-oz.) jar Major Grey's Chutney

Crusty bread or apple slices for serving

Combine cottage cheese and ½ chutney in a serving bowl and mix thoroughly. Spread remaining chutney on top of cottage cheese. Serve with wedges of crusty bread or crunchy apple slices and a spreading knife.

Variation: Mix 1 teaspoon aged balsamic vinegar into the spread for added zing.

Sweet-and-Sour Cottage Cheese Dip

This simple yet flavorful dip takes just a minute to prepare.

Serves 4

1 cup low- or nonfat cottage cheese

¼ cup sweet-and-sour sauce

¼ cup finely chopped fresh chives

Wheat crackers or Belgian endive leaves for serving

Combine cottage cheese, sweet-and-sour sauce, and 3 tablespoons chives (reserve the remaining 1 tablespoon for garnish) in a serving bowl, mix thoroughly, and chill, if possible, for 1 hour. Stir again, sprinkle top with remaining 1 tablespoon chives, and serve with wheat crackers or Belgian endive leaves as dippers.

Savoir Starter

When most people think of dip, they think of something creamy and thick that will cling to a dipper, whether it's a vegetable or a chip. To achieve that creamy dip consistency without fat, we have to be creative with mixing base components—from sour cream and cottage cheese (light, of course) to chickpeas and other vegetables.

Low-Fat Spinach Dip

As you can see, variation is the name of the game with dips. Even with the spinach theme, there are several directions you can go. This classic, even though it's out of the box and does need fridge time for the flavors to meld, is worth knowing because it's so quick to make.

Serves 6 to 8

1 (10-oz.) pkg. frozen chopped spinach, thawed and drained

1 cup low- or nonfat cottage cheese

1 cup low-fat sour cream

1 pkg. dry vegetable soup mix

Baked tortilla chips for serving

Combine spinach, cottage cheese, sour cream, and soup mix in a serving bowl and mix thoroughly. Chill for several hours, and serve with baked tortilla chips.

Spicy Healthy Chili Dip

This is a cool yet spicy variation of the classic favorite.

Serves 4

½ cup low- or nonfat cottage cheese

½ cup low-fat sour cream

1 tsp. fresh lime juice

½ tsp. chili powder

¼ tsp. ground cumin

Salt to taste

Baked tortilla chips for serving

Combine cottage cheese, sour cream, lime juice, chili powder, cumin, and salt in a serving bowl and mix thoroughly. Chill for several hours, and serve with baked tortilla chips.

Mock "Guac" (Spicy Asparagus Dip)

A longtime neighbor, Renee Crockett Rehn, inspired this tasty guacamole-looking dip.

Serves 4

½ cup sour cream

½ cup plain yogurt

1 (.7-oz.) pkg. Italian salad dressing mix

½ bunch (about 8 oz.) asparagus, tough stem ends removed, and cut into 1-inch pieces

Fresh vegetables or baked tortilla chips for serving

In a blender or food processor fitted with a metal blade, process sour cream, yogurt, salad dressing mix, and asparagus until smooth. Chill for several hours, and serve with fresh vegetables or baked tortilla chips.

Marmalade Fruit Dip

You will enjoy this creamy, tart-sweet fruit dip.

Serves 4

½ cup plain yogurt

½ cup low-fat sour cream

½ cup orange *marmalade*

1 tsp. fresh lemon juice

Sliced apples and pears for serving

Combine yogurt, sour cream, orange marmalade, and lemon juice in a serving bowl; mix thoroughly; and serve with sliced apples and pears. If fruit slices will be out for a while, rub them with a cut lemon half to delay browning.

Variation: Different flavors of marmalade or fruit preserves will work. Fruit preserves will result in a sweeter dip.

Gourmet Glossary

Marmalade is a fruit and sugar preserve that contains whole pieces of peel. Because of the peel use, we get the effect of simultaneous sweetness (from the sugar) and tartness (from the fruit's natural acids). The most common marmalades are made with citrus such as oranges and lemons and are terrific components of sweetish starters.

Creamy Chive Dip

Here we have a low-fat, savory dip that is also great as a more healthful option to top baked potatoes!

Serves 4

½ cup plain yogurt

½ cup low-fat sour cream

⅔ cup finely chopped fresh chives or 1 (.25-oz.) jar dried chives

Pinch salt

Fresh vegetables or low-fat wheat crackers for serving

Combine yogurt, sour cream, all but 1 tablespoon fresh chives (or all chives if using dried), and salt in a serving bowl and mix thoroughly. Chill for 1 hour in the fridge, if possible. Sprinkle remaining fresh chives on top (if using), and serve with fresh vegetables or low-fat wheat crackers.

Savoir Starter _____

Not all wheat crackers are created equal. A quick look at the ingredients will show you that some crackers are loaded with fats and oils, whereas others have little or none. Check the side panel on the box to discover the fat content.

Roasted Red Pepper Spread

Chickpeas, as many cooks know well, make a hearty, rich base for a spread.

Serves 6 to 8

1 (15½-oz.) can chickpeas, drained

1 cup nonfat plain yogurt

½ cup roasted red peppers, drained and cut into 1-inch pieces

2 TB. olive oil, plus more if needed

1 tsp. chopped garlic

¼ tsp. salt

Dash hot sauce (such as Tabasco)

1 TB. fresh lemon juice

1 TB. chopped fresh chives for garnish (optional)

Pita crisps for serving

In a food processor fitted with a metal blade, process chickpeas, yogurt, red peppers, olive oil, garlic, salt, and hot sauce until almost smooth. If necessary, add a little more olive oil to achieve a smooth consistency. Scrape spread into a serving bowl, stir in the lemon juice, sprinkle chives on top (if using), and serve with pita crisps.

Flavorful Bites

In this section, you'll find a short list of quick vegetable-intensive recipes.

If you like the low-fat sandwich idea in the Sliced Cucumber Sandwiches recipe that follows, don't stop with cucumbers. Also consider arugula, basil (fresh), onion (sweet), peppers (roasted), scallions, tomato and fresh basil, tomato and sweet onion (thinly sliced), tomato (thin slices), and watercress.

Sautéed Snap Peas

Take these pods for a "quick wok," and you've got an irresistible crunchy starter.

Serves 4

2 TB. olive oil

¼ cup soy sauce

1 tsp. chopped garlic

1 lb. fresh sugar snap peas

¼ tsp. kosher salt

Heat olive oil in a wok or 10-inch skillet over medium-high heat. Pour soy sauce into a small bowl, and place the bowl in the center of a serving platter. Place garlic and peas into the wok and cook, stirring, for 1 minute. Arrange pea pods on the serving plate around the bowl, sprinkle peas with salt, and serve, inviting guests to dip pea pods into soy sauce.

Variation: This works well with snow peas (flat pod peas), fresh snap beans, and other vegetables.

Quick and Cool Cukes

Now this is a great hot-weather appetizer! When I was a kid, my mom used to serve these before dinner. My brothers and I could never get enough.

Serves 4

2 small cucumbers, striped and sliced into ¼-inch sections

½ cup cold water

½ cup red wine vinegar

½ tsp. dried dill or 1 TB. fresh

3 ice cubes

Arrange cucumbers in a 12-inch shallow bowl or pie plate. Pour water and vinegar over cucumber, sprinkle with dill, and add ice cubes. For a sit-down appetizer, pass the bowl and serve cucumber slices on a plate to eat with a fork. For a delightfully drippy informal appetizer, simply allow guests to use their fingers!

Heart of Palm and Mushroom Skewers

This appetizer combines the rich textures of heart of palm and mushrooms. They disappear quickly.

Serves 6

1 (14-oz.) can hearts of palm, drained and cut into 1-inch segments	¼ cup light Italian salad dressing (your favorite)
1 (8-oz.) pkg. fresh button mushrooms, halved through the cap and stem	Salt and freshly ground black pepper, to taste

Spear one heart of palm (through the side of heart) and one mushroom piece with a toothpick. Repeat with remaining hearts of palm and mushrooms. Arrange bites on a serving plate; drizzle with Italian dressing, salt, and pepper; and serve.

Sliced Cucumber Sandwiches

Perhaps one of the most famous "finger sandwiches," this refreshing, bite-size morsel is a great appetizer.

Serves 4 to 6

1 TB. chopped fresh dill	1 English-style cucumber, striped and very thinly sliced
2 TB. light margarine, softened	
8 slices white or wheat sandwich bread, crusts removed	Salt to taste
	½ tsp. freshly ground black pepper

Combine dill and margarine in a small bowl and mix thoroughly. Spread herb margarine over 4 slices of bread. Top each slice with a layer of thinly sliced cucumber, sprinkle with salt and pepper, top with bread, and cut on the diagonal to create small triangular sandwiches. Arrange on a serving platter and serve.

 Unappetizer

Many vegetables, such as cucumbers, contain a lot of water. To prevent your appetizer sandwiches from becoming "sogwiches," prepare them just before serving.

Lean Ham and Sweet Red Pepper Bites

The soft, savory ham and the crisp sweet pepper make for a crunchy, tasty appetizer.

Serves 6

1 TB. prepared mustard

1 TB. low-fat sour cream

½ tsp. salt

½ lb. thinly sliced lean ham

2 large sweet red peppers, seeds and pith removed, and cut lengthwise into ¼-inch slices

Combine mustard, sour cream, and salt in a small bowl and mix thoroughly. Spread a thin line of mustard mixture along one side of a slice of ham about 1 inch in from the edge. Place a slice of red pepper over mustard, and roll ham over pepper to create a cylinder. Slice each cylinder in half, arrange in a circle like the spokes in a wheel and serve.

The Least You Need to Know

- ◆ Low fat definitely does not mean low flavor.
- ◆ Herbs, seasonings, and flavorful main ingredients take center stage in low-fat appetizers.
- ◆ Yes, it is possible to create a rich, creamy-tasting dip with low-fat ingredients.
- ◆ Appetizer sandwiches are loaded with low-fat possibilities.

20

Very Vegetarian

In This Chapter

- ◆ Familiar friends used in new and different ways
- ◆ Delicious mushroom-based appetizers
- ◆ Gorgeous flavorful vegetable starters
- ◆ Walnuts, pecans, and almonds—oh my!

I've taken two general approaches to the recipes in this chapter. The first is to offer "meatless alternatives" to appetizers that traditionally include meat. These tend to be healthful and often delicious, but the fact is that their premise is still about meat (or the absence thereof).

The other and more fun approach is to create hors d'oeuvres designed around vegetarian ingredients. This focus presents an opportunity to let unique flavors and seasonings shine through in ways just not possible with meat-based dishes. These mélanges of vegetables and grains can be so good that committed carnivores might have to try to imitate *them* by creating alternatives *with* meat.

Several levels of vegetarianism exist—the strict interpretation, veganism, allows no animal products—food or otherwise—whatsoever. For the purpose of this chapter, I've used a lacto-ovo vegetarian definition of vegetarian cuisine, which allows no meat but does allow animal products such as eggs, milk, and cheese.

Vegetarian Magic!

In this section, we embark on a quest for flavor … and we'll find edible treasures in our search. From legumes and fruits to mushrooms and all sorts of fresh vegetables, you'll find them here!

Although the recipes in this chapter focus exclusively on the vegetarian diet, many other recipes in Part 3 also fall in this meatless category. Check out Chapters 16 through 19 for more ideas.

Portobello-Garlic Crostini

Try these hearty, savory appetizers.

Serves 4 to 6

5 slices white or wheat sandwich bread, crusts removed, cut into 4 triangles per slice

2 to 3 TB. olive oil

1 tsp. crushed garlic

1 (6-oz.) pkg. sliced portobello mushrooms, cut into 1-inch pieces

20 fresh baby spinach leaves

2 TB. shredded Parmesan cheese

Kosher salt to taste

Preheat the broiler. Arrange bread on a baking sheet in a single layer, and broil for about 1 minute per side, until lightly browned. Meanwhile, heat olive oil and garlic in a 10-inch skillet over medium heat, add mushrooms, and sauté, shaking the pan frequently, for about 2 minutes. Arrange toast triangles on a serving platter, and place 1 spinach leaf and mushroom piece on each. Arrange crostini on a serving plate, sprinkle with a pinch of Parmesan cheese and salt and serve.

Variation: Drizzle with balsamic vinegar and/or use arugula in place of spinach for added zing.

Artichoke Hearts with Fried Sage and Garlic

To quote one taste-tester: "These are really good."

Serves 4

3 TB. olive oil

2 tsp. chopped garlic

1 (12-oz.) pkg. frozen artichoke hearts, thawed

¼ cup shredded Parmesan cheese

Kosher salt to taste

4 fresh sage leaves or ½ tsp. dried sage

Heat olive oil and garlic in a 10- to 12-inch skillet over medium-high heat until garlic begins to sizzle. Add artichoke hearts, cover, and cook for 3 minutes. Transfer artichoke hearts to a serving platter, sprinkle each with a pinch of Parmesan and kosher salt to taste. Serve with toothpicks. If you use fresh sage leaves, use them to form an X in the middle of your serving platter as a whimsical garnish.

Savoir Starter

Artichokes are available fresh, frozen, and canned or marinated and preserved in jars. Artichoke hearts and bottoms are the two preserved versions you'll find.

Tortilla Wraps with Mozzarella, Almonds, and Spinach

A rich, nutty spread that has the added benefit of being portable—perfect to carry to that party at Aunt Jean's house.

Serves 4 to 6

4 (8-inch) flour tortillas

2 cups (about 4 oz.) baby spinach leaves

2 cups (8 oz.) shredded mozzarella cheese

½ cup plus 1 TB. sliced almonds

1 cup sour cream

Place 1 tortilla on a work surface. Arrange a line of spinach leaves about 1 inch in from the tortilla side closest to you. Top with ½ cup mozzarella and 2 tablespoons almonds. Starting from this side, roll tortilla over spinach and cheese to form a cylinder. If necessary, fasten with a toothpick. Repeat with remaining tortillas and filling, place rolls on a microwave-safe plate, and heat for 1 minute or until cheese begins to melt. Spoon sour cream into a small bowl, sprinkle remaining 1 tablespoon almonds on top, and place the bowl in the center of a serving platter. Cut tortillas in half, and arrange on the platter around sour cream like the spokes on a wheel.

Warm and Chunky Mushroom Dip

Hearty and savory, this dip is a winner for mushroom lovers. The sweet onions don't need to be cooked for long for delicious flavor.

Serves 6 to 8

3 TB. olive oil

⅓ cup ¼-inch pieces sweet onion (such as Vidalia)

2 tsp. chopped garlic

1 tsp. Italian seasoning

½ tsp. dried rosemary

1 (8-oz.) pkg. sliced white mushrooms, chopped into ¼-inch-pieces

1 cup (8 oz.) light cream cheese, softened

2 tsp. fresh lemon juice

½ tsp. salt

½ tsp. freshly ground black pepper

Fresh white mushroom halves and/or tortilla chips for serving

Savoir Starter

Warm and Chunky Mushroom Dip is terrific warm, but you can eat it cold, too. It will have the consistency of a spread, so break out a knife.

Heat olive oil, onion, garlic, Italian seasoning, and rosemary in a 12-inch or larger skillet over medium-high heat, stirring, for 3 minutes.

Add chopped mushrooms, and cook for 1 minute, stirring. Remove skillet from heat, and thoroughly mix in cream cheese, lemon juice, salt, and black pepper. Scrape dip into a serving bowl, and serve with either fresh mushroom halves (for real mushroom lovers) or tortilla chips—or both.

Grape Tomato Bites with Feta and Italian Seasoning

I've raved about grape tomatoes before, so here I'll simply comment that this is yet another example of the type of delicious yet quick dish made possible by this tiny, tasty tomato.

Serves 6 to 8

1 pint grape tomatoes, cut in half

½ cup finely crumbled feta cheese

½ cup Italian salad dressing

Salt and black pepper to taste

Place tomato halves in a serving bowl. Add feta and Italian dressing, and toss to coat. Season to taste with salt and pepper, and serve in small bowls or on plates as a dinner appetizer.

Chickpea Salad

This savory sit-down hors d'oeuvre is the appetizer of choice to set the stage for a meal of grilled seafood. This is another dish that could cross the bridge between appetizer and main course.

Serves 4 to 6

1 (15-oz.) can chickpeas, drained	¼ cup olive oil
2 stalks celery, cut into ¼-inch pieces	2 TB. fresh lemon juice
1 cup chopped fresh parsley	2 anchovies
1 large carrot, shredded (about 1 cup)	½ tsp. salt
½ cup finely chopped sweet onion (such as Vidalia)	½ tsp. freshly ground black pepper
½ cup shredded Parmesan cheese	Fresh bread for serving

Combine chickpeas, celery, parsley, carrot, onion, and Parmesan cheese in a large serving bowl. In a blender, process olive oil, lemon juice, anchovies, salt, and pepper until smooth. Pour olive oil dressing over chickpea mixture, and toss to coat. Serve on small plates or bowls with fresh bread and a glass of dry white wine. (See Chapter 24 for wine suggestions.)

Three-Bean Salad

This savory vegetable appetizer/side dish has a time-honored place at the summer table. The secret is in the "chill." If you can let this hang out in the fridge overnight, you'll be rewarded with extra flavor.

Serves 8 to 10 as an appetizer dish

1 (15-oz.) can green beans, rinsed and drained	⅓ cup olive oil
1 (15-oz.) can cannellini beans, rinsed and drained	⅓ cup red wine vinegar
	1 tsp. chopped fresh dill
1 (15-oz.) can yellow (wax) beans, rinsed and drained	½ tsp. celery seed
	½ tsp. salt
½ cup granulated sugar	½ tsp. freshly ground black pepper
½ cup finely chopped sweet onion (such as Vidalia)	

Combine green beans, cannellini beans, yellow beans, sugar, onion, olive oil, vinegar, dill, celery seed, salt, and black pepper in a bowl; cover; and refrigerate for several hours. Even better—refrigerate overnight. Serve in small bowls or on plates as a dinner appetizer.

Roasted Red Pepper, Goat's Milk Cheese, and Spinach Bites

Contrasting red, white, and green and delicious flavors will draw your guests to this starter.

Serves 6 to 8

About 24 fresh baby spinach leaves, each about 2½ by 1½ inches

6 oz. fresh goat's milk cheese

¾ cup (6 oz.) roasted red peppers, drained and cut into ¼ by 1½-inch strips

1 tsp. kosher salt

Fill each spinach leaf with about 1½ teaspoons goat's milk cheese and a strip of roasted red pepper. Roll spinach leaves around filling, and fasten with toothpicks. Arrange spinach bites on a serving platter, sprinkle with kosher salt and serve.

 **Savoir Starter**

If you find large red, yellow, or green (or all three!) fresh sweet peppers at the store, cut them in half lengthwise, clean out the seeds from each half, and place these halves on a platter. Fill each one with your assembled Roasted Red Pepper, Goat's Milk Cheese, and Spinach Bites, surrounding the pepper halves with the rest. Also, to avoid the toothpicks-left-everywhere syndrome, include a small dish or cup for the used toothpicks.

Curried Pineapple Bites

These are spicy and sweet. If you really like curry flavor, use more than the called-for ½ teaspoon.

Serves 4 to 6

¼ cup honey

1 TB. sesame oil

½ tsp. curry powder

¼ cup coconut flakes

2 (8-oz.) cans pineapple chunks, drained

Combine honey, sesame oil, and curry powder in a small bowl and mix thoroughly. Spread coconut flakes on a small plate. Insert a toothpick into each pineapple chunk, dip pineapple into honey-curry mixture, and dredge in coconut flakes to coat. Arrange pineapple chunks on a platter with their toothpicks intact and serve.

Savory Spinach Spread

Spinach add... rich flavor, ...or, and hearty texture to this tasty spread.

Serves 4 to 6

1 (10-oz.) pkg. frozen chopped spinach, thawed and drained

½ cup mayonnaise

½ cup (4 oz.) cream cheese or light cream cheese, softened

1 tsp. fresh lemon juice

1 (.53-oz.) pkg. onion soup/dip mix

Sliced scallions for garnish

Crusty bread or crackers for serving

In a food processor fitted with a metal blade, process spinach, mayonnaise, cream cheese, lemon juice, and onion soup mix until smooth. Scrape dip into a serving dish, and chill to allow flavors time to meld, if possible. Garnish with sliced scallions, and spread on pieces of crusty bread or crackers.

Hors D'oeuvre History

Vegetarian dishes are a big component of the daily diet of people across the world, much more so than in the United States. Vegetarian appetizers, reflecting this reality, often offer an opportunity to travel the world via taste express.

Balsamic-Pesto Spread

If you are in a rush to set out something nice with ingredients on hand, this should do the trick.

Serves 4 to 6

1 cup cottage cheese

2 to 3 TB. prepared pesto

1 TB. balsamic vinegar

Crisp wheat crackers for serving

Combine cottage cheese, pesto, and balsamic vinegar in a serving bowl and mix thoroughly. Serve surrounded with crisp wheat crackers.

Variation: Instead of cottage cheese, use ½ cream cheese and ½ sour cream.

Call Me Nuts ...

In spite of their tiny size, nuts bring terrific flavor and nutrition to appetizers. Here are several recipes that make the most of the riches of nuts.

Several recipes in this section include the ingredient with indefinite amounts, such as "plus more olive oil if needed." The reason for this is that ingredients contain varying amounts of liquid from producer to producer; therefore, you need to have flexibility to achieve the right consistency. Otherwise, your food processor will produce something more like granola than a spread.

Toasted Walnut Spread with Apples

This simple yet flavorful appetizer seems to carry with it the comfort of a warm fire on a cool rainy night.

Serves 4 to 6

1 cup plus 1 TB. chopped walnuts	1 TB. honey
1 (15-oz.) can chickpeas, drained	½ tsp. salt
¼ cup olive oil plus more if needed	Sliced apples for serving

To toast walnuts, preheat the broiler. Spread nuts on a baking sheet in a single layer, and broil on the high rack for 2 minutes, watching closely to prevent any blackening. Stir and broil for another minute.

In a food processor fitted with a metal blade, process chickpeas, 1 cup toasted walnuts, olive oil, honey, and salt until the consistency of a thick paste. If necessary, add a little more olive oil to achieve the right consistency. Scrape spread into a serving bowl, garnish with remaining toasted walnuts, and serve on a platter surrounded by freshly sliced apples as "dippers." A lit candle on the platter adds ambiance. This, by the way, would go beautifully with a Madeira or port wine. If apple slices will be out for long, rub them with a cut lemon half to delay browning.

Variation: Add cinnamon or apple pie spice.

Walnut and Roasted Red Pepper Dip

This recipe, based on *muhammara*, or Turkish hot pepper dip, is served with flat bread or on toast.

Serves 6 to 8

¼ cup olive oil plus more if needed

½ cup ½-inch pieces onion

½ cup roasted red peppers

½ cup breadcrumbs

½ cup walnuts, toasted

1 TB. fresh lemon juice

1 TB. chopped garlic

1 tsp. hot pepper sauce (such as Tabasco)

1 tsp. ground cumin

1 tsp. salt

Pita wedges for serving

Gourmet Glossary

Muhammara is a Turkish dip or spread that varies in ingredients, although every version I've seen contains walnuts, onion, garlic, breadcrumbs, and hot peppers in some form. It's another example of a vegetable-based dish that comes loaded not only with flavor but also with history.

Heat olive oil and onion in a small skillet over medium-high heat, and cook for 3 minutes or until onions begin to soften. Meanwhile, in a food processor fitted with a metal blade, pulse red peppers, breadcrumbs, walnuts, lemon juice, garlic, hot pepper sauce, cumin, and salt a few times to chop coarsely. Add cooked onions and oil, and process until the consistency of a thick paste. If necessary, add a little more olive oil to achieve the right consistency. Scrape dip into a serving bowl, and serve with wedges of pita bread.

Toasted Almond-Apricot Spread

This rich and sweet spread is another firmly in the "comfort appetizer" category.

Serves 4 to 6

¼ lb. (about 1 cup) slivered almonds

1 cup (8 oz.) cream cheese or light cream cheese, softened

¼ cup apricot preserves

Crusty bread or wheat crackers for serving

Preheat the broiler. Spread almonds on a baking sheet in a single layer, and broil on the high rack for 2 minutes, watching closely to prevent any blackening. Stir nuts and broil for another minute. Combine cream cheese, all but 1 tablespoon toasted almonds, and apricot preserves in a serving bowl and mix thoroughly. Sprinkle spread with remaining 1 tablespoon toasted almonds, and serve surrounded by crusty bread pieces or wheat crackers.

Glazed Party Nuts

I've called for pecans here, but this will also work with almonds, walnuts, and other nuts. Work carefully and try not to spatter, as hot, liquefied sugar can cause a nasty burn.

Serves 4 to 6

3 TB. butter

¾ cup brown sugar

1 lb. pecan halves (about 3½ cups)

Heat butter, sugar, and pecans in a 10- to 12-inch skillet over medium-high heat. Cook, stirring, for 5 minutes or until sugar has liquefied and gives nuts an amber-colored coating. Spread nuts on a greased baking sheet, and cool for a few minutes. The result will be some single, coated nut pieces and some clusters. Serve from a bowl, and watch them disappear.

Variation: Add a pinch of cinnamon or a dash of vanilla to the skillet while stirring.

The Least You Need to Know

- Fast, tasty, healthy vegetarian appetizers are not only possible but also easy with a bit of knowledge and preparation.
- Vegetarian appetizers, with their breadth of ingredients and seasoning, reflect the fact that vegetarian cooking is important across the globe.
- Vegetarian appetizers present an opportunity for unique flavors and seasonings to shine through in ways not possible with meat-based dishes.
- Nuts, in both sweet and savory recipes, offer a rich and tasty element for fast appetizers.

Part 4

Practical Secrets

Finally, we'll talk about some of the best travel-worthy appetizers—those that won't spill, for which temperature isn't a critical factor, but that deliver with terrific taste. We'll also talk about the right time for warm dips or even those with a few gorgeous, flavorful drips (a party at your house or a meal with friends).

"Bites," those easy-traveling morsels, come in a great variety of combinations. We'll visit the grocery store for an insider's look at ready-made ingredients and tips on how to dress them up to make them look like they took you hours to make.

And to wrap it up, we'll look at wine and food pairing. At many social events, appetizers will be served alongside your favorite white or red wine. We'll review some of the best recipes to pick so together everything sings.

Chapter 21

Take Out or Serve In? All Appetizers Are Not Created Equal

In This Chapter

- ◆ Choosing appetizers for a car ride
- ◆ Considering your appetizer's mess factor
- ◆ "Emergency" canapés
- ◆ Setting out a classy spread

This chapter contains some of my favorite hors d'oeuvres to take to someone else's house as a host/hostess gift, to serve at a cocktail party at my own house (or any event where most of the guests will be standing), or to serve as part of a dinner party.

Take Out or Serve In?

Because there are different types of social gatherings, from sit-down dinner parties to large soirées at someone else's house, certain appetizers are naturally more appropriate for these different types of gatherings.

Keep the following characteristics in mind when deciding whether it's appropriate, for example, to take your appetizer on that 40-minute trip to Uncle Phil's:

- ◆ **Temperature A:** Is it essential that your dish be hot or cold? If so, a road trip can stop your starter, especially if it's midsummer or midwinter. Will you have access to a heat source (convenient to your host) if you need to heat up your appetizer?

- ◆ **Temperature B—food safety:** The longer your appetizer's trip, the more carefully you should consider ingredients that won't spoil or turn into "science experiments." Choose ingredients that won't be hurt by being at room temperature, or, if that's not possible, definitely use your cooler and ice for transportation.

- ◆ **Mess factor A:** Some messy appetizers are absolutely delicious but perhaps not the best choice for a trip to someone else's house. They can make a mess on the way before you even get there. I'm still trying to clean a spot off the backseat of my car …

- ◆ **Mess factor B:** If an inherent part of a dish is delicious melted drips or sauces, it sounds like something you should serve on a plate. If it's on a plate, there's a good chance that it would be better used as a "sit-down" dinner appetizer rather than served to a group of people standing up, talking, and spilling. We won't even go into the tomato sauce-on-the-white-dress saga.

- ◆ **Ease of serving:** Even quick appetizers sometimes have several steps or components (think of bread-based recipes in which the toppings need to be added just before serving), whereas others only need to be pulled out of the bag and they're ready (Figs with Chevre). The slightly more complicated ones are better served out of your own kitchen at home, so when you're taking an appetizer somewhere, keep it simple. For even more simple-to-serve appetizers, look also at the next chapter on "bites."

I think you'll find that the preferred venue of most of the recipes in this book will be pretty obvious.

Host/Hostess Gift Appetizers

Some appetizers are appealing because of their inherent texture contrast, such as creamy toppings on crisp toast. Serve those *at home* or prepare them at your host's house, which is not always an option, because after that car trip, you might create the *amazing soggy starter*.

Shrimp Balls

I first saw this time-honored starter at a community social event years ago. They were good then, and they are good now. These are very popular at parties. One step that should be done onsite, however, is to roll the balls in corn flakes just before serving to help the flakes keep their crunch.

Serves 4 to 6

1 cup crushed corn flakes	2 TB. onion flakes
1 cup (8 oz.) cream cheese or light cream cheese, softened	1 tsp. dried dill
	1 tsp. fresh lemon juice
¼ cup mayonnaise	1 (6-oz.) can tiny cocktail shrimp, drained
2 TB. prepared mustard	25 (3-inch) pretzel sticks

Spread crushed corn flakes on a plate. Combine cream cheese, mayonnaise, mustard, onion flakes, dill, and lemon juice and mix thoroughly. Gently mix in shrimp, and using your hands, form mixture into small balls about ½ inch in diameter or about the size of a large marble. Roll each ball in corn flakes to coat, skewer with pretzel stick, and set out on a serving plate.

Savoir Starter

For ensured convenience, pick out one of the many appetizers in this book for which temperature is not critical (the dish does not have to be really cold or hot, or can even be room temperature) and where the mess factor is minimized.

Corned Beef Cornucopias

I like to use packaged corned beef for this, rather than having the deli staff slice it for me, because the packaged is squared off and can be cut to form triangles. Thanks to Nancy Woods for this elegant version of an appetizer classic.

Serves 10

3 cups (24-oz.) cream cheese or light cream cheese, softened

5 TB. (heaping) prepared horseradish

1 (2½-oz.) pkg. corned beef slices, cut in half diagonally to form triangles

1 tsp. dried dill

Combine cream cheese and horseradish in a small bowl and mix thoroughly. Place a corned beef triangle on a work surface so the corner that forms a 90-degree angle (the larger one of the three) faces you. Spoon 1 teaspoon cream cheese mixture on this corner, and fold the others inward over cheese to form a cone. Arrange on a platter, sprinkle with dill, and serve.

Figs with Chopped Prosciutto

How is it that something so simple can be so elegant at the same time? I can only explain by example, and here it is.

Serves 4 to 6

¼ cup finely chopped prosciutto

2 TB. olive oil

8 oz. dried figs (about 16), stems removed, sliced in half lengthwise

Combine prosciutto and olive oil in a small bowl and mix thoroughly. On the cut side of each fig half, spoon about 1 teaspoon prosciutto mixture, arrange fig halves on a platter and serve.

Variation: Broil figs and prosciutto for 1 minute before serving warm.

Blue Chicken Ball

This one is hearty, tasty, and easy to carry. (Hey, it's a ball!)

Serves 6

1 (12-oz.) can chicken

1½ cups (12 oz.) cream cheese or light cream cheese, softened

½ cup crumbled blue cheese

3 scallions, dark green leaves removed, and finely chopped

Dash hot sauce (such as Tabasco)

½ cup slivered almonds or chopped pecans

Parsley for garnish

Crackers for serving

Break apart large chicken pieces in a bowl. Add cream cheese, blue cheese, scallions, and hot sauce and mix thoroughly. Pour almonds onto a plate. Using your hands, form chicken and cheese mixture into a large ball, and roll in almonds to coat. Chill for several hours, if possible, garnish on top with a piece of parsley, and serve with crackers and a spreading knife.

Variation: Roll into small balls about ½ inch in diameter or about the size of a large marble.

Prosciutto-Wrapped Asparagus

This popular dish is the place for those tasty thin slices of prosciutto.

Serves 8 to 12

1 (15-oz.) can asparagus spears, drained

8 oz. thin slices prosciutto, cut into 3 by 3-inch squares

Wrap each asparagus spear in a prosciutto square, and arrange on a serving plate, tips pointing out like sunrays.

Variation: Sliced ham works well in place of prosciutto in this recipe.

Favorite Cocktail Party Hors D'oeuvres

These appetizers span that narrow overlap between super-quick yet elegant to serve.

Chunky Blue Cheese Spread with Apple and Walnuts

This is a terrific spread. The tart crispness of the apples provides a refreshing counterpoint to the creamy cheese and smoky nuts. Cut the apples just before serving.

Serves 4 to 6

1 cup (8 oz.) cream cheese or light cream cheese, softened

½ cup crumbled blue cheese

1 tart apple, such as Granny Smith, cored, sliced, and cut into ¼-inch cubes

½ cup chopped walnuts

2 large heads Belgian endive, leaves separated

Combine cream cheese, blue cheese, apple, and walnuts in a small serving bowl and mix thoroughly. The result is a very chunky, hearty spread. Place the bowl on a serving platter, and arrange Belgian endive leaves around it, pointing outward on the plate like a large green flower. Add a spreading knife and serve.

Variation: If you have a few extra minutes, toast the walnuts.

Shrimp with Mustard Mayonnaise Dip

This tasty dip is an alternative to the ubiquitous cocktail sauce.

Serves 4 to 6

½ cup mayonnaise

¼ cup Dijon-style mustard

2 TB. chopped fresh chives

1 tsp. capers, drained and chopped

1 tsp. fresh lemon juice

½ lb. (31 to 40 count, about 18) cooked shrimp, peeled and deveined with tail on

Combine mayonnaise, mustard, chives, capers, and lemon juice in a serving bowl and mix thoroughly. If possible, chill for 1 hour to allow the flavors to meld. To serve, place the bowl inside a larger bowl filled with crushed ice, and arrange shrimp on the ice.

"Emergency" Crostini

Despite the name, don't expect less in terms of flavor from these super-quick crostini.

Serves 4

3 slices white or wheat sandwich bread, crusts removed, cut into 4 triangles per slice

¼ cup butter, softened

2 TB. chopped fresh parsley

1 TB. olive oil

2 TB. onion soup mix

Preheat the broiler. Arrange bread on a baking sheet in a single layer, and broil for about 1 minute on one side until lightly browned. Meanwhile, combine softened butter, parsley, olive oil, and onion soup mix in a small bowl and mix thoroughly. Remove toast from oven, flip pieces to untoasted side, and spread 1 heaping teaspoon seasoned butter on each. Broil for about 1 additional minute until butter bubbles and melts and bread is just starting to brown. Arrange toasts on a platter and serve.

 Unappetizer

Be careful if you are tempted to use more butter. This recipe allows for about 1 teaspoon butter per triangle, and I've found that more just makes the crostini taste heavy (not to mention hardens the arteries).

Pepperoni Pizza Dip

Although this is casual, it is definitely flavorful and fun!

Serves 6 to 8

1 cup (8 oz.) cream cheese or light cream cheese, softened

1 cup sour cream

1 tsp. dried oregano

¼ tsp. garlic powder

⅛ tsp. crushed red pepper flakes

½ cup pizza sauce

½ cup chopped pepperoni

¼ cup chopped green pepper

½ cup shredded mozzarella cheese

Combine cream cheese, sour cream, oregano, garlic powder, and red pepper flakes in a bowl and mix thoroughly. Scrape into a 9- or 10-inch microwave-safe quiche dish or pie plate and spread evenly. Spread pizza sauce over the top. Sprinkle with pepperoni and green pepper, and microwave on high for 3 minutes, turning the dish after the first and second minutes. Top with mozzarella, and microwave 2 more minutes or until cheese is melted and mixture is heated through.

Variation: Add 2 tablespoons sliced scallions with pepperoni and green pepper.

Red Pepper–Parmesan Dip

This colorful, piquant, and cheesy dish will get the party started on the right foot.

Serves 6 to 8

½ (5-oz.) jar roasted red peppers, drained

1 cup sour cream

1 cup (8 oz.) cream cheese or light cream cheese, softened

½ cup shredded Parmesan cheese

Dash hot pepper sauce (such as Tabasco)

Thinly sliced scallions as garnish

Tortilla chips for serving

In a food processor fitted with a metal blade, process peppers, sour cream, cream cheese, Parmesan cheese, and hot pepper sauce until almost smooth. Scrape dip into a bowl, and serve topped with sliced scallions and surrounded by tortilla chips.

Warm Blue Cheese Cheddar Dip with Slivered Almonds

This dip is rich and decadent, which will keep guests coming back for more.

Serves 4 to 6

½ cup crumbled blue cheese

⅔ cup shredded mild cheddar cheese

½ cup sour cream

½ cup (8 oz.) cream cheese or light cream cheese, softened

2 TB. Madeira or other sweet dessert wine

⅓ cup slivered almonds

Wheat crackers or Belgian endive leaves for serving

Combine blue cheese, cheddar cheese, sour cream, and cream cheese in a microwave-safe serving dish and mix thoroughly. Microwave for about 2 minutes (time will vary according to microwave power) until mixture begins to bubble. Stir in Madeira, top with slivered almonds, and serve with wheat crackers or Belgian endive leaves for dipping.

Crab Ricotta Dip with Roasted Red Peppers

This flavorful crab dip takes advantage of the smoky-sweet flavor of piquillo peppers, available at many grocery stores and Mexican markets. The bright red color is very festive, especially when set off against green chives.

Serves 6

1 (6-oz.) can flaked crabmeat

1 cup ricotta cheese

½ (5-oz.) jar roasted red or piquillo peppers, drained

⅓ cup shredded cheddar cheese

½ tsp. garlic salt

2 TB. chopped fresh chives for garnish (optional)

Pita crisps or tortilla chips for serving

In a food processor fitted with a metal blade, process crabmeat, ricotta cheese, peppers, cheddar cheese, and garlic salt until smooth. Scrap dip into a microwave-safe serving bowl, and microwave on high for 90 seconds or until dip begins to bubble. Stir, top with chives (if using), and serve with pita or tortilla chips.

Variation: Use roasted red peppers in place of piquillo peppers.

Appetizers and First Courses for a Dinner Party

Some appetizers, because of the way they are served, are just perfect for a dinner party. This section offers up several that I like. Don't forget to check out similar recipes in other chapters!

Ham Stuffed with Ricotta, Pine Nuts, and Garlic

This simple and quick "bite" is packed with flavor. For others on a similar "wrap" theme, turn to Chapter 22 or back to the "This Ham Is on a Roll: Ham-Based Starters" section in Chapter 9.

Serves 4 to 6

½ lb. deli ham, thinly sliced

½ cup ricotta cheese

¼ cup pine nuts

½ tsp. garlic salt

Savoir Starter

This is another case in which the dish is great as it is, but even better if the nuts (yes, even pine nuts) are toasted. I think just about any recipe that calls for nuts could benefit from a toasting.

Place 1 ham slice on a work surface. Spoon a line of ricotta along one side of the slice, about 1 inch in from the side closest to you. Sprinkle with pine nuts and a pinch of garlic salt. Starting from this side, roll ham over filling to form a cylinder. Insert toothpicks at ½-inch intervals, and cut through the roll at the midpoint between each toothpick. Repeat with remaining ham and filling. Arrange bites on a platter and serve.

Tropical Fruit Skewers

This playful summertime fruit appetizer is perfect for starting that outdoor barbecue … or at least setting that frame of mind.

Serves 6 to 8

½ ripe cantaloupe (about 12 oz.), carved into balls with a melon scoop

¼ ripe muskmelon (about 12 oz.), carved into balls with a melon scoop

2 (8-oz.) cans pineapple chunks

1 TB. fresh lemon juice

Amaretto liqueur (optional)

Spear 1 cantaloupe ball, 1 muskmelon ball, and 1 pineapple chunk on a skewer.

Repeat on each skewer with remaining melon balls and pineapple pieces. Arrange skewers in a pyramid on a serving platter, with approximately 6 skewers on the bottom row, 5 on the next row, 4 on the next, and so on. Drizzle fruit with lemon juice and amaretto (if using). Serve with napkins.

Vichy Soy Carrots

Served in small bowls or on plates, this is a flavorful appetizer for a sit-down meal.

Serves 6

1 (16-oz.) pkg. baby carrots

½ cup water

3 TB. soy sauce

3 TB. granulated sugar

¼ cup butter, cut into ½-tablespoon pieces

6 sprigs fresh parsley for garnish

Arrange carrots in a flat-bottomed, microwave-safe container large enough for carrots to be as close as possible to a single layer. Pour water and soy sauce over carrots, sprinkle with sugar, and scatter butter around the dish. Microwave on high for 2 minutes, stir, and microwave for 1 additional minute or until carrots begin to soften. Distribute carrots between small serving plates, garnish with parsley, and serve.

Gourmet Glossary
Vichy carrots are a classic French vegetable dish of carrots cooked in water, butter, and sugar. To add soy is, of course, to take a bit of license.

Mini Tomato and Toast Sandwiches

If the season is right, these little delights are the ultimate treatment for ripe, juicy tomatoes.

Serves 4 to 6

6 slices white or wheat sandwich bread, crusts removed

3 TB. mayonnaise

1 large (about 12 oz.) ripe tomato, cut into ¼-inch slices

12 small (1-inch) fresh basil leaves

Preheat the broiler. Arrange bread on a baking sheet and broil for about 1 minute on each side, until lightly browned. When toast is done, spread 1 tablespoon mayonnaise on 3 slices, top each with slice of tomato and 4 basil leaves, and cover with another piece of toast. Cut each sandwich on the diagonal to form 4 small triangular sandwiches. Place 2 to 3 small sandwiches on each small plate and serve.

Sautéed Mushroom Crostini

Crisp toast and savory sautéed mushrooms are a terrific starter, especially for a sit-down meal. The trick for speed is multitasking: Sauté while the toast is toasting.

Serves 6

6 slices white or wheat sandwich bread, crusts removed, cut in half diagonally

2 to 3 TB. olive oil

2 tsp. crushed garlic

1 (8-oz.) pkg. sliced white mushrooms

¼ cup sour cream

3 TB. bacon bits

2 TB. chopped fresh chives

Salt and black pepper to taste

Preheat the broiler. Arrange bread on a baking sheet in a single layer, and broil for about 1 minute on each side until lightly browned. Meanwhile, heat olive oil and garlic in a 10-inch skillet over medium heat, add mushrooms, and sauté, stirring, for about 2 minutes. Remove from heat, and stir in sour cream and bacon. Place 2 toast halves on each of 6 small serving plates, positioning the halves so the corners point inward, forming a butterfly shape. Spoon about ¼ cup mushroom mixture into the center of toast halves. Sprinkle each with chopped chives, salt, and pepper, and serve immediately with a knife and fork.

The Least You Need to Know

- The characteristics of an appetizer—related to temperature, food safety, preparation, and "mess factor"—help dictate whether a dish is more appropriate to serve in or carry out.

- Appetizers prepared for serving at dinner parties or in your own home can be served from hot to cold. If you're bringing an hors d'oeuvre to a party, it's probably best to stick with something that can safely be served closer to room temperature.

- For appetizers in which appeal is related to texture that can degrade over time (crisp toast recipes paired with high-liquid ingredients), it's best to serve them immediately. (Unless you have free reign at another home's kitchen, you should probably serve these at *your* home.)

- Don't feel that an hors d'oeuvre has to be complicated to impress. A simple, graceful appetizer with high-quality ingredients can inspire love songs.

Chapter 22

Go Ahead, Take a Bite

In This Chapter

- Simple pairings and creative presentation
- Familiar friends and new faces
- Quick, sure-fire appetizer ingredients
- Bites for the sweet tooth

Of all the appetizers out there, among the simplest and neatest are those self-contained flavor explosions that are all wrapped up and ready to eat with no additional seasoning, dipping, or heating. These morsels—what I call "bites"—are, as a rule, easy to carry. They are perfect for any occasion, from bringing to someone else's party to unveiling at your own soirée. Is it any wonder these bites are the topic of this chapter?

Wrapping Caper

The exterior of your "bite" can be more than just wrapping; your concern is with texture, flavor, and presentation. Don't forget—when these appetizers are served, the wrapping is the first thing that your guests will see. Common "suspects" include the following:

- "Leaves" (baby spinach and other fresh, flexible greens). Spinach adds texture and visual appeal but allows the flavor of fillings to shine through. Arugula, with its distinctive spiciness, contributes flavor as well.
- Deli meats (remember the related recipes in Chapter 9).
- Flat breads (flour tortillas and pita bread work wonders).
- Other creative bite-size vehicles such as mushroom caps, Belgian endive, grape tomatoes, and fruits such as dates.

Goat's Milk Cheese, Kalamata, and Baby Spinach Bites

Easy, savory, and delicious, these bites feature the dark green spinach leaves, which contrast cleanly with the white goat's milk cheese and black olives.

Serves 4 to 6

4 oz. fresh goat's milk cheese, softened

24 to 30 baby spinach leaves, each about 1 by 2 inches

½ cup pitted Kalamata olives, sliced in half lengthwise

Spread about 1 teaspoon goat's milk cheese in the center of each spinach leaf, and top each with a Kalamata olive half. Roll leaf over filling, and insert a toothpick to fasten. Arrange spinach bites on a platter and serve.

Asiago-Chicken Bites

A blast of this hearty flavor is like a ray of Tuscan sun.

Serves 6

½ lb. sliced deli chicken breast, cut into 1 by 2-inch pieces

4 oz. Asiago cheese, cut into ¼ by ¼ by 1-inch pieces

Arrange chicken pieces on a work surface in a single layer, and place a piece of Asiago in the center of each. Wrap the two ends of each chicken piece inward over cheese, and fasten with toothpicks. Arrange on a platter and serve.

Avocado Swiss Bites

For avocado lovers, this is a perfect pair.

Serves 4

1 ripe avocado	½ lb. Swiss cheese, cut into ½-inch chunks
2 TB. fresh lemon juice	Salt to taste

Cut avocado in half, and remove the pit by embedding the blade (not the tip) of a sharp knife into it. Turn the knife slowly to release the pit. Cut avocado flesh into ½-inch squares, and drizzle with lemon juice to delay browning. With a toothpick, spear a piece of Swiss cheese, then a piece of avocado. Repeat with remaining cheese and avocado. Arrange on a platter and serve, inviting guests to sprinkle each piece with salt if they desire.

Variation: Allow the guests to serve themselves by arranging avocado pieces on one side of a serving platter and Swiss cheese pieces on the other. Drizzle avocado pieces with lemon juice to delay browning, and sprinkle with salt. Serve by inviting the guests to take a toothpick, and spear a piece of Swiss cheese, then a piece of avocado.

Ham and Swiss Bites

Here we have the classic combination.

Serves 4 to 6

¼ cup whole-grain mustard	½ lb. sliced deli ham, cut into 1 by 2-inch pieces
2 TB. mayonnaise	4 oz. Swiss cheese, cut into ¼ by ¼ by 1-inch pieces

Combine mustard and mayonnaise in a small serving bowl and mix thoroughly. Place bowl in the center of a serving platter.

Arrange ham pieces on a work surface in a single layer, and place a piece of Swiss cheese in the center of each. Wrap the two ends of each ham piece inward over cheese, and fasten with toothpicks. Arrange ham bites on the platter surrounding mustard dip and serve.

Hors D'oeuvre History _____

As you've already realized, the dishes in this chapter are very simple and very quick to prepare. They are also delicious, but we have one more challenge: how to make something simple as enticing and appealing as possible. That is where presentation is important. Wherever possible in these recipes, I've provided ideas that take little extra time but add to the fun factor. For instance, set a bowl of mustard dipping sauce in the center of Ham and Swiss Bites or add an appealing big bunch of fresh grapes to the center of a platter of Pepperoni-Wrapped Grapes (recipe follows). These little touches make all the difference. Don't just take my ideas, though. Use your own creativity to think of some fun ways to present that starter!

Pepperoni-Wrapped Grapes

The cool, juicy fruit and spicy meat make a great pair.

Serves 4 to 6

½ lb. pepperoni slices

Bunch of seedless grapes for garnish

½ lb. seedless grapes, sliced in half lengthwise

Wrap a pepperoni slice around each grape half, and fasten with a toothpick. Serve these bites on a platter surrounding a bunch of grapes.

Pepperoni-Spinach Rolls

This recipe combines texture, color, and flavor.

Serves 4 to 6

½ lb. pepperoni slices

24 to 30 baby spinach leaves, each about 1 by 2 inches

Place a pepperoni slice on each spinach leaf, roll the two together to form a cylinder, and fasten with toothpicks. Arrange on a platter and serve.

Variation: Serve surrounding a small bowl of mustard dip or softened cream cheese.

Salami, Watercress, and Cream Cheese Bites

The cool crispness of the watercress is a great counterpoint to the spicy salami.

Serves 4 to 6

½ lb. thin slices salami, cut in half

½ cup (8 oz.) cream cheese or light cream cheese, softened

1 cup *watercress* sprigs

Place a piece of salami on a work surface in a single layer. Spread cream cheese along one side of salami, place a sprig of watercress in the center, and roll loosely to form a cone, with watercress sticking out the top like a feather in a pointed hat. If necessary, fasten with a toothpick. Repeat with remaining salami, cream cheese, and watercress. If the shape permits, arrange standing in a circle on a platter and serve; otherwise arrange in a wheel pattern.

Variation: Use other crisp greens, such as spinach or even *arugula*.

Spinach-Wrapped Bacon and Mushroom Bites

Bacon and mushrooms are a pair people always love.

Serves 6 to 8

2 to 3 TB. olive oil

1 tsp. crushed garlic

1 (6-oz.) pkg. sliced portobello mushrooms, cut into 1-inch pieces

30 fresh baby spinach leaves

¼ cup real bacon bits

Kosher salt to taste

Heat olive oil and garlic in a 10-inch skillet over medium heat, add mushrooms, and sauté, stir-ring, for about 2 minutes. Remove from heat, and place 1 mushroom piece in the center of each spinach leaf. Sprinkle each with some bacon bits and a pinch of salt. Roll leaves over mushroom pieces, and fasten with toothpicks. Arrange bites on a platter and serve.

Savoir Starter _____

One playful way to serve these Spinach-Wrapped Bacon and Mushroom Bites and at the same time send a signal about the ingredients is to place a large portobello mushroom cap (stem removed) on a small plate, fill the cap with the bites, and allow guests to select their bite. If necessary, fill two caps (depending on the size of the mushrooms).

Goat's Milk Cheese, Toasted Pecans, and Ham

Every now and then, you come across a recipe that makes you say "Wow!" Here's one such recipe.

Serves 4

¼ cup chopped pecans, toasted

½ lb. thin slices smoked ham, cut in half

4 oz. fresh goat's milk cheese, softened

Preheat the broiler. Spread pecans on a baking sheet in a single layer, and broil on the high rack for 2 minutes, watching closely to prevent any blackening. Stir and broil for another minute.

Meanwhile, place a slice of ham on a work surface. Spread about 1 tablespoon goat's milk cheese in a line along one side of the slice, about 1 inch in from the side closest to you. When nuts are toasted, spread about ½ tablespoon pecans over cheese. Starting from this side, roll ham over cheese and nuts to form a cylinder. Insert toothpicks at ½-inch intervals, and cut at the midpoint between each toothpick. Repeat with remaining ham, cheese, and nuts. Arrange bites on a plate and serve.

More Shrimp Starters

When it comes to entertaining, people love shrimp. In fact, when it comes to just about any occasion, people love shrimp! Here are several more of my favorite appetizers featuring the star of the sea.

Bacon, Shrimp, and Horseradish Crackers

These are tasty and quick.

Serves 6 to 8

½ cup (4 oz.) cream cheese or light cream cheese, softened

3 TB. bacon bits

2 TB. prepared horseradish

1 (6-oz.) box plain wheat crackers

1 lb. (51 to 70 count, about 30) cooked shrimp, peeled and deveined with tail off

Kosher salt to taste

Lemon wedges for garnish

Combine cream cheese, bacon bits, and horseradish and mix thoroughly. Spread about 1½ teaspoons cream cheese on each cracker, and top each with 1 shrimp. Arrange these crackers on a platter, sprinkle with salt, and serve with lemon wedges.

Miso Shrimp Bites

Sharp, savory miso adds an oriental element to this shrimp dish.

Serves 4 to 6

¼ cup miso (soybean paste, available at Asian markets, specialty stores, and in the ethnic food sections of large grocery stores)

½ lb. (51 to 70 count, about 30) cooked shrimp, peeled and deveined with tails off

40 baby spinach leaves

Spread about ½ teaspoon miso on 1 shrimp, place shrimp in the center of a leaf of spinach, roll leaf over filling, and fasten with a toothpick. Repeat with remaining spinach, miso, and shrimp. Arrange shrimp bites on a platter and serve.

Variation: Serve with a small bowl of soy sauce for dipping.

Swiss Shrimp Bites

Swiss cheese is good with ingredients from the orchard to the sea.

Serves 4

½ lb. Swiss cheese, cut into ½-inch cubes

½ lb. (31 to 40 count, about 18) cooked shrimp, peeled and deveined, tail off

4 lemon wedges

With a toothpick, first pierce a chunk of Swiss cheese and then 1 shrimp. Repeat with remaining shrimp and cheese. Arrange on a serving platter, garnish with lemon wedges, and invite guests to squeeze a few drops of lemon juice on each bite.

Richer, Fruitier, or Sweet Bites

Many fruits not only bring delicious flavor to a dish, they are a bite-size package unto themselves, needing only to be partnered with the right complementary ingredients. Here are several fruit-based suggestions.

Stuffed Dates

These rich, sweet morsels are a traditional snack at winter holiday gatherings.

Serves 4

1 (10-oz.) pkg. pitted dates

¼ cup granulated sugar

½ cup whole almonds

With a sharp knife, slit each date lengthwise to form small pockets. Pour sugar into a shallow bowl. Insert 1 almond in each date, roll date in sugar to coat, and arrange dates on a serving plate.

Variation: Instead of almonds, stuff dates with cream cheese—about ½ cup for a 10-ounce package of dates.

Turkey with Apricot and Walnuts

What a savory-sweet delight these are.

Serves 6 to 8

¼ cup chopped walnuts, toasted

1 cup (8 oz.) cream cheese or light cream cheese, softened

½ cup apricot preserves

1 lb. thin slices deli turkey breast, cut in half

Preheat the broiler. Spread walnuts on a baking sheet, and broil on high rack for 2 minutes, watching closely to prevent any blackening. Stir and broil for another minute.

Combine cream cheese, apricot preserves, and walnuts in a bowl and mix thoroughly. Place a piece of turkey on a work surface. Spread about 1 tablespoon cream cheese mixture to form a line along one side of the slice about 1 inch in from the side closest to you. Working from this side, roll turkey over cheese to form a cylinder. Insert toothpicks at ½-inch intervals, and cut at the midpoint between each toothpick. Repeat with remaining turkey and cream cheese mixture. Arrange bites on a plate and serve.

Pineapple with Goat's Milk Cheese

Sweet and savory, this is just delightful.

Serves 4 to 6

20 fresh baby spinach leaves

1 (8-oz.) can pineapple chunks, or fresh pineapple chunks

4 oz. fresh goat's milk cheese

Place 1 spinach leaf on a work surface, and top with 1 pineapple chunk and a dab of goat's milk cheese. Fold spinach leaf over pineapple, and fasten with a toothpick. Arrange on a platter and serve.

You probably saw this coming, but a fun presentation for this platter would be to have the bites surrounding a whole pineapple or a pineapple top, or arranged in a hollow pineapple shell.

Variation: Even simpler and just as tasty is to set out pineapple chunks, each with a dab of goat's milk cheese.

 Savoir Starter

Although I start with canned pineapple, if you have a few extra minutes, by all means use freshly cut pineapple chunks. The flavor is better, and that decorative pineapple top is just about the perfect garnish. After serving, let the kids grow the top as a science project.

The Least You Need to Know

◆ When working with simple appetizer combinations, presentation is critical.

◆ Indulge in whimsy when serving these and other appetizers. If you're having fun, your guests will, too.

◆ Many of these appetizers carry familiar flavors, from Ham and Swiss Bites to Bacon, Shrimp, and Horseradish Crackers, just in smaller, flavor-packed bites. This familiarity can be a good thing.

◆ Appetizers that pair savory and sweet flavors are fun, interesting, and delicious.

Chapter 23

Dress Up Store-Bought

In This Chapter

♦ Store-bought items can be the perfect place to start

♦ Go back to that friendly deli

♦ Simple is good

♦ Presentation is everything

The grocery stores are full of so-called "ready-to-go" appetizers—from vegetable dips to shrimp cocktail. The quality is often quite good, but the problem is how it looks, which could probably be summed up in one word: *plastic*. I've been to more than one event at which guests are served out of those little plastic trays—with plastic compartments for each little vegetable, shrimp, or sauce, and plastic forks for the fruit.

In this chapter, we take some of the myriad ready-made appetizers and dress them up with just a little bit of thought. The result is to send a few messages:

♦ To present by appearance that this dish took a lot more time than it really did—also known as friendly deception!

♦ To communicate a "you are worth it" message to your guests.

♦ To have a fun, attractively presented, tasty appetizer—even if it's from the store. This will get everybody in the right frame of mind to enjoy your gathering. Isn't that what it's all about?

The grocery store has a number of options when it comes to dip. We've all probably tried the salsa and the fruit dips. Actually, these old friends can work perfectly well and provide the opportunity for a bit of entertainment.

Well, Bowl Me Over!

Although the contents of an appetizer served in plastic might be the same as the contents of another served in a crystal bowl, the message it sends to guests on that continuum between "elegant" and "afterthought" is a world apart. The fact is, the contents can actually be the same. A bit of thought and an extra 30 seconds is all it takes to differentiate between the two. I can hardly claim a monopoly on ideas, but I hope you'll find here some suggestions into which you, too, can plant your flag, er, toothpick.

Fruit Dip

Serving your dip out of fresh fruit gives added visual appeal.

Serves 4

½ cantaloupe, seeds removed

1 (16-oz.) pkg. fruit dip

1 (32-oz.) pkg. mixed fresh fruit, cut into chunks

> **Savoir Starter**
> Fruit tricks we've used before are even more useful with store-bought fare when you want to send that "homemade" message. A quick drizzling of fresh lemon juice or amaretto (only ½ teaspoon is needed) enhances the flavor appeal of fresh fruit.

Place cleaned cantaloupe half on a plate. Fill cantaloupe bowl with fruit dip, and top with a decorative piece of fruit from your mixed fruit package (a cherry is always nice). Drain mixed fruit, and reserve any juices for another use. Pour fruit chunks into a serving bowl, and place this bowl next to cantaloupe bowl. If fruit dip runs low, replenish with what's left in the plastic container.

Variation: Although the precut fruit mixes save time, fruit dips can be served with a wide variety of fruits. Sliced apple or pear, whole strawberries, grapes—you name it—are all great.

> **Unappetizer**
> When serving store-cut fruit for dipping, be sure to remove the fruit pieces from the juice in that container. Otherwise, your fruit dip becomes a drippy fruit mess. Waste-nothing tip: If you're looking for an excuse to make the perfect breakfast bread in that bread machine hiding in your closet, the juice from store-cut fruit is a terrific liquid base.

Specialty Salsas

What's your favorite salsa? Here's one idea to get you started.

Serves 4 to 6

1 pineapple

1 (12-oz.) jar pineapple salsa

1 (12-oz.) bag tortilla chips

Cut pineapple in half crosswise, about halfway down from the top. Cut out the core. Fill the resulting hollow with salsa, and set pineapple top next to it to give the impression that you just took off the top and found salsa inside. Serve with a basket of tortilla chips.

Salsa "Tasting Tray"

Want fun and learning at the same time? We can do that.

Serves 8 to 10

Assorted specialty salsas, such as 2 varieties of fruit salsa, 1 mild tomato salsa, and salsa verde (green salsa)

Tortilla chips for serving

Place about 1 cup of each salsa variety in a different bowl. If you have a matching set of serving bowls, this is the perfect time to use them. Arrange the bowls in a line, backed up by a basket or bowl mounded with tortilla chips. If you really want to make the "class" effect, place a small card in front of each salsa with its name.

Unappetizer

Salsa ingredients now come in many palate-pleasing variations, with hot-pepper heat that varies from barely there to *volcanic*. Unless heat is the theme of your party, I'd suggest that you stick with the milder stuff or clearly label the Insanely Hot Sauce and serve an alternative alongside. You don't want to smoke out your guests.

A Tisket, a Tasket, a Toothpick, and a Basket

Been wondering what to do with that basket that's been lurking in your closet? Use it to serve food! Somehow a basket transmits thoughts of open skies, a picnic, a casual gathering, and fun. Here are several appetizer suggestions with a basket in mind.

Specialty Chips

Need a twist on the "bowl of chips"? These days, chips are made out of a wide variety of vegetables, and the flavors are quite different. Dill dip makes a relatively mild accompaniment that complements the chips.

Serves 6 to 8

1 (16-oz.) pkg. prepared dill dip

Several varieties of chips (such as sweet potato, vegetable, blue corn tortilla, and taro)

Savoir Starter
Small baskets lined with colorful cloth napkins make appealing serving containers for chips.

Place dip in a serving bowl. Serve chips around dip bowl in separate baskets lined with cloth napkins.

Cheesy Salsa Dip

Is this too easy? Yes.

Serves 6 to 8

1 (12-oz.) jar prepared salsa (your favorite)

1 cup (8 oz.) cream cheese or light cream cheese, softened

1 cup shredded Monterey Jack or Mexican-style cheese

Tortillas for serving

Combine salsa and cream cheese in a serving bowl and mix thoroughly. Top with shredded cheese, and serve with tortilla chips.

Olive Oil Tasting

All around the Mediterranean, people serve fresh, crusty bread with nothing more complicated than fresh *extra-virgin olive oil*. This fruity, peppery, and delicious liquid differs widely from producer to producer and from country to country. The closest analogy might be to a wine tasting, and there are almost as many olive oils as there are wines! This is another "learning experience" that just happens to be fun along the way.

Serves 6 to 8

Several types of extra-virgin olive oil (as a start, consider a California, Spanish, Italian, and Greek Kalamata olive oil)

1 loaf fresh Italian bread, sliced into 1-inch rounds (cut slices in half if bread is more than 3 inches in diameter)

Pour about ¼ cup of each olive oil into separate small serving bowls, and arrange in a U, centering on a basket lined with a cloth napkin or bowl piled with pieces of fresh bread for dipping.

> **Gourmet Glossary**
> **Olive oil** is produced by crushing or pressing olives. **Extra-virgin olive oil** is the oil produced from the first pressing of a batch of olives (oil is also produced from other pressings after the first). Extra-virgin olive oil is generally considered the most flavorful and highest quality. This is the type you want when your focus is on the oil itself. Be sure the label on the bottle says "extra virgin."

Classic Shrimp Cocktail

This is an upward adjustment from the plastic shrimp ring at your local grocery store.

Serves 4 to 6

Shaved ice

Several sprigs fresh parsley for garnish

One prepared "shrimp ring," including cocktail sauce

Lemon wedges for garnish

Mound shaved ice in a large bowl so ice comes up almost to the top. Nestle a small serving bowl in the center of the ice, and pour cocktail sauce into the bowl. Arrange shrimp on top of shaved ice around the bowl, and garnish with parsley sprigs and lemon wedges. Now, that looks a lot better, doesn't it?

Guacamole Salsa Swirl

Rich colorful flavors of guacamole and salsa make for an irresistible dip.

Serves 6 to 8

1 (12-oz.) jar prepared salsa (your favorite)

1 (10-oz.) pkg. prepared guacamole (you can also make it, but that won't be under the "store-bought" category)

½ cup sour cream

Tortilla chips for serving

Pour salsa and guacamole into a serving bowl, and stir a few times to create a swirl effect. Spoon sour cream on the center of dip, and serve with tortilla chips.

> **Unappetizer**
>
> When serving tortilla chips as dippers, the focus is usually intended to be on the flavors of the dip (such as salsa). For this reason, highly seasoned or flavored chips are not a good idea. Stick with plain, lightly salted chips. Some chips are made from different grains or even different varieties of the same grain (such as blue, yellow, and white corn tortilla chips). As long as these aren't highly seasoned, they're great to use!

Garlic Toast with Tomato Dipping Sauce

Crisp toast … warm, savory tomato sauce—all is right with the world.

Serves 6 to 8

1 loaf store-made garlic bread (available in the bakery section of grocery stores)

1 (14- to 15-oz.) can pizza sauce

2 TB. shredded Parmesan cheese

Preheat the broiler. Cut garlic bread into rounds about 1½ inch wide, and place it garlic side up on a baking sheet. Broil for about 2 minutes or until bread begins to brown and crisp. Meanwhile, pour pizza sauce into a serving bowl, and microwave for 1 minute or until warm.

Serve toasted garlic bread in a basket lined with a cloth napkin. Sprinkle Parmesan on top of warm pizza sauce, and place that bowl next to bread. Invite your guests to "dip in," and watch the whole thing vanish.

Hummus Platter

Fast, tasty, and healthy—this platter is all three.

Serves 6 to 8

1 (16-oz.) pkg. hummus (available in grocery stores)

2 pieces fresh pita bread, each sliced pizza-style into 8 wedges

1 (16-oz.) pkg. precut vegetable sticks, such as cucumber, carrots, and celery (or cut these yourself)

1 cup black olives

Scrape hummus into a serving bowl; set the bowl on a large platter; arrange pita, vegetables, and olives around the platter; and serve.

Variation: For a fun variation, use a new small flowerpot to hold the fresh vegetables and pita bread.

Lightning Salsa Sour Cream Dip

Here is another appetizer that is just too easy!

Serves 6 to 8

1 (12-oz.) jar prepared salsa (your favorite)

1 cup (8 oz.) sour cream

1 TB. chopped scallions or chopped fresh chives for garnish (optional)

Tortilla chips for serving

Combine salsa and sour cream in a serving bowl. Top with chopped scallions or chives (if using), and serve with tortilla chips.

Sausage Rounds with Mustard Dip

Hearty and flavorful, these sausage bites are easy to fix.

Serves 4

½ cup whole-grain mustard

½ cup mayonnaise

½ lb. cooked sausage, such as knockwurst or herbed chicken sausage

Combine mustard and mayonnaise in a small serving bowl, and place bowl in the center of a serving platter. Slice sausage into ½-inch rounds, insert a toothpick into each, arrange on a platter surrounding mayonnaise-mustard sauce and serve.

Variation: Heat sausage pieces in the microwave for a minute and serve warm.

Tapenade Platter

Tapenade is a thick, chunky spread filled with savory ingredients such as olives, lemon juice, and anchovies. Adventuresome grocery and gourmet stores are likely to have different versions focusing on specific ingredients, from olives to peppers and mushrooms. Keep a jar for those occasions when you need something classy and *quick*.

Serves 6

1 (10-oz.) pkg. prepared tapenade

2 pieces fresh pita bread, each sliced pizza-style into 8 wedges

Scrape tapenade into a serving bowl, and set bowl on a serving platter. Surround with fresh pita wedges. Provide a spreading knife to spread tapenade on pita.

Variation: Toast points, wheat crackers, or melba toast will also work fine in place of pita.

The Deli Is My Friend (Again)

The deli at your local grocery store is a gold mine for quick appetizers. Here are just some of the "nuggets."

Mini Meatballs with Blue Cheese Dipping Sauce

This is a good reason to like your deli.

Serves 4 to 6

1 lb. small (1-oz. or smaller) meatballs	Salt and freshly ground black pepper
½ tsp. hot pepper sauce (such as Tabasco) (optional)	1 cup chunky blue cheese dressing

Arrange meatballs on a platter, leaving space in the center of the platter for a small bowl, and microwave on high for 2 minutes or until warm. Sprinkle with hot pepper sauce (if using), salt, and pepper, and insert a toothpick into each meatball. Pour blue cheese dressing into a small bowl, place the bowl in the center of the platter and serve.

Chicken Salad Spread

Take advantage of prepared ingredients like tasty chicken salad. If you love it in a sandwich, why not as a chunky spread?

Serves 6 to 8

½ lb. deli chicken salad	Freshly ground black pepper
2 TB. finely chopped fresh parsley for garnish	4 heads Belgian endive leaves, separated

Scrape chicken salad into a serving bowl, and sprinkle with parsley and freshly ground black pepper. Place the bowl on a platter, and surround with Belgian endive leaves arranged pointing out, as though the bowl of spread were the center of a flower.

Seafood Salad Canapés

Seafood salad sings a siren song.

Serves 6 to 8

½ lb. deli seafood salad

4 slices white or wheat sandwich bread, crusts removed, cut into 4 triangles per slice

2 TB. finely chopped fresh chives for garnish

Spread about 1 tablespoon seafood salad onto each piece of bread, arrange on a platter, garnish with chives and serve.

Variation: Prepare with 4 additional slices of bread as small cocktail sandwiches. Also consider serving this spread with toast for added texture.

Ham Salad Crostini

This is delicious any time.

Serves 6 to 8

4 pieces bread, crusts removed, cut into 4 triangles per slice

½ lb. deli ham salad

¼ cup shredded Parmesan cheese

2 TB. finely chopped fresh parsley for garnish

Preheat the broiler. Arrange bread on a baking sheet, and broil for about 1 minute on each side until lightly browned. Remove from oven. Spread about 1 tablespoon ham salad on each, sprinkle with Parmesan cheese, and arrange on a serving tray. Sprinkle a pinch of parsley on each and serve.

The Least You Need to Know

- Some attention to your presentation of store-bought items makes all the difference.
- As the source for many quick appetizers, the deli is (still) your friend.
- Creative use of nonfood items, from scooped-out cantaloupe shells to flower pots, will communicate "fun" and put a smile on your guests' faces.
- Even when you're using off-the-shelf items, you can create a fun, tasty, and sometimes even educational appetizer.

Chapter 24

Wine-Friendly Appetizers

In This Chapter

- Wine with hors d'oeuvres—a natural pair
- Appetizer and wine chart
- Favorite recipes
- Wine hot list: reliable producers and recommended wines

In this chapter, we'll review some of the basics of matching food with wine, provide some suggestions for appetizers and recipes for different types, and finish up with a detailed listing of wine suggestions. My hope is that, after you're through with this chapter, you'll be able to choose with confidence. (The list of reliable wine producers might just help, too!)

Good Matches

First, let's start with a basic observation about appetizers: They typically come before a meal. Although there are exceptions to everything, this basic truth affects our approach to the ingredients in appetizers and, as a result, the wines that best match these hors d'oeuvres. For example, although there certainly are beef appetizers, I've found that there are many more on the lighter side of the scale, based on dairy products, seafood, vegetables and fruits, or white meats. So when it comes to wines, our choices reflect this. Generally, this means we choose to serve white wines or light reds.

Basic Wine and Appetizer Pairing

	Light White	Rich White	Light Red	Rich Red	Sweet
Light seafood	X	X			
Rich seafood	X	X	X		
White meats	X	X	X		
Rich meats				X	
Spicy dishes					X
Sweet dishes					X

Appetizers for Light Whites

Light white wines include Sauvignon Blanc, Pinot Grigio, and others. These are often available at a low price relative to other white wines and offer characteristically refreshing tart flavors of grapefruit and green apple. These are often great wines for relatively light foods.

Savoir Starter _____

Despite all the advice of "what goes with what," it's not a bad idea to give your guests a choice of a white and a red. A lot of people have a favorite wine they will pick regardless of the food served—and happy guests mean a happy host.

Recipes in this book that will go well with light white wines include the following:

- ◆ Recipes featuring goat's milk cheese (throughout the book, especially Chapter 12)
- ◆ Ginger-Lemon Goat Cheese (Chapter 5)
- ◆ Shrimp recipes (particularly Chapter 8) (Shrimp recipes can also be good matches with sweeter whites.)

Also try the following recipes.

Endive with Herbed Goat's Milk Cheese

Savory herbs and flavorful goat's milk cheese are a delicious match with a dry white wine.

Serves 4 to 6

6 oz. fresh goat's milk cheese, softened

1 tsp. fresh lemon juice

½ tsp. dried rosemary

Pinch dried thyme

3 heads Belgian endive, leaves separated

Pinch freshly ground black pepper

Lemon slices for garnish

Combine goat's milk cheese, lemon juice, rosemary, and thyme in a small bowl and mix thoroughly. If possible, let this mixture chill for 1 hour. Place about 1 teaspoon herbed cheese on the thick end of each large Belgian endive leaf, arrange leaves in concentric circles filling side in on a large platter, and sprinkle with black pepper. Place one lemon slice in the center of the platter and others around the perimeter and serve.

Chicken and Goat's Milk Cheese Bites

These quick bites are simple yet tasty.

Serves 6 to 8

1 lb. thin slices deli roast chicken (or turkey), cut in half

8 oz. fresh goat's milk cheese, softened

Salt and freshly ground black pepper, to taste

Place a piece of chicken on a work surface. Spread goat's milk cheese in a line along one side of the slice, about 1 inch in from the side closest to you. Starting from this side, roll chicken over cheese to form a cylinder. Insert toothpicks at ½-inch intervals, and cut through the roll at the midpoint between each toothpick. Repeat with remaining chicken and cheese. Arrange on a serving plate, season to taste with salt and black pepper and serve.

Shrimp with Lemon Cream Cheese

Light, tasty seafood and flavors of citrus and creamy cheese beg to be accompanied with a tasty Sauvignon Blanc.

Serves 4 to 6

Shaved ice

½ cup (4 oz.) cream cheese, softened

1 TB. prepared horseradish

1 TB. fresh lemon juice

¼ cup minced sweet onion (about ½ medium)

½ lb. (31 to 40 count, about 18) cooked shrimp, peeled and deveined with tail on

Lemon wedges for garnish

Mound shaved ice in a large (12-inch) bowl so ice comes up almost to the top. In a small (4-inch) bowl, combine cream cheese, horseradish, lemon juice, and onion and mix thoroughly. Nestle this bowl in the center of the ice. Arrange shrimp on top of shaved ice around the bowl, garnish with lemon wedges, and serve with a knife for guests to spread a dab of cream cheese on shrimp.

Appetizers for Rich Whites

Chardonnay is the prime suspect here. You can also consider Riesling and Gewürztraminer, although these two tend to be in a category by themselves because of their usually higher residual sugar. Chardonnay is often characterized by buttery, even creamy notes and is generally a good match for lighter fares, such as seafood and mildly seasoned poultry and pork.

Recipes in this book that will go well with rich white wines include the following:

◆ Melted Brie with Crisp Apple Slices (Chapter 3)

◆ Warm Crab-Parmesan Dip (Chapter 4)

◆ Chickpea and Sun-Dried Tomato Dip (Chapter 4)

◆ Apple and German Sausage Spread (Chapter 5—a Riesling)

◆ Derek's Curry Ball (Chapter 5—a Riesling)

◆ Salmon recipes (Chapter 7)

◆ Crab-based recipes (particularly Chapter 8)

◆ Quesadillas (Chapter 10)

Also try the following recipes.

Quick Crab Balls

Crab cakes are delicious, and these tiny, quick versions preserve that rich flavor.

Serves 6

¼ cup canola oil

¼ cup breadcrumbs

1 egg

1 TB. mayonnaise

1 tsp. Worcestershire sauce

½ tsp. celery seed

Dash hot pepper sauce (such as Tabasco)

Pinch salt

1 (6-oz.) can crabmeat

Lemon wedges for garnish

Heat canola oil in a 12-inch skillet over medium heat. Combine breadcrumbs, egg, mayonnaise, Worcestershire sauce, celery seed, hot pepper sauce, and salt in a bowl and mix thoroughly. Mix in crabmeat, and, using your hands, form into balls about 1 inch across. As you make the balls, carefully place them into the skillet. Cook the balls for about 2 minutes per side or until browned and cooked through the center. Remove crab balls to a serving platter, garnish with lemon wedges, and serve with toothpicks.

Spicy Thai Peanut and Chicken Spread

This one is tailor-made for wines with a bit of residual sweetness, such as a German Riesling or Gewürztraminer.

Serves 6 to 8

1 (8-oz.) jar peanut dipping sauce (or use the Celery and Banana Chips with Peanut Sauce recipe in Chapter 14)

1 (12-oz.) can chunk chicken

¼ cup sesame oil

2 scallions, dark green parts removed, and chopped

2 TB. shelled peanuts for garnish

Fresh vegetable sticks or crusty bread for serving

In a food processor fitted with a metal blade, process peanut sauce, chicken, sesame oil, and scallions until almost smooth. Scrape spread into a serving bowl, scatter peanuts on top, and serve with fresh vegetable sticks or crusty bread.

Garlic Goat's Milk Cheese Spread

The toasted garlic flavors and the creamy tang of the goat's milk cheese are a symphony for the taste buds.

Serves 4

2 TB. olive oil

1 TB. chopped garlic

8 oz. fresh goat's milk cheese, softened

2 scallions, dark green leaves removed, and sliced into ⅛-inch pieces, for garnish

Crusty bread for serving

Heat olive oil in an 8- to 10-inch skillet over medium heat. Add garlic and cook for 1 minute, stirring, until garlic pieces begin to brown and crisp, being careful not to let them blacken. Remove skillet from heat. Place goat's milk cheese into a serving bowl, pour garlic and oil over it, and mix thoroughly. Scatter scallion pieces on top, and serve spread with pieces of crusty bread.

Seafood Salad Spread

This spread takes good advantage of store-bought seafood salad.

Serves 6 to 8

½ lb. deli seafood salad

½ cup (4 oz.) cream cheese or light cream cheese, softened

1 tsp. fresh lemon juice

¼ tsp. freshly ground black pepper

2 TB. finely chopped fresh parsley for garnish

3 heads Belgian endives, leaves separated

In a food processor fitted with a metal blade, pulse seafood salad, cream cheese, lemon juice, and black pepper for about 10 seconds to achieve a chunky consistency. Scrape spread into a serving bowl, and sprinkle with parsley. Place the bowl on a serving platter, and surround with Belgian endive leaves radiating out from the bowl like petals of a flower. Provide a spreading knife and serve.

Sherried Shrimp

Succulent shrimp with a hint of sherry make for an elegant hors d'oeuvre.

Serves 4

3 TB. olive oil

1 tsp. chopped garlic

2 TB. sherry

½ lb. (31 to 40 count) cooked shrimp, shelled and deveined with tail removed

1 tsp. fresh lemon juice

2 TB. toasted coconut flakes

Salt and freshly ground black pepper to taste

Heat olive oil, garlic, and sherry in a 10- to 12-inch skillet over medium-high heat. Add shrimp and heat, stirring, for 1 to 2 minutes. Remove shrimp to a serving plate; drizzle with lemon juice; sprinkle with coconut, salt, and pepper; insert toothpicks and serve.

> **Savoir Starter**
>
> Toast coconut the way you would toast nuts. Preheat the broiler, spread coconut on a baking tray, and toast under the broiler for about a minute or so.

Fromage Forte (Strong Cheese)

I first read about this dish in Steven Jenkins's terrific book, *Cheese Primer*. It's such a flavorful way to use leftover cheese. When I've cheerfully informed guests that they are eating leftovers, they have pretended to be offended—and then reached for thirds.

Serves 6 to 8

8 pieces bread, crusts removed, cut into 4 triangles per slice

1 lb. leftover cheese pieces (blue, brie, cheddar, Provolone—the more the better), unappetizing bits discarded

½ cup white wine

2 TB. chopped garlic

½ tsp. freshly ground black pepper

Preheat the broiler. Arrange bread on a baking sheet in a single layer, and broil for about 1 minute on each side until lightly browned. Meanwhile, in a food processor fitted with a metal blade, process cheese, wine, garlic, and black pepper. You might have to cut larger, harder pieces of cheese into small chunks first so the food processor blade doesn't get stuck. Remove toast from oven, but keep it on the baking sheet. Spread 1 tablespoon or so cheese mixture on each toast triangle, broil for an additional minute, then serve to sighs of appreciation.

Appetizers for Light Reds

Light and medium-bodied reds, such as Gamay (in Beaujolais), some Merlot, some Pinot Noir, Sangiovese (the grape in Chianti), and others are—in the less-than-$15 range—generally pleasant and easy drinking with characteristics of ripe cherries, chocolate, toffee, and vanilla. These versatile wines are good with a range of foods, with the sweet spot (no pun intended) being with lighter meats.

Recipes in this book that will go well with light red wines include the following:

Savoir Starter
Chianti, the famous Sangiovese-based wine from central Italy, is a natural match with tomato dishes such as bruschetta.

- Romano-Bacon Dip (Chapter 4)
- Warm Dijon-Ham Spread (Chapter 5)
- Quick Bruschetta (Chapter 6)
- Chicken-based recipes (particularly Chapter 9)
- Ham-based recipes (particularly Chapter 9)

Also try the following recipes.

Broiled Mushroom Caps Stuffed with Bacon and Cheddar Cheese

A bit of separately cooked magic, this looks like it spent a half-hour in the oven.

Serves 6 to 8

1 (8-oz.) pkg. button mushrooms, stems removed

2 TB. olive oil

1 cup shredded cheddar cheese

¼ cup bacon bits

¼ cup plain breadcrumbs

¼ cup mayonnaise

½ tsp. garlic salt

Preheat the broiler. Place mushroom caps in a microwave-safe bowl, pour olive oil over them, and toss to coat. Arrange mushroom caps on a baking sheet, and broil for about 2 minutes on each side. Meanwhile, in the same bowl in which you tossed mushrooms, combine cheddar cheese, bacon pieces, breadcrumbs, mayonnaise, and garlic salt. Microwave for 2 minutes or until melted.

Remove caps from the broiler, and turn hollow side up. Place 1 tablespoon melted cheese mixture in each, arrange on a platter and serve.

Prosciutto Bites with Cream Cheese and Toasted Pine Nuts

This salty, savory aged ham blends perfectly with toasted nuts.

Serves 4

½ lb. thin slices prosciutto, cut in half

¼ cup (2 oz.) cream cheese or light cream cheese, softened

3 TB. pine nuts, toasted

Place 1 prosciutto piece on a work surface. Spread cream cheese in a line along one side, about 1 inch in from the side, and sprinkle with pine nuts. Starting from this side, roll prosciutto over cheese to form a cylinder. Insert toothpicks at ½-inch intervals, and cut through the cylinder at the midpoint between each toothpick. Repeat with remaining prosciutto, cream cheese, and nuts. Arrange pieces on a platter and serve.

Unappetizer

A classic match might be Chianti with pasta dishes, but there is also a lesson to learn here. Chianti, which tends to have tart fruit, can stand up to acidic tomato sauce. That same sauce, on the other hand, might obliterate a ripe, fruity Pinot Noir. Pick a similarly acidic, or tannic, wine with highly acidic dishes (like with like).

Hot Cheddar-Onion Dip

A classic, this dip is so easy to prepare.

Serves 4

8 oz. shredded sharp cheddar cheese

¼ cup finely chopped *sweet onion*

¾ cup mayonnaise

¼ tsp. freshly ground black pepper

Tortilla chips, crackers, or crusty bread for serving

Combine cheese, onion, mayonnaise, and black pepper in a microwave-safe serving dish and mix thoroughly. Microwave on high for 3 minutes or until bubbling. Stir, then serve with tortilla chips, good crackers, or crusty bread.

Gourmet Glossary

Regular table onions have plenty of that tart, eye-watering quality that requires ample cooking to reduce. **Sweet onions** are an important ingredient in quick appetizers because they are not quite so sharp and can be used uncooked (in moderation) in recipes. Sweet onions include well-known names such as Vidalia and Spanish.

Appetizers for Rich Reds

Grapes like Cabernet Sauvignon, Syrah/Shiraz, and Zinfandel yield flavor-packed, assertive red wines with characteristics of ripe fruit, spice, even chocolate and oak. They can overpower many foods but often are good matches for rich meats or meat dishes such as steaks and stews.

Recipes in this book that will go well with rich red wines include the following:

◆ Mushroom "Pâté" (Chapter 5)

◆ Beef-based recipes (particularly Chapter 9)

Appetizers for Sweet Wines

Sweet wines have a lot of residual sugar and can be made from many grape varietals—from otherwise light whites (Sauvignon Blanc makes the world-famous sweet white wine of Sauternes) to rich reds. These powerful wines need careful pairing and are often at their best with correspondingly sweet foods.

Recipes in this book that will go well with sweet wines include the following:

◆ Blue Cheese and Chopped Pecan Spread (Chapter 5)

◆ Sautéed Balsamic Pears (Chapter 18)

◆ Cream Cheese with Dried Mediterranean Fruits (Chapter 18)

◆ Dates Stuffed with Chutney Cheese Spread (Chapter 18)

◆ Fruit and Cream Platter (Chapter 18)

Also try the following recipe.

Madeira Cream Fruit Dip

This is a creamy, irresistible fruit dip. The optional addition of heavy cream loosens up the dip just a bit.

Serves 4 to 6

1 (8-oz.) pkg. *mascarpone*

2 TB. Madeira

1 TB. honey

1 TB. heavy or whipping cream (optional)

1 ripe pear, seeds removed, and sliced

2 cups ripe red pitted cherries

2 cups ripe strawberries

Mix mascarpone, Madeira, honey, and cream (if using) in a small bowl, and surround with pear, cherries, and strawberries for dipping. If pear slices will be out for long, rub them with a cut lemon half to delay browning.

Variation: Try other fruits with this delicious dip such as apple slices or pineapple pieces.

Gourmet Glossary

Mascarpone is a thick, buttery, rich, cheese that resembles cream. It is traditionally from Italy (although versions using the same name are made in the United States). It is perhaps one of the most delicious and decadent cheeses to use as a base for desserts or for a fruit dip.

Favorite Food Wines

Ongoing reviews and food and wine information are available at my website, www. tastingtimes.com (© Tod Dimmick and TastingTimes.com; reprinted with permission).

Reliable Producers

To give you a decent shot at a sure winner, here are several dependable sources—wine producers I've found to sell good-quality, reasonably priced wines across the board:

- Bogle (United States)
- Chateau Ste. Michelle (United States)
- Coppola (United States)
- DuBoeuf (France)
- Hogue (United States)
- J. Lohr (United States)
- Joseph Phelps (United States)
- Lindemans (Australia)
- Louis Jadot (France)
- Penfolds (Australia)
- Rabbit Ridge (United States)
- Renwood (United States)
- Rosemount (Australia)
- Ruffino (Italy)
- Tyrrell's (Australia)
- Yellow Tail (Australia)

> **Savoir Starter**
> Plenty of tasty, high-quality wines exist that can be purchased for less than $15 and often less than $10.

Wine Hot List

I've listed here some of my favorite wines from recent tastings. To make your search easier, I've listed them by country. (Wines are often listed by country in wine stores.)

You won't find all these wines in every store, which is why I've included a decent-size list. Keep in mind the previous list of reliable producers!

We tasted these wines with food, as the notes often reflect. The "grade" is a subjective measure of quality and price (I've only included here wines I highly recommend):

A = Yum. Worth *searching* for.

B = Very good. Worth buying again.

C = Fine, but not worth buying again.

Listings are in the following order:

♦ Winery/producer

♦ Region of origin

♦ *Varietal*

♦ *Vintage*

♦ Approximate price

♦ Description

Prices listed were current at the time of this writing.

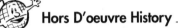

Hors D'oeuvre History

These notes relate to specific wines of specific vintages. By the time you take a look at your local wine store, you might be looking at a 2003, say, rather than a 2001 or 2002. That's okay. Wine from a different vintage won't taste exactly the same, but the characteristics will be similar.

Gourmet Glossary

The **vintage** is the year in which the grapes were harvested and, usually, in which the wine was produced. A 2002 Chardonnay means that the grapes were harvested in 2002. A **varietal** is the type of grape used to make a wine, such as Cabernet Sauvignon, Merlot, or Chardonnay. Many producers, often in the "New World"—Australia, South America, the United States, etc.—bottle primarily varietal-based wine. Other producers, often in Europe, produce primarily *blends*, which contain several different varietals in one wine. A Bordeaux blend, for example, often contains both Cabernet Sauvignon and Merlot.

Australia

Black Swan Vineyards, South Eastern Australia, Shiraz, 2002, $6: *Spicy blackberry and a bowl of ripe fruits with a hint of pepper. Perfect with cheeseburgers.* **B+**

Marquis Philips, South Eastern Australia, Shiraz, Cabernet, Merlot, 2000, $15: *Wow. Cornucopia of jammy, ripe fruits, chocolate, and butter cream. Gorgeous.* **A**

New Zealand

Sacred Hill, Hawkes Bay, Sauvignon Blanc, 2000, $11: *Tangerine rind, tart peach, tart fruits, refreshing, and delicious.* **A–**

Reynolds Vineyards, New South Wales, Sauvignon Blanc, 2002, $12: *Peach, lemon essence ... and all the other citrus. Very tasty.* **B+**

South America

Norton, Mendoza, Sauvignon Blanc, 2001, Argentina, $9: *Grapefruit, melon, peach, and nutmeg. Gorgeous. Run, don't walk, to get this.* **A–**

Santa Rita, Lontue Valley, Merlot, 2000, Chile, $7: *Ripe cherries and vanilla, pleasant, and easy drinking. This is a good wine for the price.* **B**

France

Noblens, Macon Villages, "Petit Roi," 2001, $9: *Almonds, pineapple, and cream. Refreshing and much too easy to drink. If only American Chardonnay tasted like this ...* **B+**

Domaine Le Clos Des Cazaux, Vacqueyras, 1999, $10: *Dusty blueberry, sinewy cherry, and earth (that's a good thing).* **B+**

J&F Lurton, D'Oc Vin De Pays, Sauvignon Blanc, 2000, $6: *Clean, fresh, citrus, and lemon. Very tasty, and perfect with seafood.* **B+**

Louis Jadot, Beaujolais-Villages, Gamay, 2000, $10: *Leather, clove, earth, and strawberry. Delicious.* **A–**

E. Guigal, Cotes du Rhône (white), 2000, $10: *Creamy tropical fruits, pineapple, vanilla, and orange peel. This is very tasty stuff. I will buy it again.* **B+**

Savoir Starter

For entertaining, keep an eye out for "magnums" (double-size) bottles. These bottles are unusual for their size and sometimes even give you better value for the money. Several Australian, French, Italian, domestic, and others on the reliable producers list offer these larger bottles.

Italy

Vignarco, Orvieto Classico, 2001, $10: *Grassy, flinty, lemon-lime, and honeydew. Coming off several unremarkable Orvietos, this was like seeing the sun after a week of rain. Delicious.* **A–**

San Fabiano Calcinaia, Chianti Classico, 2000, $15: *Ripe plums, chocolate, and earth. Somehow this wine elevated a simple roast chicken to haute cuisine.* **A–**

Ruffino, Chianti, Sangiovese, 2000, $7: *Juicy cherry, juicy fruits. Hard not to drink it quickly. Factor in the price and this is an* **A–.**

Spain

Castillo Labastida, Rioja, 2001, $7.50: *One of my favorite wine concepts: berries and cream. Can you taste it? Soft, ripe plums. Grilled pork was the match this time.* **B+**

Portugal

Tonel 22, Dao, 1999, $6: *A whiff of cloves, grass, earth, and dried cherry. There's a lot here—for not much money.* **B+**

Famega, Vinho Verde, 2001, Portugal, $7: *Citrus, effervescence—perfect with pasta tossed with scallops.* **B**

United States

Sutton Wines, Sonoma County, "Table Wine," Chardonnay, 2001, $10: *Cream, nutmeg, vanilla, and lemon. Delicious.* **A–**

Four Vines Cellars, California, "Old Vine Cuvee," Zinfandel, 2000, $10: *Super-ripe blackberries, cherries, and raspberries.* **B+**

Renwood, California, "Select Series" Viognier, 2001, $9: *Tropical fruits, pineapple, nutmeg, and vanilla. How did they pack all this into a $9 bottle of wine?* **A–**

Joseph Phelps, California, "Le Mistral," 1999, $12: *Very berry! Fruity, yet at the same time dusty with a hint of sage. Nice job creating a wine with a sense of the Old Country.* **A–**

Chateau Ste. Michelle, Columbia Valley, "Horsehead Vineyard" Sauvignon Blanc, 2000, $9: *Grapefruit, kiwi. Succulent.* **A–**

Cline, California, Zinfandel, 2000, $10: *Raspberry syrup, Twizzlers, cough drops. This is a "big" tasty wine. The poem on the back is the perfect, slightly risqué toast.* **A–**

Dry Creek Vineyards, California, Chenin Blanc, 2000, $10: *Gardenia notes, tropical fruits, and gulpably delicious. Perfect with seafood.* **B+**

The Least You Need to Know

◆ When planning wines to go with hors d'oeuvres, think "like with like": lighter flavors such as seafood with lighter wines such as Sauvignon Blanc.

◆ Respect your guests' preferences by providing options, usually both a red and a white, even if most of the appetizers say "white" to you.

- Don't feel compelled to spend more than $10 or $15 for a bottle of wine. In that range, you'll find a world of food-friendly opportunities.

- Familiarize yourself with this chapter's short list of dependable wine producers, and look for them at your wine store.

- Don't get hung up on finding the perfect match. The fact is, if you like it, *it's the right match!*

Appendix A

Glossary

accoutrement   An accoutrement is an accompaniment, trapping, or garnish. When we talk about appetizers, accoutrements are the garnishes.

al dente   Italian for "to the tooth." Refers to pasta (or other ingredient such as rice) that is neither soft nor hard, but just slightly firm against the teeth. This, according to many pasta aficionados, is the perfect way to cook pasta.

all-purpose flour   Flour that contains only the inner part of the wheat grain. Usable for all purposes from cakes to gravies.

allspice   Named for its flavor echoes of several spices (cinnamon, cloves, nutmeg), ground allspice berries are used in many desserts and in rich marinades and stews.

almonds   Mild, sweet, and crunchy nuts that combine nicely with creamy and sweet food items.

amaretto   A popular almond liqueur.

americano   A popular coffee drink of espresso mixed with hot water.

anchovies (also **sardines**)   Tiny, flavorful salt- or oil-cured fish that typically come in cans. The strong flavor from these salted fish is a critical element in many recipes. Anchovies are a traditional garnish for Caesar salad, the dressing of which contains anchovy paste.

andouille sausage   A sausage made with highly seasoned pork chitterlings and tripe, and a standard component of many Cajun dishes. *Andouillette* is a similar sausage, although smaller and usually grilled.

antipasto   A classic Italian-style appetizer plate including an assortment of prepared meats, cheeses, and vegetables such as prosciutto, capicolla, mozzarella, mushrooms, and olives.

arabica   The variety of coffee bean most often used for high-quality coffee.

arborio rice   A plump Italian rice used, among other purposes, for risotto.

artichoke hearts   The center part of the artichoke flower, often found canned in grocery stores and used as a stand-alone vegetable dish or as a flavorful base for appetizers or main courses. Marinated artichoke hearts are a nice accent to many dishes.

arugula   A spicy-peppery garden plant with leaves that resemble a dandelion and have a distinctive—and very sharp—flavor.

au gratin   The quick broiling of a dish before serving to brown the top ingredients. The term is often used as part of a recipe name and implies cheese and a creamy sauce.

au jus   French for "with juice," an expression that refers to a dish that is served with juices that result from cooking (as in roast beef).

baba ghanouj   A Middle Eastern–style spread composed of eggplant, lemon juice, garlic, olive oil, and tahini.

baby corn   This small version of corn on the cob, eaten whole, is a popular ingredient in Southeast Asian–style cooking. In the United States, baby corn is often imported preserved and/or pickled from Southeast Asia.

bake   To cook in a dry oven. Baking is one of the most popular methods of cooking and is used for everything from roasts, vegetables, and other main courses to desserts such as cakes and pies. Dry-heat cooking often results in a crisping of the exterior of the food being cooked. Moist-heat cooking, through methods such as steaming, poaching, etc., brings a much different, moist quality to the food.

baking pans   Pans used for baking potatoes to chicken, cookies to croutons.

balsamic vinegar   Vinegar produced primarily in Modena, Italy from a specific type of grape and aged in wood barrels. It is heavier, darker, and sweeter than most vinegars.

bamboo shoots   Crunchy, tasty white parts of the growing bamboo plant, often purchased canned.

barbecue   This is a loaded word, with different, zealous definitions in different parts of the country. In some cases it is synonymous with grilling (quick-cooking over high heat); in others, to barbecue is to cook something long and slow in a rich liquid (barbecue sauce).

basil   A flavorful, almost sweet, resinous herb delicious with tomatoes and used in all kinds of Italian, Mediterranean, and Asian-style dishes.

baste   To keep foods moist during cooking by spooning, brushing, or drizzling with a liquid.

beat   To quickly mix substances.

Belgian endive   A plant that resembles a small, elongated, tightly packed head of romaine lettuce. The thick, crunchy leaves can be broken off and used with dips and spreads.

blanche   To place a food in boiling water for about 1 minute (or less) to partially cook the exterior and then submerge in or rinse with ice water to halt the cooking and fix the color. This is a common method for preparing some vegetables such as asparagus for serving and also for preparing foods for freezing.

blend   To completely mix something, usually with a blender or food processor, more slowly than beating.

boil   To heat a liquid to a point where water is forced to turn into steam, causing the liquid to bubble. To boil something is to insert it into boiling water. A rapid boil is when a lot of bubbles form on the surface of the liquid.

bok choy (also **Chinese cabbage**)   A member of the cabbage family with thick stems, crisp texture, and fresh flavor. It is perfect for stir-frying.

bouillon   Dried essence of stock from chicken, beef, vegetable, or other ingredients. This is a popular starting ingredient for soups as it adds flavor (and often a lot of salt).

bouquet   The aroma or fragrance of a wine.

bouquet garni   A collection of herbs including bay leaf, parsley, thyme, and others. Traditionally, these herbs are tied in a bunch or packaged in cheesecloth for cooking and subsequent removal. Bouquet garni is often found in the spice section of your grocery store and through specialty spice vendors.

braise   To cook with the introduction of some liquid, usually over an extended period of time.

bread flour   Wheat flour used for bread and other recipes.

breadcrumbs   Tiny pieces of crumbled dry bread. Breadcrumbs are an important component in many recipes, often as thickeners and stuffings, and are also used as a coating, for example with breaded chicken breasts.

brie   A creamy cow's milk cheese from France with a soft, edible rind and a mild flavor.

brine   A highly salted, often seasoned, liquid that is used to flavor and preserve foods. To brine a food is to soak, or preserve, it by submerging it in brine. The salt in the brine penetrates the fibers of the meat and makes it moist and tender.

broil   To cook in a dry oven under the overhead high-heat element.

broth   *See* stock.

brown   To cook in a skillet, turning, until the surface is brown in color, to lock in the juices.

brown rice   Whole-grain rice with a characteristic brown color from the bran coating; more nutritious and flavorful than white rice.

Cajun cooking   A style of cooking originating in Louisiana that combines French and Southern characteristics and includes many highly seasoned stews and meats.

cake flour   A high-starch, soft, and fine flour used primarily for cakes.

canapés   Bite-size hors d'oeuvres made up of any number of ingredients but prepared individually and usually served on a small piece of bread or toast.

capers   Usually sold preserved in jars, capers are the flavorful buds of a Mediterranean plant. The most common size is *nonpareil* (about the size of a small pea); others are larger, including the grape-size caper berries produced in Spain.

capicolla   Seasoned, aged pork shoulder; a traditional component of antipasto dishes.

cappuccino   A coffee drink consisting of equal parts espresso and steamed milk topped with milk foam.

caramelize   The term's original meaning is to cook sugar over low heat until it develops a sweet caramel flavor; however, the term is increasingly gaining use to describe cooking vegetables (especially onions) or meat in butter or oil over low heat until they soften, render their sugars, and sweeten, and develop a caramel color. Caramelized onions are a popular addition to many recipes, especially as a pizza topping.

caraway   A distinctive spicy seed used for bread, pork, cheese, and cabbage dishes. It is known to reduce stomach upset, which is why it is often paired with, for example, sauerkraut.

cardamom   An intense, sweet-smelling spice, common to Indian cooking, used in baking and coffee.

casserole dishes   Primarily used in baking, these covered containers hold liquids and solids together and keep moisture around ingredients that might otherwise dry out.

cayenne   A fiery spice made from (hot) chili peppers, especially the Cayenne chili, a slender, red, and very hot pepper.

ceviche   A seafood dish in which fresh fish or seafood is marinated for several hours in highly acidic lemon or lime juice, tomato, onion, and cilantro. The acid "cooks" the seafood.

cheddar   The ubiquitous hard, cow's milk cheese with a rich, buttery flavor that ranges from mellow to sharp. Originally produced in England, cheddar is now produced worldwide.

cheese boards or **cheese trays**   A collection of three or four mixed-flavor cheeses arranged on a tray, platter, or even cutting board. One classic example would be at least one cheese made from cow's, sheep's, and goat's milk. Often restaurants will offer a selection of cheeses as a "cheese flight," or course.

chevre Goat cheese, a typically creamy-salty soft cheese delicious by itself or paired with fruits or chutney. These vary in style from mild and creamy to aged, firm, and flavorful. *Artisanal* goat cheeses are usually more expensive and sold in smaller quantities; these are often delicious by themselves. Other goat cheeses produced in quantity are less expensive and often more appropriate for combining with fruit or herbs.

chickpeas (also **garbanzo beans**) The base ingredient in hummus, chickpeas are high in fiber and low in fat, making this a delicious and healthful component of many appetizers and main dishes.

chili peppers (also **chile peppers**) Any one of many different "hot" peppers, ranging in intensity from the relatively mild ancho pepper to the blisteringly hot habanero.

chili powder A seasoning blend that includes chili pepper, cumin, garlic, and oregano. Proportions vary among different versions, but they all offer a warm, rich flavor.

chives A member of the onion family, chives are found at the grocery store as bunches of long leaves that resemble the green tops of onions. They provide an easy onion flavor to any dish. Chives are very easy to grow, and many people have them in their garden.

chop To cut into pieces, usually qualified by an adverb such as "*coarsely* chopped," or by a size measurement such as "chopped into ½-inch pieces." "Finely chopped" is much closer to mince.

chorizo A spiced pork sausage eaten alone and as a component in many recipes.

cider vinegar Vinegar produced from apple cider, popular in North America.

cilantro A member of the parsley family and used in Mexican cooking and some Asian dishes. Cilantro is what gives some salsas their unique flavor. Use in moderation, as the flavor can overwhelm.

cinnamon A sweet, rich, aromatic spice commonly used in baking or desserts. Cinnamon can also be used for delicious and interesting entrées.

cloves A sweet, strong, almost wintergreen-flavor spice used in baking and with meats such as ham.

coat To cover all sides of a food with a liquid, sauce, or solid.

cookie sheet A large, thin, flat tray used for baking cookies and other foods.

core To remove the unappetizing middle membranes and seeds of fruit and vegetables.

coriander A rich, warm, spicy herb used in all types of recipes, from African to South American, from entrées to desserts.

cottage cheese A mild, creamy-texture cheese made from curds from fresh cow's milk cheese. Curds vary in size; containers will indicate, for example, "small curd" or "large curd." In its low-fat and nonfat forms, cottage cheese is a useful component of low-fat dips, spreads, and other recipes.

count On packaging of seafood or other foods that come in small sizes, you'll often see a reference to the count, how many of that item compose 1 pound. For example, 31 to 40 count shrimp are appetizer shrimp often served with cocktail sauce; 51 to 60 are much smaller.

coulis A thick paste, often made with vegetables or fruits, used as a sauce for many recipes.

couscous Granular semolina (durum wheat) that is cooked and used in many Mediterranean and North African dishes.

cream To blend an ingredient to get a soft, creamy liquid or substance.

crimini mushrooms A relative of the white button mushroom but brown in color and with a richer flavor. *See also* portobello mushrooms.

croutons Pieces of bread, usually between ¼ and ½ inch in size, that are sometimes seasoned and then baked, broiled, or fried to a crisp texture.

crudités Fresh vegetables served as an appetizer, often all together on one tray.

cuisine A style of cooking, typically reflecting a country or region (such as "Spanish cuisine"), a blending of flavors and cuisines (called "fusion"), or an updated style (such as "New Latin").

cumin A fiery, smoky-tasting spice popular in Middle-Eastern and Indian dishes. Cumin is a seed; ground cumin seed is the most common form of the spice used in cooking.

curing A method of preserving uncooked foods, usually meats or fish, by either salting and smoking or pickling.

curry A general term referring to rich, spicy, Indian-style sauces and the dishes prepared with them. In the West, the term also refers to powdered spice blends whose common ingredients include hot pepper, nutmeg, cumin, cinnamon, pepper, and turmeric.

custard A cooked mixture of eggs and milk. Custards are a popular base for desserts.

dash A dash refers to a few drops, usually of a liquid, that is released by a quick shake of, for example, a bottle of hot sauce.

daube A French slow-cooked dish of meat, vegetables, and wine.

deglaze To scrape up the bits of meat and seasoning left in a pan or skillet after cooking by adding a liquid such as wine or broth and creating a flavorful stock that can be used to create sauces.

demi-sec French for "half-dry." Refers to wine that contains residual sugar and has noticeable sweetness.

demitasse French for "half-cup." Refers to a small cup, usually of coffee.

devein The removal of the dark vein from the back of a large shrimp with a sharp knife.

dice   To cut into small cubes about ¼-inch square.

digestif   French for "aides the digestion." It has now come to mean a strong drink or liqueur, such as cognac or brandy, taken after dinner as a presumed aid to digestion.

Dijon mustard   Hearty, spicy mustard made in the style of the Dijon region of France.

dill   A slightly tangy, unique herb that is perfect for eggs, cheese dishes, and, of course, vegetables (pickles!).

dolce   Italian for "sweet." Refers to desserts as well as styles of a food (*Gorgonzola dolce* is a style of Gorgonzola cheese).

double boiler   A set of two pots designed to nest together, one inside the other, and provide consistent, moist heat for foods that need delicate treatment. The bottom pot holds water (not quite touching the bottom of the top pot); the top pot holds the ingredient you want to heat.

dough   A soft, pliable mixture of liquid and flour that is the intermediate step, prior to cooking, for many bread or baked-goods recipes such as cookies or bread.

dredge   To cover a piece of food with a dry substance such as flour or corn meal.

dressing   A liquid mixture usually containing oil, vinegar, and herbs used for seasoning salads and other foods. Also the solid dish commonly called "stuffing" used to stuff turkey and other foods.

drizzle   To lightly sprinkle drops of a liquid over food. Drizzling is often the finishing touch to a dish.

dry   In the context of wine, a wine that has been vinified to contain little or no residual sugar.

dust   To sprinkle a dry substance, often a seasoning, over a food or dish.

emulsion   A combination of liquid ingredients that are mixed together thoroughly to form a third liquid. Classic examples are salad dressings and mayonnaise. Creation of an emulsion must be done carefully and rapidly to ensure that particles of one ingredient are suspended in the other.

entrée   The main dish in a meal.

espresso   Strong coffee made by forcing steam through finely ground coffee beans.

étouffée   Cajun for "smothered." This savory, rich sauce (often made with crayfish) is served over rice.

extra-virgin olive oil   *See* olive oil.

falafel   Middle Eastern hand food composed of seasoned, ground chickpeas formed into balls, cooked, and often used as a filling for pita bread.

fennel In seed form, a fragrant, licorice-tasting herb. The bulbs have a much milder flavor and a celerylike crunch and are used as a vegetable in salads or cooked recipes.

feta This white, crumbly, salty cheese is popular in Greek cooking, on salads, and on its own. Traditional feta is usually made with sheep's milk, but feta-style cheese can be made from sheep's, cow's, or goat's milk. Its sharp flavor is especially nice with bitter, cured black olives.

fillet A piece of meat or seafood with the bones removed.

fish basket A grill-top metal frame that holds a whole fish intact, making it easier to turn.

fish poacher A long, rectangular pan with a separate metal basket designed to hold a fish either above boiling water for steaming or in simmering liquid for poaching. Fish poachers come in varying sizes up to 24 inches, although an 18-inch version will cover all but the largest meals.

flake To break into thin sections, as with fish.

floret The flower or bud end of broccoli or cauliflower.

flour Grains ground into a meal. Wheat is perhaps the most common flour, an essential component in many breads. Flour is also made from oats, rye, buckwheat, soybeans, etc. Different types of flour serve different purposes. *See also* all-purpose flour; bread flour; cake flour; whole-wheat flour.

foie gras A goose liver from specially grown geese, foie gras is considered quite a delicacy for many. *Pâté de foie gras* contains mostly goose liver with pork liver or other ingredients added.

fricassee A dish, usually meat, cut into pieces and cooked in a liquid or sauce.

fritter A food such as apples or corn coated or mixed with batter and deep-fried for a crispy, crunchy exterior.

fry Pan-cooking over high heat with butter or oil.

fusion To blend two or more styles of cooking, such as Chinese and French.

garam masala A famous Indian seasoning mix, rich with cinnamon, pepper, nutmeg, cardamom, and other spices.

garlic A member of the onion family, a pungent and flavorful element in many savory dishes. A garlic bulb, the form in which garlic is often sold, contains multiple cloves. Each clove, when chopped, provides about 1 teaspoon garlic.

garnish An embellishment not vital to the dish but added to enhance visual appeal.

ginger Available in fresh root or powdered form, ginger adds a pungent, sweet, and spicy quality to a dish. It is a very popular element of many Asian and Indian dishes, among others.

goulash   A rich, Hungarian-style meat-and-vegetable stew seasoned with paprika, among other spices.

grate   To shave into tiny pieces using a sharp rasp or grater.

grill   To cook over high heat, usually over charcoal or gas.

grind   To reduce a large, hard substance, often a seasoning such as peppercorns, to the consistency of sand.

grits   Coarsely ground grains, usually corn.

Gruyère   A rich, sharp cow's milk cheese with a nutty flavor made in Switzerland.

gyoza (also **pot stickers**)   Small, usually 1½- to 2-inch-long, Chinese dumplings filled with chicken, seafood, or vegetables. They are traditionally served with soy sauce for dipping.

handful   An unscientific measurement term that refers to the amount of an ingredient you can hold in your hand.

haute cuisine   French for "high cooking." Refers to painstakingly prepared, sometimes exotic, delicious, and complex meals (such as one might find at a high-end traditional French restaurant).

Havarti   A creamy, Danish, mild cow's milk cheese perhaps most enjoyed in its herbed versions such as Havarti with dill.

hazelnut (also **filbert**)   A sweet nut popular in desserts and, to a lesser degree, in savory dishes.

hearts of palm   Firm, elongated, off-white cylinders from the inside of a palm tree stem tip. They are delicious in many recipes.

herbes de Provence   A seasoning mix including basil, fennel, marjoram, rosemary, sage, and thyme.

herbs   The leaves of flavorful plants characterized by fresh, pungent aromas and flavors, such as parsley, sage, rosemary, and thyme.

hors d'oeuvre   French for "outside of work" (the "work" being the main meal). An hors d'oeuvre can be any dish served as a starter before the meal.

horseradish   A sharp, spicy root that forms the flavor base in many condiments from cocktail sauce to sharp mustards. It is a natural match with roast beef. The form generally found in grocery stores is prepared horseradish, which contains vinegar and oil, among other ingredients. If you come across pure horseradish, use it much more sparingly than the prepared version, or try cutting it with sour cream.

hummus   A thick, Middle Eastern spread made of puréed chickpeas (garbanzo beans), lemon juice, olive oil, garlic, and often tahini (sesame seed paste).

infusion   A liquid in which flavorful ingredients such as herbs have been soaked or steeped to extract that flavor into the liquid.

Italian seasoning (also **spaghetti sauce seasoning**)   The ubiquitous grocery store blend, which includes basil, oregano, rosemary, and thyme, is a useful seasoning for quick flavor that evokes the "Old Country" in sauces, meatballs, soups, and vegetable dishes.

jicama   A juicy, crunchy, sweet, Central American vegetable that is eaten both raw and cooked. It is available in many large grocery stores as well as from specialty vendors. If you can't find jicama, try substituting sliced water chestnuts.

julienne   To slice into very thin pieces.

latte   A coffee drink with one part espresso and two parts steamed milk.

liver   The nutritious and flavorful organ meat from all types of fowl and animals.

macchiato   An espresso drink consisting of one shot espresso with a dollop of foamed or steamed milk.

macerate   To mix sugar or another sweetener with fruit. The fruit softens, and its juice is released to mix with the sweetener.

marinate   To soak meat, seafood, or other food in a seasoned sauce, called a marinade, which is high in acid content. The acids break down the muscle of the meat, making it tender and adding flavor.

marjoram   A sweet herb, a cousin of and similar to oregano, popular in Greek, Spanish, and Italian dishes.

marmalade   A fruit-and-sugar preserve that contains whole pieces of fruit peel, to achieve simultaneous sweetness (from the sugar) and tartness (from the fruit's natural acids). The most common marmalades are made with citrus fruits such as orange and lemon.

mascarpone   A thick, creamy, spreadable cheese, traditionally from Italy, although versions using the same name are made in the United States. It is perhaps one of the most delicious and decadent dessert toppings for fruit.

medallion   A small round cut, usually of meat or vegetables such as carrots or cucumbers.

meld   A combination of *melt* and *weld*, many cooks use this term to describe how flavors blend and spread over time throughout dips and spreads. Melding is often why recipes call for overnight refrigeration and is also why some dishes taste better as leftovers.

meringue   A baked mixture of sugar and beaten egg whites, often used as a dessert topping.

mesclun   Mixed salad greens, usually containing lettuce and assorted greens such as arugula, cress, endive, and others.

mince   To cut into very small pieces smaller than diced pieces, about ⅛ inch or smaller.

mirin   A thick, sweet wine or liqueur made from rice. Mirin is an important component in many Japanese-style dishes such as teriyaki.

miso   A fermented, flavorful soybean paste. It is a key ingredient in many Japanese dishes.

mold   A decorative, shaped metal pan in which contents, such as mousse or gelatin, set up and take the shape of the pan.

muhammara   A classic Turkish dip or spread that contains walnuts, onion, garlic, bread-crumbs, and hot peppers.

mull (or **mulled**)   To heat a liquid with the addition of spices and sometimes sweeteners.

mushrooms   Any one of a huge variety of *edible* fungi (note emphasis on "edible"; there are also poisonous mushrooms). *See also* crimini mushrooms; porcini mushrooms; portobello mushrooms; shiitake mushrooms; white mushrooms.

nouvelle cuisine   *Nouvelle* is French for "new." Refers to a style of cooking that is relatively light in flavor and consistency.

nut   A shell-covered seed (or fruit) whose meat is rich in flavor and nutrition. A critical component in many dishes, many nuts are tasty on their own as well. *See also* almonds; hazelnuts; pecans; walnuts.

nutmeg   A sweet, fragrant, musky spice used primarily in baking.

oenophile   A person who loves wine; often an enthusiast who collects or enjoys tasting and learning about wine.

olivada   A simple spread composed of olives, olive oil, and pepper that carries a wealth of flavor.

olive oil   A fragrant liquid produced by crushing or pressing olives. Extra-virgin olive oil is the oil produced from the first pressing of a batch of olives; oil is also produced from other pressings after the first. Extra-virgin olive oil is generally considered the most flavorful and highest quality and is the type you want to use when your focus is on the oil itself. Be sure the bottle label reads "extra-virgin."

olives   The fruit of the olive tree commonly grown on all sides of the Mediterranean. There are many varieties of olives but two general types: green and black. Black olives are also called ripe olives.

oregano   A fragrant, slightly astringent herb used in Greek, Spanish, and Italian dishes.

oxidation   The browning of fruit flesh that happens over time and with exposure to air. Although it's best to prepare fresh fruit dishes just before serving, sometimes that's not possible. If you need to cut apples in advance, minimize oxidation by rubbing the cut surfaces with a lemon half.

paella   A grand Spanish dish of rice, shellfish, onion, meats, rich broth, and herbs.

pan-broil   Quick-cooking over high heat in a skillet with a minimum of butter or oil. (Frying, on the other hand, uses more butter or oil.)

pancetta   Salted, seasoned bacon; an important element in many Italian-style dishes.

paprika   A rich, red, warm, earthy spice that also lends a rich red color to many dishes.

parboil   To partially cook in boiling water or broth. Parboiling is similar to blanching, although blanched foods are quickly cooled with cold water.

pare   To scrape away the skin of a food, usually a vegetable or fruit, as part of preparation for serving or cooking.

Parmesan   A hard, dry, flavorful cheese primarily used grated or shredded as a seasoning for Italian-style dishes.

parsley   A fresh-tasting green leafy herb used to add color and interest to just about any savory dish. Often used as a garnish just before serving.

pâté   A savory loaf that contains meats, spices, and often a lot of fat, served cold spread or sliced on crusty bread or crackers. In traditional French cuisine a pâté has a pastry crust.

peanuts   The nutritious and high-fat seeds of the peanut plant (a relative of the pea) that are sold shelled or unshelled and in a variety of preparations, including peanut butter and peanut oil. Some people are allergic to peanuts, so be cautious with their inclusion in recipes.

pecans   Rich, buttery nuts native to North America. Their flavor, a terrific addition to appetizers, is at least partially due to their high unsaturated fat content.

pepper   A biting and pungent seasoning, freshly ground pepper is a must for many dishes and adds an extra level of flavor and taste.

peppercorns   Large, round, dried berries that are ground to produce pepper.

pesto   A thick spread or sauce of Italian origin made with fresh basil leaves, garlic, olive oil, pine nuts, and Parmesan cheese. Other new versions are made with other herbs. Rich and flavorful, pesto can be made at home or purchased in a grocery store and used on anything from appetizers to pasta and other main dishes.

pickle   A food, usually a vegetable such as a cucumber, that has been pickled in brine.

pilaf   A rice dish in which the rice is browned in butter or oil, then cooked in a flavorful liquid such as a broth, often with the addition of meats or vegetables and seasonings. The rice absorbs the broth, resulting in a savory dish.

pinch   An unscientific measurement term that refers to the amount of an ingredient—typically a dry, granular substance such as an herb or seasoning—you can hold between your finger and thumb.

pine nuts (also **pignoli** or **piñon**)   Nuts grown on pine trees, that are rich (read: high fat), flavorful, and, yes, a bit pine-y. Pine nuts are a traditional component of pesto and add a wonderful hearty crunch to many other recipes.

pinzimonio   An Italian vegetable dish in which combinations of sliced vegetables are served with olive oil, vinegar, salt, and pepper.

pita bread   A flat, hollow wheat bread of Middle Eastern origin that can be used for sandwiches or cut pizza-style, into wedges. Pita bread is terrific soft with dips or baked or broiled as a vehicle for other ingredients.

pizza stone   Preheated with the oven, a pizza stone cooks a crust to a delicious, crispy, pizza-parlor texture. It also holds heat well, so a pizza removed from the oven on the stone will stay hot for as long as a half-hour at the table. It can also be used for other baking needs, including bread.

plantain   A relative of the banana, a plantain is larger, milder in flavor, and used as a staple in many Latin American dishes. Certain forms are starchy and must be cooked.

poach   To cook a food in simmering liquid, such as water, wine, or broth.

porcini mushrooms   Rich and flavorful mushrooms used in rice and Italian-style dishes.

portobello mushrooms   A mature and larger form of the smaller crimini mushroom, portobellos are brownish, chewy, and flavorful. They are trendy served as whole caps, grilled, and as thin sautéed slices. *See also* crimini mushrooms.

pot stickers   *See* gyoza.

preheat   To turn on an oven, broiler, or other cooking appliance in advance of cooking so the temperature will be at the desired level when the assembled dish is ready for cooking.

presentation   The appealing arrangement of a dish or food on the plate.

prosciutto   Dry, salt-cured ham that originated in Italy. Prosciutto is popular in many simple dishes in which its unique flavor is allowed to shine.

purée   To reduce a food to a thick, creamy texture, usually using a blender or food processor.

raclette   A famous cheese-intensive Swiss and French dish using raclette cheese (a richly flavored relative of Swiss cheese). As the cheese melts, it is scraped off the wedge. It is then combined with potatoes, pickles, and tiny onions and served with crusty dark bread.

ragout (pronounced *rag-OO*)   A thick, spicy stew.

red pepper flakes   Hot yet rich, crushed red pepper, used in moderation, brings flavor and interest to many savory dishes.

reduce   To heat a broth or sauce to remove some of the water content, resulting in more concentrated flavor and color.

refried beans (also **refritos**)   Twice-cooked beans—most often pinto beans—softened into a thick paste and often seasoned with peppers and spices. Most refried beans include lard, but many fat-free, lard-free versions are available.

render   To cook a meat to the point where its fat melts and can be removed.

reserve   To hold a specified ingredient for another use later in the recipe.

rice vinegar   Vinegar produced from fermented rice or rice wine, popular in Asian-style dishes.

risotto   A popular Italian rice dish made by browning arborio rice in butter or oil, then slowly adding liquid to cook the rice, resulting in a creamy texture.

roast   To cook something uncovered in an oven.

robusta   The variety of coffee bean most often found in commercial ground coffee.

Roquefort   A world-famous (French) creamy but sharp sheep's milk cheese containing blue lines of mold, making it a "blue cheese."

rosemary   A pungent, sweet herb used with chicken, pork, fish, and especially lamb. A little of it goes a long way.

roux   A mixture of butter or another fat source and flour used to thicken liquids such as sauces.

saffron   A famous spice made from stamens of crocus flowers. Saffron lends a dramatic yellow color and distinctive flavor to a dish. Only a tiny amount needs to be used, which is good because saffron is very expensive.

sage   An herb with a fruity, lemon-rind scent and "sunny" flavor. It is a terrific addition to many dishes.

salsa   A style of mixing fresh vegetables and/or fresh fruit in a coarse chop. Salsa can be spicy or not, fruit-based or not, and served as a starter on its own (with chips, for example) or as a companion to a main course.

satay (also **sate**)   A popular Southeast Asian dish of broiled skewers of fish or meat, often served with peanut sauce.

sauté   Pan-cooking over lower heat than used for frying. The cooking medium is fat, and the cook stirs the food and shakes the pan continually. In French, the term means "to jump."

savory   A popular herb with a fresh, woody taste.

scant   A measurement modification that specifies "include no extra," as in 1 scant teaspoon.

Scoville scale   A scale used to measure the "hot" in hot peppers. The lower the Scoville units, the more mild the pepper. Ancho peppers, which are mildly hot, are about 3,000 Scovilles; Thai hot peppers are about 6,000; and some of the more daring peppers such as Tears of Fire and habanero are 30,000 Scovilles or more.

scrapple   A sausagelike mixture of seasoned pork and cornmeal that is formed into loaves and sliced for cooking.

sear   To quickly brown the exterior of a food over high heat to preserve interior moisture (that's why many meat recipes involve searing).

search engine   An Internet tool that, based on keywords you type, helps find related websites on the topic you searched for. A good search engine such as Google or Yahoo! will suggest sites that are close to what you seek.

shallot   A member of the onion family that grows in a bulb somewhat like garlic and has a milder onion flavor.

shellfish   A broad range of seafood, including clams, mussels, oysters, crabs, shrimp, and lobster. Some people are allergic to shellfish, so care should be taken with its inclusion in recipes.

shiitake mushrooms   Large (up to eight inches or more), dark-brown mushrooms originally from the Far East with a hearty, meaty flavor that can be grilled or used as a component in other recipes and as a flavoring source for broth.

short-grain rice   A starchy rice popular for Asian-style dishes because it readily clumps for eating with chopsticks.

shred   To cut into many long, thin slices.

simmer   To boil gently so the liquid barely bubbles.

skewers   Thin wooden or metal sticks, usually about eight inches long, that are perfect for grilled dishes such as kebabs, dipping food pieces into hot sauces, or serving single-bite food items with a bit of panache.

skillet (also **frying pan**)   A generally heavy, flat metal pan with a handle designed to cook food over heat on a stovetop or campfire.

slice   To cut into thin pieces.

slow cooker   An electric countertop device with a lidded container that maintains a low temperature and slowly cooks its contents, often over several hours or a full day.

sommelier   A member of a restaurant's staff devoted to storing, recommending, and serving wine with the meal.

steam   To suspend a food over boiling water and allow the heat of the steam (water vapor) to cook the food. Steaming is a very quick cooking method that preserves flavor and texture of a food.

stew   To slowly cook pieces of food submerged in a liquid. Also, a dish that has been prepared by this method.

sticky rice (or **glutinous rice**)   *See* short-grain rice.

Stilton The famous English blue cheese, delicious with toasted nuts and renowned for its pairing with Port wine.

stir-fry To cook food in a wok or skillet over high heat, moving and turning the food quickly to cook all sides. Usually involves food cut into small pieces.

stock A flavorful broth made by cooking meats and/or vegetables with seasonings until the liquid absorbs these flavors. This liquid is then strained and the solids discarded. Stock can be eaten by itself or used as a base for soups, stews, sauces, risotto, or many other recipes.

stripe To scrape off a fruit's or vegetable's skin in lengthwise strokes, leaving a "stripe" of the skin between each scrape.

succotash A cooked vegetable dish usually made of corn and peppers.

sweetbreads The thymus gland from common food animals, most popularly from veal. They are prized for their creamy, delicate texture.

Tabasco sauce A popular brand of Louisiana hot pepper sauce used in usually small portions to season savory food. The name also refers to a type of hot pepper from Tabasco, a state in Mexico that is used to make this sauce.

tahini A paste made from sesame seeds that is used to flavor many Middle Eastern recipes, especially baba ghanouj and hummus.

tamarind A sweet, pungent, flavorful fruit used in Indian and Southeast Asian–style sauces and curries.

tapenade A thick, chunky spread made from savory ingredients such as olives, lemon juice, and anchovies. Adventuresome grocery and gourmet stores are likely to have different versions focusing on specific ingredients, from olives to peppers and mushrooms.

taro A popular root vegetable that is similar to the potato and is used in African and Caribbean cuisines.

tarragon A sour-sweet, rich-smelling herb perfect with seafood, vegetables (especially asparagus), chicken, and pork.

teriyaki A delicious Japanese sauce composed of soy sauce, rice wine, ginger, and sugar. It works beautifully with seafood as well as most meats.

terroir All the elements that affect a grapevine in the vineyard, including the sun, wind, soil, and climate. All the external factors that affect how that vine grows are respected for the role they play in the grapes used to make a wine.

thyme A minty, zesty herb whose leaves are used in a wide range of recipes.

toast To heat something, usually bread, so it is browned and crisp.

toast points (also **toast triangles**) Pieces of toast with the crusts removed that are then cut on the diagonal from each corner, resulting in four triangle-shape pieces.

tofu   A cheeselike substance made from soybeans and soy milk. Flavorful and nutritious, tofu is an important component of foods across the globe, especially from the Far East.

tomatillo   A small, round fruit with a distinctive spicy flavor. It resembles the tomato but is actually closer botanically to the gooseberry. Tomatillos are a traditional component of many south-of-the-border dishes. To use, remove the papery outer skin, rinse off any sticky residue, and chop like a tomato.

tripe   The stomach of a cow.

turmeric   A spicy, pungent yellow root used in many dishes, especially Indian cuisine, for color and flavor. Turmeric is the source of the brilliant yellow color in many prepared mustards.

twist   A twist (as in lemon or other citrus fruit twist) is simply an attractive way to garnish an appetizer or other dish. Cut a thin, about $1/8$-inch-thick cross-section slice of a lemon, for example. Then take that slice and cut from the center out to the edge of the slice on one side. Pick up the piece of lemon and pull apart the two cut ends in opposite directions.

varietal   The type of grape used to make a wine, such as Cabernet Sauvignon, Merlot, or Chardonnay.

veal   Meat from a calf, generally characterized by mild flavor and tenderness. Certain cuts of veal, such as cutlets and scaloppini, are well suited to quick-cooking.

vegetable steamer   An insert for a large saucepan. Also a special pot with tiny holes in the bottom designed to fit on another pot to hold food to be steamed above boiling water. The insert is generally less expensive and resembles a metal poppy flower that expands to touch the sides of the pot and has small legs. *See also* steam.

vehicle   A food that is used to scoop or dip another ingredient, such as vegetables or pitas with dip.

venison   Meat from deer or other large wild game animals.

vichy   A classic French vegetable dish of carrots cooked in water, butter, and sugar.

vindaloo   A famous spicy Indian curry dish.

vinegar   An acidic liquid widely used as dressing and seasoning. Many cuisines use vinegars made from different source materials. *See also* balsamic vinegar; cider vinegar; rice vinegar; white vinegar; wine vinegar.

vintage   The year in which the grapes were harvested and, usually, in which the wine was produced. A 2002 Sauvignon Blanc means that the grapes were harvested in 2002.

walnuts   Grown worldwide, walnuts bring a rich, slightly woody flavor to all types of food. For the quick cook, walnuts are available chopped and ready to go at your grocery store. They are delicious toasted and make fine accompaniments to cheeses.

wasabi   Japanese horseradish, a fiery, pungent condiment used with many Japanese-style dishes, including sushi. Most often sold as a powder; add water to create a paste.

water chestnuts Actually a tuber, water chestnuts are a popular element in many types of Asian-style cooking. The flesh is white, crunchy, and juicy, and the vegetable holds its texture whether cool or hot.

whisk To rapidly mix, introducing air to the mixture.

white mushrooms Ubiquitous button mushrooms. When fresh, they will have an earthy smell and an appealing "soft crunch." White mushrooms are delicious raw in salads, marinated, sautéed, and as component ingredients in many recipes.

white vinegar The most common type of vinegar found on grocery store shelves. It is produced from grain.

whole-wheat flour—Wheat flour that contains the entire grain.

wild rice Actually a grass resembling rice with a rich, nutty flavor, popular as an unusual and nutritious side dish.

wine vinegar Vinegar produced from red or white wine.

wok A wonderful tool for quick-cooking. Unfortunately, it is only suitable for use on a gas cooktop, unless you purchase a plug-in electric version, which might not have the important rapid heating characteristic of a wok over a gas flame. Large enough to hold an entire meal, different enough to inspire interest, a wok brings fun to a meal.

Worcestershire sauce Originally developed in India and containing tamarind, this spicy sauce is used as a seasoning for many meats and other dishes.

yeast Tiny fungi that, when mixed with water, sugar, flour, and heat, release carbon dioxide bubbles, which, in turn, raise bread. The yeast also provides that wonderful warm, rich smell and flavor.

zest Small slivers of peel, usually from a citrus fruit such as lemon, lime, or orange.

zester A small kitchen tool used to scrape zest off a fruit. A small grater also works fine.

References

Books

Barrett, Judith. *From an Italian Garden*. New York: Macmillan, 1992.

Carpenter, Hugh, and Teri Sandison. *Fast Appetizers*. Berkeley: Ten Speed Press, 1999.

Casas, Penelope. *Tapas: The Little Dishes of Spain*. New York: Knopf, 1985.

Chalmers, Irena. *Good Old Food*. Hauppauge: Barron's Educational Services, 1993.

Child, Julia. *The French Chef Cookbook, Thirtieth Anniversary Edition*. New York: Ballantine, 1998.

Creasy, Rosalind. *The Edible Flower Garden*. Boston: Periplus, 1999.

Cunningham, Marion. *The Fanny Farmer Cookbook*. New York: Alfred A. Knopf, 1990.

Dimmick, Tod. *The Complete Idiot's Guide to 20-Minute Meals*. Indianapolis: Alpha Books, 2002.

Gardiner, Anne, and Sue Wilson. *The Inquisitive Cook*. New York: Henry Holt, 1998.

Garten, Ina. *The Barefoot Contessa Cookbook*. New York: Clarkson Potter, 1999.

Gorman, Donna, and Elizabeth Heyert. *The Artful Table*. New York: William Morrow and Company, 1998.

Green, Henrietta. *Farmer's Market Cookbook*. London: Kyle Cathie, 2001.

Harlow, Joan S. *The Loaf and Ladle Cookbook*. Camden: Down East Books, 1983.

Herbst, Sharon Tyler. *Food Lover's Companion*. Hauppauge: Barron's Educational Series, 2001.

Loomis, Susan Herrmann. *Farmhouse Cookbook*. New York: Workman Publishing, 1991.

Jenkins, Steven. *Cheese Primer*. New York: Workman Publishing, 1996.

Katzen, Mollie. *Moosewood Cookbook*. Berkeley: Ten Speed Press, 1977.

Kropotkin, Igor, and Marjorie Kropotkin. *The Inn Cookbook*. Secaucus: Castle, 1983.

Lanchester, John. *The Debt to Pleasure*. New York: Henry Holt, 1996.

MacMillan, Diane D. *The Portable Feast*. San Francisco: 101 Productions, 1984.

Mayes, Francis. *Under the Tuscan Sun*. New York: Broadway Books, 1997.

Mayle, Peter. *A Year in Provence*. New York: Vintage Books, 1991.

McNair, James. *Pizza*. San Francisco: Chronicle Books, 1987.

Murphy, Margaret Deeds. *The Boston Globe Cookbook, Third Edition*. Chester: Globe Pequot Press, 1990.

Oliver, Jamie. *The Naked Chef*. London: Michael Joseph, 1999.

Ostmann, Barbara Gibbs, and Jane L. Baker. *The Recipe Writer's Handbook*. New York: John Wiley & Sons, 2001.

Richardson, Ferrier, ed. *Scotland on a Plate*. Edinburgh: Black & White Publishing, 2001.

Rodgers, Rick. *Dip It!* New York: William Morrow and Company, 2002.

Rosso, Julee, and Sheila Lukins. *The New Basics Cookbook*. New York: Workman Publishing, 1989.

———. *The Silver Palate Cookbook*. New York: Workman Publishing, 1982.

———. *The Silver Palate Good Times Cookbook*. New York: Workman Publishing, 1985.

Scicolone, Michele. *The Antipasto Table*. New York: William Morrow and Company, 1991.

Seranne, Ann, ed. *The Western Junior League Cookbook*. New York: McKay, 1979.

Stewart, Martha. *Entertaining*. New York: Clarkson N. Potter, 1982.

Tudor, Tasha. *The Tasha Tudor Cookbook*. Boston: Little, Brown, 1993.

Urvater, Michele. *Monday to Friday Cookbook*. New York: Workman Publishing, 1991.

Wells, Patricia. *Bistro Cooking*. New York: Workman Publishing, 1989.

Magazines

Saveur
www.saveur.com

Cooking Light
www.cookinglight.com

Bon Appétit
www.bonappetit.com

Cook's Illustrated
www.cooksillustrated.com

Wine Spectator
www.winespectator.com

Food & Wine
www.foodandwine.com

Fine Cooking
www.taunton.com/finecooking/index.asp

Favorite Food Websites

Following are selected cooking-related web pages reviewed by Tod Dimmick in his
e-mail newsletter for WZ.com. (© Copyright WZ.com Inc., reprinted with permission.)

General Recipe Sites (with Plenty of Information on Appetizers)

AllRecipes, All the Time

www.allrecipes.com
AllRecipes draws on a massive database of recipes and provides advice on techniques, meal
planning, and more. The "by ingredient" search engine enables mix-and-match creativity;
think shrimp and pasta or apples and cream. Type them in, the inspiration flows, and you
can save your favorites to your personal recipe box.

Sam Cooks

www.samcooks.com
Longtime gourmet columnist for *Wine Spectator* Sam Gugino has constructed a clean,
information-packed site for the intelligent cook. Check out "Cooking to Beat the Clock"
and "Eat Fresh, Stay Healthy: An A to Z Guide to Fruits and Vegetables."

Epicurious

www.epicurious.com
Epicurious claims more than 13,000 recipes, drawing from years of *Gourmet* and *Bon
Appétit,* among other sources. Try visiting the search engine with random ingredients you
have on hand that need a "common destiny." You'll be surprised what you come up with;
ground turkey and sun-dried tomato meatloaf is a surprising delight I make every winter.
Assemble your favorites, and create your own personal recipe file.

Cooking Light

www.cookinglight.com
Tips, recipes, and themes (French, Italian, celebration menus, and so on) are given for those
of us who want taste and quality but who also might be concerned with what we eat.

Eat Smart

www.usaweekend.com/food/carper_archive/index.html

This collection of articles from Jean Carper, well-known columnist for *USA Weekend*, covers everything from vitamins and whole grains to avoiding carcinogens when grilling. I need those tips.

Tastes Great, Less Fat

lowfatcooking.about.com

Trevy Little hosts a detailed page of resources on the low-fat theme. Categories include the expected salads as well as imaginative entries for beef, pasta, lamb, and more.

Fatfree

www.fatfree.com/recipes/sauces

Find the antidote here for some of the richer foods we eat. Can there be a fat-free alfredo?

Reluctant Gourmet

www.reluctantgourmet.com

Reluctant Gourmet is refreshing for its modesty. The site covers tasks simply and completely—from cooking techniques (how to braise) to a glossary of gourmet terms. I grin as soon as I see the photo on the home page. You'll see what I mean.

Southern Living

www.southernliving.com

For comfort food with a regional slant from *Southern Living*, click on the Foods link. Tantalizing recipes throughout make it tough to decide where to start.

Cook's Thesaurus

www.foodsubs.com

Cook's Thesaurus contains a truly massive gourmet glossary. Ever wonder where that cut of beef is from? Voilà! There it is—with diagrams. Each section provides guidance on substitutions, which is very useful if you cook with what's on hand.

Global Gourmet

www.globalgourmet.com

Global Gourmet will draw you in to articles on everything from "Holiday Helpers" to "I Love Chocolate."

Sites Focused on Quick Cooking

My Meals

www.my-meals.com

This site includes a section devoted to recipes requiring 30 minutes or less. Some are very basic, whereas others are decidedly less so. What about Hot Carameled Apples with Pie Crust Dippers?

Simple Pleasures

www.allfood.com/mmeal.cfm

Minutemeals challenges the assertion that cooking quickly requires sacrifice of quality and taste. The listing of complete holiday menus is especially soothing.

Theme Cuisine

All Fins, All the Time

www.seafoodrecipe.com

This subset of the AllRecipes site has got it all, organized by cooking method, ethnic origin, and specific undersea creature.

Vegetarian Times

www.vegetariantimes.com

Vegetarian never looked so good as the collection of mouthwatering recipes here.

Vegetarian Across the Globe

www.ivu.org/recipes/regions.html

The International Vegetarian Union offers a multitude of recipes divided by region of the world and by type of cuisine. From tofu to curry, chili to portobello bruschetta, it's here—plus everything you ever wanted to know about vegetarianism.

White Meat

www.eatchicken.com

This is a chicken lover's paradise, with information from technique to recipes and poultry statistics. Follow the Show a Little Leg link to Peruvian Grilled Chicken Thighs with Tomato Cilantro Sauce.

Penzey's Spices

www.penzeys.com

Each recipe makes use of one or more assertive, characteristic spices. Check out Grilled Asparagus using bold cracked pepper. I'm a big fan of these guys.

Holy Guacamole

recipes.alastra.com/Mexican

Wow! Talk about *Encyclopedia Mexicana!* Nothing fancy, but check out how many kinds of guacamole there are—that's just for starters.

Food and Wine Sites

TastingTimes

www.tastingtimes.com

The author's own site offers a growing section on food and wine pairing, wine menus, and recipes. It also features a free e-mail newsletter, the *wine minute*, with recommendations under $15.

Start Simple

www.adwfoodandwine.com/index.asp

Here's a basic chart, courtesy of Clos du Bois, explaining matches that work and why.

EatDrinkDine

www.eatdrinkdine.com

What a great site! Sommelier Evan Goldstein offers a wonderfully complete yet easy to use page that you can approach from "Start with Food" or "Start with Wine."

Mondavi

www.robertmondavi.com/FoodWine/index.asp

This is a friendly database of neatly organized menus, with suggested wines. Try Butter-nut Squash Risotto with a friendly Merlot—it's a winner.

Wine and the Good Life

www.winespectator.com

Winespectator.com, one of the largest wine-related sites on the web, offers a mountain of information on wine, travel, restaurants, and more.

Wine Sauce

www.corkcuisine.com

A fun site for lovers of food and wine, it includes history, recipes, and a wealth of wine and food tips.

Favorite Vendors

Here are a few of my favorite vendors:

Trader Joe's

www.traderjoes.com

This national chain offers an eclectic yet tempting array of ingredients helpful to the cook in a hurry.

King Arthur Flour

www.kingarthurflour.com

This mail- and Internet-order company provides a huge range of specialty flours and baking ingredients. Add a little buckwheat flour to quick pancakes, and you'll never go back.

Penzey's Spices

www.penzeys.com

Another mail- and Internet-order company, it has a huge selection of top-quality herbs and spices, as well as a recipe-filled catalog to salivate over.

Your Local Farmer's Market

www.ams.usda.gov/farmersmarkets/map.htm

You'll know the one down the street from you better than I. A farm stand is the place to go for the freshest, tastiest farm produce—key ingredients of healthful 5-minute cuisine. This link takes you to a U.S. map where you can find the market nearest you.

Index